TRIBES OF NORTH-EAST INDIA
Biological and Cultural Perspectives

TRIBES OF NORTH-EAST INDIA

Biological and Cultural Perspectives

Editor

SARTHAK SENGUPTA

GYAN

Tribes of North East India

ISBN: 81-212-0463-1

Reprinted in 2012 in India by
Gyan Publishing House
23, Main Ansari Road, Daryaganj,
New Delhi - 110002
Phones : 23282060, 23261060
Fax : (011) 23285914
E-mail : books@gyanbooks.com
Website: gyanbooks.com

Printed in India by Artxel,

to the sacred memory of my father-in-law
Late JITENDRA NATH BARUAH

PREFACE

The present work is an attempt to contribute to the growing literature on the biological and cultural perspectives of the tribes of North East India. During last few decades, social scientists have increasingly turned their attention towards the development and problems of the tribes of India and literature on the subject at present is voluminous. However, in recent years, a tendency has been observed among many social scientists to avoid precise and clear cut definition of the term *'tribe'* employed by them in their studies. It is true that the definition of *tribe* in the Indian context appears to be in an inconstant state, as the word has been perceived variously. The word can be defined at different level having different perspectives. On academic parlance the *tribe* can be defined on theoretical level. Definition of the term may be on historical, anthropological or on sociological context. There is yet another approach to the definition of tribe which is charged with ideological orientation - the Marxian approach. However, in the present context of India, most of the attributes of the above mentioned approaches have lost their significance and existence. Defining *tribe* in terms of single set of attributes is thus, immensely difficult. Again, if we strictly follow the above indicators, probably many groups which are scheduled as tribals would cease to remain as tribal while some other non-scheduled groups may easily claim the scheduled status.

In contemporary India, the Scheduled Tribes are basically a politico-administrative category and are devoid of any academic definition. In the present compilation, therefore, the word *'tribe'* refers to those communities which are declared as such by the Constitution of India. It would not be out of place to mention here that Government of India declared that only those who were in the list of 'primitive tribe' in the Census Report of 1931 were to be included in the list of Scheduled Tribes. For Constitution, Scheduled Tribe are those which are backward and which deserve special provision for development. The problem of specifying the members of Scheduled Tribes (art 342) though entrusted to the President of India, the Constitution however, did not define the Scheduled Tribes. At present the tribes so specified in the order number about 450 approximately, and about 130 such communities inhabit in North East India.

North East India, the earswhile greater Assam, presently the land of seven sisters covers political units namely the states of Arunachal Pradesh, Assam, Manipur, Meghalaya, Mizoram, Nagaland and Tripura and is located between latitude 20° and 22° North and longitude 89°46' and 97°5' East. It has an area of 2,55,082 sq. km., having a hilly and wild topography. The indigenous inhabitants of this region, who are mostly tribes, are bewildering in their variety, ethnicity, culture and folklore. The area is endowed with rich resources of land, water, forests, and minerals etc., and perched at the confluence of countries like China and Tibet in the north, Myanmar in the east and north and Bangladesh in the west. This region is connected with the rest of India by a narrow corridor between Nepal and Bangladesh. This has greatly enhanced its strategic importance.

It is estimated that out of approximately 31'4 million people living in North East India, about 8'1 millions of them are made up of tribal people of the hills and plains. At present, in four of the seven states in North East India, tribals are in majority. Arunachal Pradesh which attained statehood from Union Territory status only in 1984, alone accounts for some twentyfour major tribal groups and these constitute about 70.0% of the total population. Tribes living in the states of Assam are categorised into fourteen hill tribes and nine plains tribes and the state accounted for merely 11.0% tribal population. Manipur is abode of twentyeight tribal groups which makes up approximately 28.0% of the toral population. Meghalaya which came into being in 1972 is a tribal dominated (81.0% to the total population) state and noted for its three matriarchal tribal groups besides others. Mizoram, the land of Mizos which also was born in 1972, is again dominated (94.0%) by the tribals. Nagaland which was made a separate state in 1963 where tribal population constitute more than 84.0% and is inhabited by thirteen major tribes and sub-tribes speaking different dialects. Among the Nagas, there are sixteen distinctly recognised tribal groups. In Tripura, where Scheduled Tribe constituted 29.0% of the total population, is the home of nineteen different Scheduled Tribes (Census, 1981).

North East India is the land of co-existence of the extreme forms of both tradition land modernity. Ethnically the tribes of North East belong to the Indo-Mongoloid racial stock. The tribal people of this region speak languages of different divisions and sub-divisions of the Sino-Tibetan linguistic family. However, a few speak Mon-Khmer (Austro-Asiatic) languages. In some tribes, the literacy rate is remarkably low. Again few tribes could take their literacy rate to a respectable stage which is much above national level. Majority of the tribes are patriarchal while, matriarchal tribal societies also exist in few pockets. Some are in transitional stage.

Traditionally the tribes of North East are *jhum* (shifting) cultivators, while many of them are settled cultivators and as good peasants as others. Market economy prevails but barter trade also exists. Simple family system is the basic norm although extended family system is also followed by some. Cross cousin marriage is almost a common factor. Certain tribal groups have stratified society. Chieftainship is prevalent among some, while others prefer to be ruled by a village council. Though a large number of them was brought under the orbit of institutionalised religion like Buddhism, Hinduism (both Vaishnavism and Brahmanical) and Christianity, yet many still practice traditional religion based on magico-religious practices. Most of the festivals are celebrated by them centering round agricultural activities.

Many tribal groups of the region cannot be considered as fixed or static category as tribe - caste transformations in some areas have been in operation till very recent times. However, very recently a tendency of revivification and consolidation of traditional awareness has come in this process. Ethnic tensions resulting from economic and cultural imbalances between tribes and others are also discernible here. Of late, tremendous upsurge of primordial sentiments in the form of 'tribal movement' and 'insurgency' have also been noticed. The boundaries of several tribal communities are no longer well defined. If some tribes live in the remote inaccessible rugged and hostile regions, where linkages with wider society were non existant, on the other hand many others since historical times have been living in close proximity to and have maintained close socio-political contact with the non-tribal people of neighbouring area. During freedom struggle score of North East tribes join the nationalist movement. Many tribes live on international boundaries and share ethnic and cultural affinities with other people accross the frontier.

The history of tribal studies in North East India is quite old. There were works reported mainly by British officers, travellers, missionaries, etc., which appears from the second quarter of the last century. Most of these studies however, suffer from personal bias and other methodological grounds. Even today, empirical studies on the various tribal people of North East India surprisingly remain as rarity. No serious attempt has yet been made to make the available basic information about the tribal groups of the region upto date and recording of new information about hitherto least known groups. During the last few decades there have been a renewed academic interest on tribal studies based on authentic researches by few social scientists. The repository is still insufficient to elicit any clear socio-cultural or historical picture of the region.

The present volume is an compilation of work to combine the studies and analysis of celebrated anthropologists, sociologists, political scientists, administrators on the tribes of North East India. The scholars who have contributed these articles have long standing experience with tribal situation of North East India.

As the title of the book suggests, it encompasses a wide range of tribal panorama of North East India. The papers which follow are undoubtedly unique in their own way and do refer to the broad canvass of the compilation in one way or another.

The book opens with an article by Prof. R.K.Kar, who

introduces in a nutshell the whole canvass of the book and lessens the burden of the editor from writing a separate introduction. A brief description has been given for some important tribal groups of each of the north eastern states. The discourse have been delimited to the ethnological, philosophical, linguistic, mythological and historical aspects of the population with special emphasis on tracing the origin and affinity of the different groups of people. In next article, Prof. B. Pakem discussed in details the constraints in the application of tribal research findings in North East India in planning, development and administration and the role of social scientists. He also critically reviewed and assessed the position of social policy research to the solution of contemporary social problems and the amelioration of the social ills.

In one article, Prof. S.N. Ratha, deals with the aboriginals of Arunachal Pradesh in a very interesting way. Another is the work of Dr. J. Sarkar who deals with further descriptive account of the society and culture of tribals of Arunachal Pradesh and presents exhaustive picture of the life, society and culture change among these tribes.

Tribal ethnography is the prime concern in anthropology. It is fitting that two articles in this volume in essence an ethnographic account, one on the Sonowal of Assam (by K. Barua) and the other on the Jamatia of Tripura (by D. Mandal). Both the authors make a careful observation and truthful reporting of social structure, kinship, clan, phratry; ceremonies relating to birth, marriage, and death; different social strata; faith and superstition etc., in detail.

The world view, in essence, is a set of inferences or assumptions that the people derive or make about their own world and the world around them as well as other people. The concept of world around the Lisu tribe of Arunachal Pradesh and as they conceive it, is from the pen of Dr. A. Maitra who has dealt with the topic in detail.

The existence of age old institutions of Chieftainship among the Noctes and Wanchos of Arunachal Pradesh and its continuity and change in the event of the introduction of the Statutory Panchayat System is meticulously described by Dr. P.C. Dutta. Dr. D. K.

Duarah's article on Apatani kinship system is an important contribution to a hitherto unstudied virgin area. Based on empirical data, the concept and cause of disease, the indigenous method of treatment and health practices including documentation of medicinal herbs and application of animal items in folk medicine with particular reference to the Idu Mishmis of Arunachal Pradesh have been portrayed by Dr. S. S. Duttachoudhury and Dr. G.C. Ghosh.

The economy of the Karbi tribe of Assam is the subject matter of Dr. B.K. Medhi. Under the economic condition, the author discusses agriculture, shifting *(jhum)* cultivation, animal husbandry, sericulture and the various other professions of the people. The system of land management, pattern of ownership and also the mechanism of production vary from one tribal community to another. Dr. B.N. Bordoloi's study in this context present in the framework of nature-land-man relations, its continuity and change among the hill tribes of Assam in general and Zeme Naga in particular. Dr. T. K. Bhattacharjee has attempted to study the problems of land alienation with particular reference to hill tribes of Assam. Special provision of Sixth Schedule, Rules and Regulations and the role of District Council to safeguard the interest of the tribals thereon are carefully assessed and stated very clearly through his articles.

Few contributions in the volume deal with the demographic aspects such as index of selection intensity among the matrilinial Pnar tribe of Meghalaya (by M. Banerjee, D. Choudhury, D. Adak), dermatoglyphic features of the Lakher (Mara) tribes of Mizoram (by N.N. Sengupta), morpho-genetic characters among the Mao and Maram Naga of Manipur (by M. Mani Babu). One essay having bearing on micro-evolutionary dynamics among the Deoris of Assam is by Dr. S. Sengupta and H.B. Chetry, where a comparative study of different segments of the tribe has been attempted.

Continuity and change in the traditional way of life among the Naga community is also reflected in two thought provoking articles. The process of cultural fusion and fission that are going on among the Chakhesang, Pochury, Zeliangrong and Yimchunger Naga for political power and economic benefit is highlighted by Dr. N. Saha and Dr. S.S. Mishra through their paper. Dr. J.K.K. Saikia has dealt in her article with the Angami Naga tribe and their religions in past and present. Their conversion to Christianity and its impact on socio-economic and cultural life of the tribe has been examined.

Dr. R.P. Athparia through his article has shown the political institutions of the Chakma, a numerically small tribe of North East India. He examines how the political institutions in them took shape in the course of history.

North East India is a region where the social scientists investigate not only the lives and behaviour of tribal communities but also the tensions and conflicts prevailing among various ethnic groups. Studies in tribal ethnicity and identity in last two decades are increasingly becoming important in several states in North East India, where numerous tribal communities have made their homeland. In the concluding article, Dr. J. Ganchoudhury attempts to examine the dynamics of ethnicity and identity orientation among tribal populations in the states of Tripura in North East India.

Obviously, the present treatise do not claim or aspire even to cover the whole gamut of bio-cultural perspective of North East Indian tribes within its limited space. It touches upon only some important segments of the vast and varied area of the canvass. I am well aware of the lapse and lacunae the present compilation contains. It is not free from the thematic inconsistency with regard to various states of North East India. The reason, the present compilation cannot be made comprehensive and presented as a volume of assorted research articles because it proved impossible for a number of would be contributors to meet the deadline set.

I personally owe a debt of profound gratitude to all those scholarly contributors for so kindly responding to my request and readily contributed to this book through their articles. A few articles included in this volume were originally published in various journals. However, they have been modified or expanded for the present publication. I would like to thank the editor and publisher of these journals for permitting me to include these articles in this volume.

I also take this opportunity to express my deep appreciation to my wife Kaveeta and my sons Sushruta and Samrat for their unlimited confidence, tolerance and encouragement; to my nephew

Caesar Sengupta for cartographic works ; to Mrs. Neelanjana Barua for her efforts to prepare the typescript ; to my research students for secretarial assistance rendered by them. My thanks are also due to Messrs M.N. Dutta and Shovan Sengupta and Mrs. Priti Sengupta for their kind help in my academic persuit. Before I close down my pen, I must thank Gyan Publishing House, New Delhi for undertaking its publication expeditiously. They really deserve my special appreciation.

My endeavour will be rewarded if the book proves to be informative and useful, and arouse interest to scholars and researchers as well as administrators and policy makers.

Department of Anthropology SARTHAK SENGUPTA
Dibrugarh University
Dibrugarh, Assam

Contents

List of Contributors

1. Dr. Dipak Kumar Adak
Department of Anthropology
Gauhati University
Gopinath Bordoloi Nagar
Guwahati, Assam, 781 014

2. Dr. Rajendra Prasad Athparia
Anthropological Survey of India
North East Regional Centre
Shillong, Meghalaya, 793001

3. Ms. Mrinmayi Banerji,
Anthropological Survey of India
North East Regional Centre
Shillong, Meghalaya, 793 001

Sri Kalyan Baruah
Department of Anthropology
Dudhnoi College
Dudhnoi, Goalpara, Assam, 783 124

5. Dr. Tanmay Bhattacharjee
Department of Political Science
Haflong Government College
North Cachar, Assam, 788 819

6. Dr. B.N. Bordoloi
Director,
Assam Institute of Research for Tribals
and Scheduled Castes Guwahati, Assam, 781 022

7. Sri Harka Bahadur Chetry
Department of Anthropology
Dibrugarh University
Dibrugarh, Assam, 786 004

8. Dr. Dipesh Choudhury
Anthropological Survey of India
North East Regional Centre
Shillong, Meghalaya, 793 001

9. Dr. S. S. Datta Chaudhury
Anthropological Survey of India
Indian Museum
27, Jawaharlal Nehru Road
Calcutta, West Bengal, 700 016

10. Dr. Dwijendra Kumar Duarah
Assistant Director (Cultural)
Directorate of Research
Government of Arunachal Pradesh
Itanagar, Arunachal Pradesh, 791 111

11. Dr. Parul Ch. Dutta
Director
Directorate of Research

Government of Arunachal Pradesh
Itanagar, Arunachal Pradesh, 791 111

12. Dr. Jagdish Ganchaudhury
Department of Political Science
Bir Bikram Evening College
Government of Tripura
Agartala, Tripura, 799 004

13. Dr. Guru Charan Ghosh
Anthropological Survey of India
Indian Museum 27, Jawaharlal Nehru Road
Calcutta, West Bengal, 700 016

14. Professor Dr. R. K. Kar
Department of Anthropology
Dibrugarh University
Dibrugarh, Assam, 786 004

15. Dr. Asim Maitra
Anthropological Survey of India
Indian Museum
27, Jawaharlal Nehru Road
Calcutta, West Bengal, 700 016

16. Dr. Debabrata Mandal
Anthropological Survey of India
Indian Museum
27, Jawaharlal Nehru Road
Calcutta, West Bengal, 700 016

17. Shri Mayanglambam Manibabu
Department of Anthropology
Manipur University
Canchipur, Manipur

18. Dr. Birinchi Kumar Medhi
Department of Anthropology
Guhati University
Gopinath Bordoloi Nagar
Guwahati, Assam, 781 014

19. Dr. Sudhanshu Sekhar Mishra
North Eastern Institute of Anthropological Research
Moimoon Mahal, Arboothnot Road
Shillong, Meghalaya, 793 003

20. Professor Dr. B. Pakem
Vice Chancellor
North Eastern Hill University
Shillong, Meghalaya, 793 001

21. Professor, Dr. Satya Narayan Ratha
Department of Anthropology and Sociology
Sambalpur University
Jyoti Vihar, Burla
Sambalpur, Orissa, 768 019

22. Dr. Nareswar Saha
Anthropological Survey of India
North East Regional Centre
Shillong, Meghalaya, 793 001

23. Dr. Jogamaya K.K. Saikia
Department of Humanities
Regional Engineering College
Silchar, Assam, 788 010

24. Dr. Jayanta Sarkar
Anthropological Survey of India
Indian Museum
27, Jawaharlal Nehru Road
Calcutta, West Bengal, 700 016

25. Shri Nipendra Nath Sengupta
Anthropological Survey of India
North East Regional Centre
Shillong, Meghalaya, 793 001

26. Dr. Sarthak Sengupta
Department of Anthropology
Dibrugarh University
Dibrugarh, Assam, 786 004

1

The Tribes of North-East India : An Overview

R.K. KAR

The Civilization of India is the joint creation of her diverse peoples; Arynan, Dravidian, Austric (Kol) and Mongoloid.

Rabindra Nath Tagore, in one of his great poems *Bharat-tirtha* ('The Sacred Waters of India') has sung of India as the Ocean where Humanity in all its diversity has merged and united. The poem goes as :

> *Keha nahi jane, kar ahwane, kato manusher dhara durvara srote elo kotha ha' te samudre ha' lo hara hethay Aryya, hetha Anaryya, hethay Dravida, Chin Saka-Huna-dal Pathan-Mogal ek dehe ha' lo lin Paschim aji khuliyache dwar, setha ha' te sabe ane upahar dibe ar nibe, milabe milibe, jabe naphire ei Bharater maha-manaver sagara-tire.*

In the poem he says, "No one knows at whose call so many streams of men flowed in resistless tides from places unknown and were lost in one sea; here the Aryan and non-Aryan, the Dravidian, Chinese, the bands of the Sakas and Hunas, and the Pathan and Mughal have become combined in one body. The door to the West has also been opened, and they bring presents from there : they will give and they will take, they will unite and be united, and will never go away, -in this ocean shore of the Great Humanity of Bharata or India".

The poem, in noble poetic language sums up the main trend of India's history in the past and of India's destiny in the future-how there has been a synthesis of races and cultures in the past leading to the creation and characterization of a composite Indian people and a composite Indian civilisation, diverse in its origin but united in its ideals and aspirations-ideals and aspirations which are acceptable to all mankind; and how India looks forward to a still greater unification of all mankind, both within her shores and outside (Chatterji, 1974 : 1).

As a matter of fact, from time immemorial peoples of different races and languages and cultures have come to India, and in course of time have settled down here for a peaceful comingling and cultural as well as racial fusion with their predecessors in the land.

North-east India is not an exception to this process. North-East India is commonly conceived of as the land of seven sister states, namely Assam, Meghalaya, Arunachal Pradesh, Nagaland, Manipur, Mizoram and Tripura. The land is considered by many scholars as a clultural corridor between India and South East Asia and has a tremendous strategical importance, not only because of its geography but also because of its history, demography and culture.

According to 1991 census, the total population of the region is around 31.4 million who are distributed over an area of around 2.6 lakh sq. km.

North East India Provides shelter to numerous populations of various ethnic affiliations having different social structures and cultural heritages. There is a rich assembly of tribal cultures and communities in this rugged expanse of the eastern Himalayas. All told there, are upwards of 130 major tribal groups in North-Eastern India, including the few inhabiting the plains areas. In other words, one third of the total number of listed tribes for the whole of India are to be found in this region (Table 1).

The ethnic affinities among population groups can be studied at various levels. At the broadest level, the whole mankind can be grouped into three or four categories like Caucasoids, Mongoloids and Negroids etc. On the other hand one can attempt to see differences between sub-groups of a small tribe at micro-level, these being caused because of relative isolation from one another. The affinities can be observed on the basis of a number of criteria. For example, (i) biological differences (ii) variations in cultural patterns (iii) linguistic similarities and (iv) geographical location. Besides, history and mythology are also important factors in discussing the origin and unity of human groups. History, however, was unknown to the early inhabitants of North East India. It started only with the Ahom invasion in 1228 A.D. Earlier periods can be reconstructed from a few ancient inscriptions, from the observation of a Chinese traveller, and some dubious and fragmentary references in the *Mahabharat,* and in the *Puranas* and *Tantras* and other similar records. Some general indications regarding the ancient movements of the people, however can be suggested by philological and ethnographical considerations.

From ethnic point of view the people of North East India may conveniently be divided into two broad groups : the 'Indid' and the 'Mongoloid'. 'Indid' group mostly comprises the Hindu castes and the Muslims, who may be considered as Caucasic in origin, while the 'Mongoloid' group includes the various tribes, both hill and plains tribes and also other Mongoloid populations that have not been referred to as tribes. Prior to these two ethnic groups, representatives of another ethnic group called the Australoid also came to this region. Perhaps the Mongoloid groups have completely absorbed this conjecturable autocthonous population of this region. The Vedic Aryans could also recognize these two types whom they referred to as the *Nisadas, Sabaras, Pulindas* (for the Australoids) and *Kiratas* (for the Mongoloids).

North-western China between the headwaters of Hoang Ho and the Yang-taze Kiang rivers is supposed to be the original homeland of the Mongoloid populations, wherefrom they migrated southward and west-ward during the pre-historic time. Migration took place in succession. But, it appears that certain large scale movements started in the early part of the first millennium B.C. First they moved south-ward to reach north of Burma where they bifurcated; one group moved further south and came down to Burma and then to South-east Asia, while the other moved towards the Brahmaputra valley. One section, however, migrated towards west following the sub-Himalayan tract to reach Nepal and other areas.

It is generally agreed that the Mongoloids, mentioned as the *Kiratas* in ancient Sanskrit literatures of India, once occupied practically the whole of the north-eastern region. It has, for instance been surmised that long ago one section of the Indo-Mongoloids, namely, the Bodo-speakers spread over the whole of the Brahmaputra valley. North Bengal as well as East Bengal (now Bangladesh) giving rise to various groups whom we know to-day as Bodo-Kachari, Garo, Hajong, Tripuri, etc. (Chaterjee, 1951 : 27-28). The diverse Mongoloid groups which eventually settled down in different habitats and ecological settings of the north-eastern region thus crystallised into discrete entities that we call tribes today.

It has been noted earlier that the non-tribal plains-men of North-East India are mostly Caucasoid origin. But, because of prolonged interaction with neighbouring Mongoloid populations through inter-marriages and assimilation, particularly with those who have been living in the plains and in the adjoining areas, Mongoloid features are not uncommon among them. Similarly, it is no wonder that certain Caucasoid ethnic strains have also entered into the tribal population of North East India.

In the present paper discussions have conveniently been confined mainly to the Mongoloid tribal population of the region. Further, the discourse has been delimited to the ethnological, philological, linguistic, mithological and historical aspects of the populations, Biological variations and the process of micro-evolution operating on various groups have not been brought within the purview of the discussion. Relative emphasis, in the paper has been laid on tracing the origin and affinity of the different groups of people.

The Mongoloids are characterised by yellow or yellow- brown skin and wavy and coarse head hair. Their eyes are black or dark-brown in colour. The eye-slit is oblique. One of the typical characteristics of the Mongoloid is the presence of Mongolian fold in their eyes. Their face is broad and zygomatic arches are very prominent. Another important feature is scanty growth of facial and body hairs.

The Indo-Mongoloids of North East India speak different languages of Sino-Tibetan linguistic group. This group of languages has been divided into two broad branches-Tibeto-Burman and Siamese-Chinese. The Siamese-Chinese branch includes in it Siamese, and its connected speeches or dialects like *Davi* or *Thai*. The Ahom, Khamti, Khamyang, Aiton, Phakial, Turung, etc., living in different parts of North-East India speak languages belonging to this *Thai* sub-division. The other Indo-Mongoloids of North-East India except the Khasi and the Pnar, speak languages of Tibeto-Burman branch. One of the sub-divisions of the Tibeto-Burman is North-Assam groups of languages spoken by the tribes of Arunachal and some parts of Assam. These tribes are Aka, Adi, Mishing, Nishi, Mishmi, etc. Another sub-division of Tibeto-Burman is formed by Assam Burma group, which includes the speeches of North and East Bengal, Assam and Burma. These include (i) the Bodo speeches-Bodo, Mech, Rabha, Garo, Kachari, Tipra and few more, (ii) the Naga dialects-Ao, Angami, Sema, Tangkhul, Sangtam, Konyak, Lotha, Mao and Kabui, etc., (iii) the Kuki Chin speeches of Manipur, Tripura and Mizoram, the most important of which is Meitei or Manipur which is quite an advanced literary speech.

Linguistically, the Khasi with their sub-division stand apart from other tribes of North-East India, because they speak a dialect of the Mon-Khmer linguistic group which belongs to Austro-Asiatic language family. Thus, it is interesting to note that the Austric speaking Khasi are living in an isolated pocket encircled by peoples who speak Tibeto-Burman languages.

The Mongoloid population of North-East India may conveniently be grouped under following categories : (i) Arunachal tribes,

(ii) Bodos, (iii) Khasis, (iv) Lushai-Kukis, (v) Nagas, and (vi) Others. This grouping has been done on the basis of the other factor like linguistic affinity, cultural similarity and common territory.

Arunachal Pradesh provides shelter to a large number of Mongoloid tribes. Central Arunachal tribes inhabiting eastern Kameng, Subansiri, Siang and Lohit districts form one broad ethnic groups. These are Aka, Nishi, Tagin, Hill Miri, Apatani, Adi and Mishmi. The Mishing of Assam plains are akin to this group. The Monpa and Sherdukpen of western Arunachal Pradesh are close to Tibetan and Bhutanese. The Nocte and Wancho of eastern Arunachal show similarities with the Naga. Some Shan tribes, e.g., the Khamti are found in the eastern part.

The tribes of Arunachal Pradesh are believed to have come from the North, i.e., the Tibetan region, and North-East. With regard to their movement in that region, different groups, however, nourish different stories. One legend, e.g., tells that the Nishi and the Mishings are descendants of two brothers. The Nishi preferred to live in the hills while the Mishing came down to settle in the river valleys. One section of the Mishing, called the Hill Miri, however, live in the hills and they are very much akin to the Nishi. The tribes of Tirap district, more particularly the Nocte and Wancho appear to have migrated to the region not from north but from east and south east.

The Bodos were the first among Tibeto-Burman speakers to enter this region. They may perhaps be described as the aborigines, or the earliest known inhabitants of Assam. They were probably the most important section of the Indo- Mongoloid people in Eastern India. Once they settled and ruled over the entire Brahmaputra valley and spread in the west up to North Bengal, and in the south they occupied Cachar, Sylhet and Mymensingh districts. They are undoubtedly of trans-Himalayan origin, but it is uncertain by what route and stages they reached the valley (Baines 1976 : 128). It is generally agreed that the home of these Tibeto-Burman speakers was the north west China from where they moved south wards to enter North East India and hills and valleys of South East Asia.

Certain legends are prevalent among some of the Bodo tribes. Playfair (1909) has elaborately dealt with the migratory routes of the Garo from their ancestral home land Tibet to their present habitat Garo hills. The Rabhas also maintain legendary stories about their migration. Das (1960) reports that the ancestors of the Rabha tribe migrated from the sub-Himalayan region; north of Tezpur towards the Brahmaputra valley.

Thus, the traditional stories prevalent among the Garo and the Rabha point to Tibet or eastern sub-Himalayan region, as their ancestral home. Playfair analysed certain cultural elements found among the Garo which confirm traditional link between the Garo and their ancestors in the Tibetan region.

It has been noted earlier that the people from those regions come to north-eastern India not in one migration but in successive waves. One such migration probably brought the Kacharis to North East India. Endle (1911) is also of the opinion that the original home of the Kacharis is Tibet and China.

Taking Brahmaputra as the dividing line, the Bodo groups may be divided into two divisions : northern and southern. In the legends of the Garo and the Rabha we find that the ancestors of the Bodo crossed Brahmaputra to reach its southern bank. The Garos occupy the southern bank. A section of the population migrated further south towards east to take the name of Dimasa. Another group moved further south-west to reach Tripura and the adjoining areas where they are referred to as Hill Tripura. Still another group settled in Nowgong district (Assam) and are known as Tiwa (Lalung).

In the eastern Assam we come across some sections of the Kachari like Sonowal, Jharua and Thengal who were brought there by the eastward expansion of the Kachari. It is believed that all the ancestors of the Bodo did not cross the Brahmaputra. This is supported by some legends also. Some of the Kachari, Rabha, Mech and Koch, etc. were left behind. These groups at present occupy different regions of the northern bank of Brahmaputra.

The Khasis belong to Mon-khmer linguistic group. The available information suggests their migration from south east Asia. They might belong to a wave of Austric speakers, who initially migrated towards east and intermingled with the Mongoloid population of south Chinese area. These people are Mongoloid but have retained the austric speech. There are some tribes in Burma, Thailand and Kampuchia who share these characteristics with Khasis. On the other hand some tribes of Western and Central Himalayas like the Kinnaura and Limbu have elements of austric speech in their dialects. These might be the remnants of the austric speakers, who once inhabited the the vast areas of the sub-continent (Chaterjee, 1951).

With regard to the origin and migration of the Khasis, Das (1978) has suggested two possibilities. One is that they are an Australoid population speaking austric language but have undergone remarkable changes in physical features, because of strong intrusive Mongoloid strains. The other possibility is that the Khasis are Mongoloid. They came down from the same area of dispersion of the Tibeto-Burman speakers. But they adopted austric language, most probably while they were in northern Burma from where they migrated to their present habitat. Das (1978) further opines that the Khasis are the earliest settlers in this part of the country. It may be relevantly noted here that Endle (1911) and others consider Kacharis as the original settlers in North East India.

In the southern Manipur and Mizoram we encounter Lushai-Kuki tribes, which are closer to Chin and Burma. The Meithei of Manipur valley show intermediate characteristic between the Naga and the Lushai-Kuki. They are however, the dominating people of Manipur. Some Kuki-Chin tribes like the Aimol, Hmar, Paite, Thado and Vaipheis and also Naga tribe like the Kabui, besides other small populations live in the State of Manipur.

The Lushai-Kuki also came from north east and south east. In this connection it may be noted that one branch of the ancestral Tibeto Burman group migrated southward to reach as far as south east Asia. Some sections of these migrants perhaps are the ancestors of the Naga and the Lushai Kuki tribes. Perhaps the Naga came earlier. They were followed by the Lushai-Kuki.

The Naga is a generic name for a group of tribes inhabiting Nagaland, northern Manipur and bordering districts of Assam and Arunachal Pradesh. The various Naga groups include Ao, Angami, Sema, Konyak, Lotha, Phom, Chang, Rengma, and others. The heterogenity among the Nagas may be because of prolonged in-breeding and lack of intermixture within the Naga group of tribes.

All the Naga tribes have legends which refer to their movements in North East India. In the monographs written on various groups, these legends have been incorportated by respective author. Taking into consideration all the Naga tribes as a whole, it may perhaps be said that the Naga came to this region from north-east, east and south-east. Oliver (1958) maintains, "Though they trace their ancestry from north-west China and north-east Tibet, but seem to have reached their present habitat by the southern routes,driven by Lushai-Kuki tribes".

The most numerically dominant original inhabitants of Tripura are the Tripuri (Tippera). Then we find the Chakma. The Magh, another tribe of Tripura are migrants from Burma. The Riangs were originally inhabitants of Mizoram, but now live in Tripura. Besides these tribes some members of the Kuki-Chin group like Purum, Thado, Vaiphei, Paite and Jamatia and also Tankhual Naga who have migrated from the adjoining areas are found in Tripura.

The early history of Tripura is clouded in mystery and romance. The tale is told in the *Rajmala* that gives the story of Tripura kings and their subjects. People (both tribal and non-tribal) from the British India started migrating to Tripura towards the second half of the nineteenth century.

Of the various tribes and clans, only the Durlongs, who came from eastern Burma some three centuries ago via the Mizo Hills and now confined largely to Kailasahar, claim to be indigenous to Tripura. The rest are by and large southern Kukis who migrated to Tripura from Lungleh a couple of centuries back following the large scale invasion of Mizo Hills from tracts in Burma. The Lushais first came to Tripura in 1912 after the terrible Mizoram famine in 1911.

Saigal (1978 : 93) observes that the Tripuris can be subdivided into five sections, namely, Old Tripuris, Deshi Tripuris Riangs, Jamatias and Noatias. The Deshi Tripuris have almost completely submerged their identity with the Bengalis.

There is a story that in the old days the Riangs lived in the Maiyanithlang area of Lushai Hills, bordering on and stretching into the Arakans of Burma. Most probably at that time they spoke in a tongue closely related to the Austro-Asiatic family of languages. In the 14th century they migrated to Chittagong Hill Tracts, and later on to Hill Tipperah (now Tripura).

The Chakmas and the Maghs are all Buddhist. In the oldest book (*Agartara*) of the Chakmas, it is mentioned that the Chakmas came originally from Champaknagar (opinions, however, differ as to whether the place falls in Bihar or Cambodia). About their origin L.G. Loeffler has put forward a theory that the Sak tribe, a small tribe living on the borders of Chittagong Hill Tracts and the Arakans, descended from the same people as the Chakmas (cited in Saigal, *ibid.* : 108). From a linguistic study of the Sak language he concluded that they are related to the Kadu of upper Burma and to the Loi of Manipur. He asserts that during the 15th to 17th century the main group of the Sak population appear to have adopted Bengali culture and language and become Chakmas in the modern sense of the term.

While dwelling back on the people of Assam, the Karbi of the Karbi Anglong district is an interesting tribe in the sense that though they belong to Assam-Burma group of Tibeto-Burman linguistic family they can neither be put under Bodo nor any other linguistic group. Grierson (1904) classed them as an intermediate group between the Bodo and the Western Naga on the basis of language. Again, some others want to suggest that Karbi language shows mixture of Austric and Bodo language, though they undoubtedly belong to Tibeto-Burman linguistic family. According to some scholars the Karbi language has some similarities with certain Naga dialects on the one hand and Lushai-Kuki dialects on the other. Lyall (1881), however, maintained that the Karbis are more akin to the Bodo than the Khasis. Among the Karbis also several traditional stories of migration are in prevalence. It is believed that they also came from the north in one of the waves of migration.

In this context, it may be noted that many of the groups in North East India tend to trace their line of descent from certain mythological heroes of the Hindus. Thus, the Kacharis claim their descent from the marriage of Bhim with Hirimba as described in *Mahabharata*. This suggests an early contact of some of the north-eastern population with Caucasoid people.

It needs be borne in mind that in comparatively recent years as well as in the long past there were movements of different groups from one area to another in this region of the country. In some cases they spread over larger areas, while in other cases they were confined to a circumscribed territory of their own.

Further, contrary to popular notions, the numerous culturally or politically autonomous communities lived in a situation of contact and communication with their neighbouring populations. This is authenticated by the myths and legends of various communities as well as history. Insead of isolation, most of the communities imbibed and absorbed inspirations emanating from many different quarters. This is e.g., exemplified by the fact of adoption of Buddhism of the Tibetan variety by tribes like the Monpa and the Sherdukpen of Western Arunachal Pradesh, and of the South East Asian variety by tribes like the Tai Khampti and the Singpho of the eastern and south-eastern parts of the same State. In the State of Manipur, the evolution of the Meitei society in the Imphal Valley through the forging together of tribal groups of Kuki-Chin linguistic stock provides another example. "In the Assam-Meghalaya region many of the autonomous groups were integrated into the Hindu social order long before the advent of the British and the process continued well into this century" (Bhagabati, 1988 : 4). "One may, for example, find a continum between the interior Hill Garos (a matrilineal tribe of Meghalaya) upto the Hinduised Koch, Hajong or Rajbanshi of the foot hills and the plains" (Sinha, 1967 : XIV).

Until recently, formal acceptance of Hinduism was a common occurrence among many of the Bodo-speaking tribal groups of Assam. In the plains of Assam, infact, the tribal groups such as the Bodo-Kachari, Rabha, Mech, Hojai, Lalung and the Deuri Chutiya had, for centuries, provided the main source of Hindu population, through a process of conversion and subsequent sanskritization. The continums from the tribal base to the Hindu caste and can still be seen in many a cases. For instance, the Hindu Chutiya caste is said to be the consequence of progressive sanskritization of the former Chutiya tribe, whose priestly section, the Deori, still preserves the traditional tribal culture and recognised as a scheduled tribe of the Assam plains (Saikia 1976 : 1-2). An indication of the manner in which indigenous tribesmen were converted to Hinduism and then absorbed into a remarkably open caste system is found in the Census Report of 1891 (Gait, 1892 : 225). Through giving up former habits and customs such as eating pork and other forbidden food and drinking strong liquor, undergoing *prayachit* (atonement) and receiving *saran bhajan* (religious instruction and mode of worship) from a Vaishnavite *Gosai* (preacher), the aboriginals could gain admittance into the Hindu society. In Manipur where Hinduism became the principal religion of the Meiteis by a royal edict in 1705, the inhabitants of a village could be elevated en masse, if the *Raja* so decided (Johnstone, 1896 : 84).

It thus apparent that fission, fusion and diffusion in both racial and cultural fronts, and both micro and macro levels, have since long been in operation in shaping the present population scenario of North East India.

REFERENCES

BAINES, A.,1976. *Ethnography*, Delhi : Concept Publishing Company (First published in 1912).

BHAGABATI, A.C.,1988. Tribal transformation in Assam and North east India : An appraisal of emerging ideological dimensions, *Presidential address, section of Anthropology and Archaeology, Indian Science Congress Association*, 75th Session, Pune.

CHATERJEE, S.K.,1974. *Kirata-Janakriti*, Calcutta : Asiatic Society of Bengal.

DAS, B. M.,1960. *Ethnic affinities of the Rabha*, Department of Publication : Gauhati University.

DAS, B. M.,1978. *Variation in physical characteristics in the Khasi population of North east India*, Gauhati : Dutta Barua and Co.

DAS, B. M.,1984. 'Some aspects of Physical anthropology of the tribes of North east India'. In *The Tribes of North East India*. Edited by S. Karotemprel, Shillong : Vendrame Missiological Institute.

DAS, B. M.,1986. *Asomar Manuh : Projati aru Sanskriti : Eti Dristipat*. (In Assamese), Dibrugarh : Assam College Teachers Association, DHSK College Unit.

DAS, B.M.; P.B. DAS : R. DAS,1980. *A Comparative study of physical anthropology of five mongoloid populations of Assam*, Gauhati : Gauhati University, Department of Anthropology (Mimeographed).

ENDLE, S.,1911. *The Kacharis*, Delhi (reprinted in 1975).

GAIT, E.,1926. *A History of Assam*, Calcutta : Thacker, Spink and Co.

GAIT, E. A.,1892.*Census of India 1891*. Shillong : Assam Secretariat Press.

GRIERSON, G. A. 1904. *Linguistic Survey of India*, Calcutta.

JASWAL, I.J.S.,1984. 'Tribes of North East India : Ethnic and Population Aspects'. In *The Tribes of North East India*, Edited by S. Karotemprel, Shillong : Vendrame Missiological Institute.

JOHNSTONE, J.,1896. *Manipur and Naga Hills*, (Reprinted in 1971), Delhi : Vikas Publishing House.

KAR, R.K.,1981. The Bodo relationship terms, *The Eastern Anthropologists*, 34,1 : 37-46.

OLIVIER, G.,1958. Physical Anthropology of Nagas of Assam, *Man In India*, 38 : 1-33

PLAYFAIR, A., 1909. *The Garos*, Gauhati (reprinted in 1975).

SAIGAL, O.,1978. *Tripura : Its History and Culture*, Delhi : Concept Publishing Company.

SAIKIA, P. C.,1976. *The Dibongyas*, Delhi : B.R. Publishing Corporation.

SINHA, S.,1967. 'Social integration of the Hill Tribes and the Plainsmen', In *A Common Perspective for North East India*, Edited by R. Mitra and B. Das Gupta, Culcutta Pannalal Das Gupta.

Table 1

Distribution of Some Important Tribes in Different States of North East India

State	*Important tribes*		
I. Arunachal Pradesh	1.	Adi	
		i.	Ashing
		ii.	Bogum
		iii.	Bokar
		iv.	Bori
		v.	Botng
		vi.	Gallong
		vii.	Komkar
		viii.	Karka

State	*Important tribes*
	ix. Lodung
	x. Milang
	xi. Minyong
	xii. Padam
	xiii. Pailibo
	xiv. Pangi
	xv. Pasi
	xvi. Ramo
	xvii. Shimong`
	xviii. Tangam
	2. Aka
	3. Apatani
	4. Bangni
	5. Khamba
	6. Khampti
	7. Khowa
	8. Memba
	9. Miji
	10. Hill Miri
	11. Mishing/Miri
	12. Mishmi
	13. Monpa
	14. Na
	15. Nishi (Dafla)
	16. Nocte
	17. Sherdukpen
	18. Sulung
	19. Singpho
	20. Tagin
	21. Tangsa
	22. Wancho
	23. Yobin (Lisu
	24. Zakhring (Meyor)
II. Assam	*In the autonomous districts :*
	1. Chakma
	2. Dimasa, Kachari
	3. Garo
	4. Hajong
	5. Hmar
	6. Khasi, Jaintia, Synteng, Pnar, War, Bhoi, Lyngngam
	7. Any Kuki Tribes
	8. Lakher
	9. Man (Tai speaking)
	10. Any Mizo (Lushai) tribes
	11. Mikir

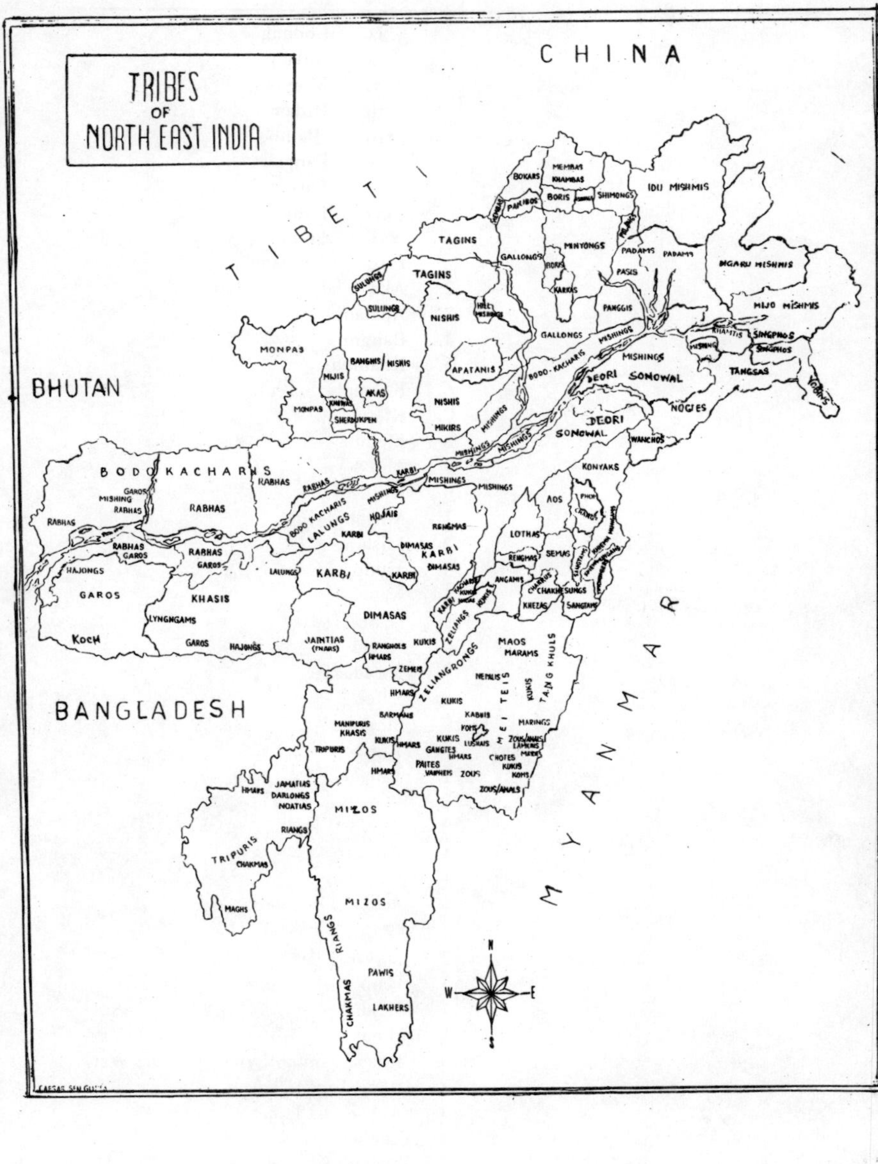
TRIBES
OF
NORTH EAST INDIA
CHINA
TIBET
BHUTAN
BANGLADESH
MYANMAR
MEMBAS
KHAMBAS
BOKARS
BORIS
SHIMONGS
IDU MISHMIS
TAGINS
MINYONGS
GALLONGS
PADAMS
PASIS
DIGARU MISHMIS
MIJU MISHMIS
SULUNGS
NISHIS
PANGGIS
KHAMTIS
SINGPHOS
MONPAS
BANGNIS/NISHIS
APATANIS
BODO-KACHARIS
MISHINGS
DEORI
SONOWAL
TANGSAS
MIJIS
AKAS
SHERDUKPEN
MIKIRS
NOCTES
WANCHOS
KONYAKS
BODO KACHARIS
RABHAS
GAROS
MISHING
KARBI
HOJAIS
RENGMAS
AOS
LALUNGS
DIMASAS
LOTHAS
SEMAS
HAJONGS
KHASIS
ANGAMIS
CHAKHESANGS
KHEZAS
SANGTAMS
LYNGNGAMS
JAINTIAS
(PNARS)
ZELIANGS
ZELIANGRONGS
MAOS
MARAMS
KOCH
RANGHOLS
HMARS
KUKIS
ZEMEIS
NEPALIS
MEITEIS
TANGKHULS
KABUIS
MARINGS
MANIPURIS
BARMANS
TRIPURIS
PAITES
VAIPHEIS
ZOUS
CHOTES
KOMS
ZOUS/AMALS
JAMATIAS
DARLONGS
NOATIAS
MIZOS
RIANGS
CHAKMAS
MAGHS
PAWIS
LAKHERS
N
S
E
W

State	*Important tribes*
	12. Any Naga tribes
	13. Pawi
	14. Syntheng
	In the state of Assam excluding the autonomous districts :
	1. Barmans in Cachar
	2. Boro, Borokachari
	3. Deori
	4. Hojai
	5. Kachari, Sonowal
	6. Lalung (Tiwa)
	7. Mech
	8. Miri (Mishing)
	9. Rabha
III. Manipur	
	1. Aimol
	2. Anal
	3. Angami
	4. Chiru
	5. Chothe (Purum)
	6. Gangte
	7. Hmar
	8. Kabui
	9. Kacha Naga
	10. Koirao
	11. Koireng
	12. Kom
	13. Lamgang
	14. Mao
	15. Maram
	16. Maring
	17. Mizo (Lushai)
	18. Monsang
	19. Moyon
	20. Paite
	21. Ralte
	22. Sema
	23. SimteA
	24. Sahte
	25. Tangkhul
	26. Thadou
	27. Vaiphai
	28. Zou
IV. Meghalaya	
	1. Bhoi
	2. Boro
	3. Chakma

State	*Important tribes*
	4. Dimasa (Kachari)
	5. Garo
	6. Hajong
	7. Hmar
	8. Jaintia
	9. Karbi (Mikir)
	10. Khasi
	11. Koch
	12. Kuki
	13. Lakher
	14. Lyngngam
	15. Man (Tai speaking)
	16. Mizo (Lushai)
	17. Naga
	18. Pawi
	19. Pnar
	20. Rabha, Raba
	21. Synteng
	22. War
V. Mizoram	
	1. Chakma
	2. Dimasa, Kachari
	3. Garo
	4. Hajong
	5. Hmar
	6. Khasi, Jaintia, Synteng, Pnar, War, Bhoi, Lyngngam
	7. Any Kuki tribes :
	i. Biate, Biete
	ii. Chngsan
	iii. Chongloi
	iv. Doungel
	v. Gamalhou
	vi. Gangte
	vii. Guite
	viii. Hanneng
	ix. Haokip, Haupit
	x. Haolai
	xi. Hengna
	xii. Hongsungh
	xiii. Hrangkhwal, Rangkhol
	xiv. Jongbe
	xv. Khawchung
	xvi. Khawathlang, Khothalong
	xvii. Khelma
	xviii. Kholhou

State	*Important tribes*
	xix. Kipgen
	xx. Kuki
	xxi. Lengthang
	xxii. Lhangum
	xxiii. Lhoujem
	xxiv. Lhouvun
	xxv. Lupheng
	xxvi. Mangjel
	xxvii. Misao
	xxviii. Riang]
	xxix. Sairhem
	xxx. Selnam
	xxxi. Singson
	xxxii. Sitlhou
	xxxiii. Sukte
	xxxiv. Thado
	xxxv. Thangngeu
	xxxvi. Uibuh
	xxxvii. Vaiphei
	8. Lekher
	9. Man (Tai speaking)
	10. Any Mizo (Lushai) tribe
	11. Karbi
	12. Any Naga tribe
	13. Pawi
VI. Nagaland	
	1. Adi
	2. Aka
	3. Dimasa (Kachari)
	4. Galong
	5. Garo
	6. Khasi and Jaintia
	7. Khowa
	8. Kuki
	9. Karbi (Mikir)
	10. Mizo
	11. Any Naga tribe
	i. Ao
	ii. Angami
	iii. Chakhesang
	iv. Chang
	v. Chiru
	vi. Khiemnungan
	vii. Konyak
	viii. Lotha

State	*Important tribes*
	ix. Makwari
	x. Phom
	xi. Rengma
	xii. Sangtam
	xiii. Sema
	xiv. Tikhir
	xv. Yimchungre
	xvi. Zeliang
	12. Synteng
	13. Momba
VII. Tripura	
	1. Bhil
	2. Bhutiya
	3. Chaimal
	4. Chakma
	5. Garo
	6. Halam
	7. Jamatia
	8. Khasia
	9. Kuki tribes
	10. Lepcha
	11. Lushai
	12. Magh/Mog
	13. Munda
	14. Noatia
	15. Orang/Oraon
	16. Riang
	17. Santal
	18. Tripura, Tripuri or Tippera
	19. Uchai/Ochoi

2

Application of Results of Tribal-Research Studies in North-East India in Planning, Development and Administration

B. PAKEM

Tribal research in North East India was first conducted by British administrators, missionaries, soldiers, travellers and businessmen. But most of these studies and researches were in the field of anthropology. A number of monographs and official reports on the various tribes and communities of the region were written by them. Such research studies, while including the social, economic, political and cultural aspects of the society had left some important questions unanswered. The question of social responsibility of the monographs and official reports had been raised because it is quite natural for

Reproduced by the permission of the authority of the Journal of North-East India Council for Social Science Research, Volume 10, Number 2, 1986, pp. 1-11.

colonial admintrators and their ilk who did not have any such social responsibility to the various problems of North East India. Whatever responsibility that they might have was mainly administrative responsibility. That is, they worked in the interest of colonial administration only. In some cases, there had been even personal bias in their study and research.

After independence, a spurt of developmental activities was carried on by the Government of Free India. Without much caring for proper research, huge amount of expenditures had been made. The result was that the direction of little development was not commensurate with huge investment. The findings of the Commission on Scheduled Castes and Scheduled Tribes was quite significant in this connection. It had rightly observed that the welfare approach of the 1950s was exercised through the development schemes of the Five Year Plans, the concept of community development and the democratic decentralisation under the Panchayati Raj but failed to alleviate the Socio-economic and political problems of the Indian tribal people in general and of the hill people of North East India in patrticular. While the above attempts are quite alright, nwhat the hill people are really interested in is not so much about the Five Year Plans. Community Development, or Panchayati Raj as in the solution of their problems relating to rights in land, rights in forests, the doing away with exploitation by money-lenders, the evil effects of industrialisation, health, education and communication on the tribal life.

The first flush of enthusiasm after independence equally affected the generations of scholars, researchers, and investigators. While they are quite aware of their social responsibility of the fierce competition between the traditional society and the modern society made them more baffled as much as the tribal people of the region themselves. The onset of a transitional period between traditions and modernisation has further aggravated the problems. In such a situation researchers, scholars and investigators with all the scientific tools of research at their command may not really come nearer the goal of scientific truth. In the absence of scientific truth, the question of application of results of research studies in planning, development and administration does not simply arise.

A researcher's primary goal is to explore and gain understanding of human behaviour and social life. This understanding helps all concerned to gain not only an understanding of but also a greater control over human behaviour and social life. The knowledge thus gained further helps in the construction of a theory or in the practice of an art. Research therefore, helps us to pursue both knowledge for knowledge sake called pure or basic research and knowledge in the betterment of human destiny called applied or practical research.

Earlier we have referred to the question of social responsibility in research. It is in the field of applied or practical research that the question of social responsibility of the scholars, researchers and investigators studying social, economic and political problems of North East India is more keenly felt. If the earlier researchers of the British period on North East India with limited empirical social research could contribute much to the advantage of colonial administration as well as to the world of knowledge, there is no doubt that our present researchers and investigators can do much in that we have more access to modern scientific tools, concepts and theories.

A scientific study, in the last analysis, is simply a means to an end. The end is to solve a problem whether practical, theoretical or methodological. In the present study it is the solution of a practical problem that lies uppermost in our mind. We can accomplish this by means of both scientific method which is logical and scientific technique which is statistical as well as by philosophical scientific endeavour. In addition to training and experience in the arts and science of research, all researchers and investigators in North East India require proper personal conduct and value in their relationships with informants. This is what is called "sensitivity to human relations" on the part of researchers and investigators.

This is very important in the context of North East India. The British administrators and scholars managed to do without it a century ago. Today we have to face a distant relationship between researchers and the people in the region because of research activities devoid of sensitivity to human relations. That is why, sometimes, we have to question the validity of research findings of the British period, apparently based on impressionistic views. For example, their census figures require a further research into the occurrence and relationships of certain facts behind their figures. After all facts and figures do not speak for themselves. They have to be analysed and interpreted. In thus analysing and interpreting we will gain more insight and knowledge if we penetrate into the secret of their occurrence and their relationships. Today a lot of acrimonious debate about the question of similarities or differences between North East India and the rest of the country had been raised in the academic platform precisely for the same reason of lack of sensitivity to human relations in North East India on the part of the researchers and investigators. Other issues like the side-stream joining the main-stream or the question of provincial nationalism being branded as sub-nationalism, or as outright anti-nationalism had touched the sentiments of the people of the region. Or talk about integration with all its ramifications, the same end result ensues. Even development activities have been questioned and put them under searching querries by the sons of the soil : how far developmental activities help in building up the sense of the pride and participation of the hill people of the region.

Social policy research, therefore, maintains that the social scientists should apply their work to the solution of contemporary social problems and the amelioration of the social ills. But this role is a controversial one. Pure and basic researchers hold that the primary role of social science is the persue of knowledge in discovering and verifying the principles of social behaviour which may not be immediately useful in programmes for improvement of social life and social relations. On the other hand, whether by desire or by force of circumstances considerable social research activity is interwined with efforts to identify, understand, and apply research findings in relation with planning, development and administration.

An attempt has been made to define social policy research by Freeman and Sherwood (1968) in their book *'Social Research and Social Policy'*. Social policy research refers to th.e u'se of meth.ods and findings of social research in the development and carrying out of communal efforts to improve social and physical environment of the members of the community and to better their psychological and physical lives. Thus social policy research is not different from other types of social investigations either in terms of empirical perspective or research principles and techniques. Social policy research can be distinguished from basic or pure research only in the selection of the problems and the goals of research. In other words, "Social policy research can be thought of as the application of general social research methods under a particular set of circumstances and towards certain specific ends by individuals with training in the social sciences and an orientation towards the solution of social problems".

Social policy research is not so very new. In Western countries, particularly in the United States of America, it began in the 1930s. Since then social sciences, have grown enormously. Traditional activities like teaching and basic research have expanded as much as opportunities for applied research. It is no wonder then that by the 1960s and onwards some social scientists began to demand that members of their respective disciplines take notice of the social policy role. It is in this setting that development of social policy research develops in India.

The different roles of the social policy researchers may take place at four levels. First, the scope of a researcher's involvement in overall policy development which corresponds to the role of comprehensive participation. Second, the scope of involvement may be restricted to some specific parts corresponding to fragmented participation in policy development. Third, the base from which the researcher operates is also an important aspect of the role of a researcher in his intention. Even if his intention is not toward policy development, his work often filters into the policy-making process. This is called "serendepitous participation". Thus, at all levels the different roles of social policy researchers indicate not only a policy-oriented but also an action-oriented research.

Further, like any other scientific enquiry including basic or pure research, social research is subject to the same requisites of tools, crafts and philosophy of scientific endeavours. Social research, therefore, contains three basic functions of scientific enquiry-description, prediction and causal analysis. All the three functions are very important to the accumulation of knowledge in the fields of social relations and social processes. Descriptive science deals with facts, distinction among phenomena and with counting and meaning of facts and phenomena. Definition, observations and classifications are fundamental to descriptive science. There are two basic descriptive tasks-static and dynamic descriptions. On the one hand, static description deals with momentary aspects of phenomena as in the observations of conditions, events characteristics, behaviour and the properties of things at any point of time. On the other, dynamic description deals with changing aspect as in giving the summary or interpretation of a series of two or more static descriptions relating to conditions, events, characteristics, behaviour and the properties of things.

The second function of scientific enquiry deals with prediction. Scientific prediction is made either on the basis of theories which is called deductive prediction or on the basis of observed relationship among variables which is called inductive prediction. In social sciences there has been little progress in deductive prediction through the production of theoretical system. However, various attempts have been made to develop inductive prediction through the collection and analysis of information based on variables that may either be dependent or independent which may again be either quantitative or qualitative.

From this follows the third function of scientific research. That is the function of finding out the possibility of a causal connection between the dependent or independent variables in scientific predictions or the connections caused by co-related variables or some other variables or set of variables. Causal analysis helps us in understanding the linkages among phenomena. True considerable dispute has been caused in social research about social processes and social behaviour cannot come solely from causal experiment but also through a phenomenological explanation of human nature.

The above three functions of research correspond and to three processes of policy development-planning, programme development and implementation, and evaluation. In the planning process an assessment of the empirical situation is required. This assessment may be achieved either from impressionistic views of the policy-maker or from a result of a systematic research enquiry by technically qualified investigators. These qualified investigators are those who have been trained in collecting research informations with some kind of measurement of data through surveys, records, case studies, field investigations and experimental research on social behaviour or social conditions and norms.

The next step in the process of policy development is programme development and execution. This stage refers to the design of specific interventions and emoliorative activities based on informations, analyses, decisions and recommendations produced in the planning phase. It is at this stage that constant use of hypotheses and models are restored to.

The third and final process of policy development is evaluations. It would be poor social policy to plan and execute programmes without any provision for their evaluation. Evaluation provides the basis for the policy-makers decision either to continue, modify, expand or eliminate programmes towards the amelioration of social life. Evaluation consists of two activities, the assessment of how well a programme is carried out an measuring its impact. The first activity is carried out through anthropological or field investigations. And the second activity can be assessed through systematic empirical research either through planned experimental manipulation of events or behaviour or through the systematic behaviour of natural occurrences. In order to design evaluation experiment a knowledge of the target population and the impact model is necessary. Social planners are most dependent upon social researchers for finding out the target population and designing the impact model since the technicalities of evaluation and the conduct of evaluation assessments require the skills and the orientation of the qualified or trained researchers and investigators.

North Eastern India is the region where the social scientists investigate not only the lives and behaviour of tribal communities but also the tensions and conflicts prevailing among various, non-tribal ethnic groups. The impact of development activities of a modern State on these communities and groups as well as on policy - makers themselves constitute yet another field of studies for social scientists. In such a situation the social scientists can fruitfully apply among others the impact model and the target population studies of social research.

However, in India, particularly in North East India, we are facing a number of constraints in applying the results of research findings in the field of planning, development and administration. Myron Weiner (1979) in his study on "Social Science Research and Public Policy in India" pointed out that unless research centres are free from governmental restrictions not much progress could be made in the desired direction.

In India we have different types of social science research centres. First, there are research centres and research institutions called Councils, Institutes, Organisations, Bureaus, Units, Cells, or Directorates within Central or State Governments. These includes Bureaus of Economics and Statistics within Finance or Planning Ministries or Departments, State Councils for Education Research and Training within Education Departments, Tribal Research Institutes of the Home Ministry and the Departments of Education, Agricultural Informations of the Agricultural Ministry and Departments. But these research centres confined their research more in the field of data collection similar to the Anthropological Survey of India rather than the application of results of research studies in policy-making and administration. This is quite natural since their researchers are Government employees with inherent limitations rather than academic researchers with certain amount of academic freedom which is most needed for more objectivity in research.

The second type of research in social sciences has a link with autonomous research institutions like the New Delhi based Indian Institute of Public Administration, National Council for Educational Research and Training, Institute of Applied Man-Power, National Council of Applied Economic Research and Indian Council of Social Science Research. The last named Council encouraged the establishment of regional research institutions. These regional research centres include the Institute of Social and Economic Change (Bangalore), Centre for Development Studies (Trivandrum), Madras Institute of Development Studies (Madras), A.N. Sinha Institute of Social Studies (Patna), Gandhi Institute (Varanasi), Centre for Studies in Social Sciences (Calcutta), Sardar Patel Institute of Economics and Social Research (Ahmedabad), Public Enterprise Institute (Hyderabad) and Giri Institute of Social Sciences (Lucknow). During the last few years serious attempts have also been made to establish one such Centre in Guwahati, Assam. Some older centres like the Tata Institute of Social Sciences (Bombay) and Gokhale

Institute of Politics and Economics (Pune) are collaborating with the Indian Council of Social Science Research, while the centres like Indian Institute of Education (Pune) are revived recently. All these institutes are located outside government departments or ministries. They are more important than government research centres because officials recognised that these institutions are getting financial assistance not only from the Central and State Governments but also from international funding agencies like the Ford Foundations and the U.N.O.

In North East India, however, we have yet to have autonomous research centres as in the rest of the country. A branch of the Indian Council of Social Science Research has been recently set up for the North-Eastern region with its head-quarters located in the North-Eastern Hill University, Shillong. The branch definitely requires more time in order to enable it to function more effectively. The general environment of the University and the temper of academic research in the University seem to have affected the Indian Council of Social Science Research branch in Shillong. Another non-government research institutions, the North East India Council for Social Science Research located in Shillong has no parent body. It has to struggle against heavy odds. But there is hope for a better future for this purely non-government organisations since it is receiving presently certain financial assistance from various State Governments in the region and other resources both local and national. Other autonomous research centres are also growing in the region. With liberal financial assistance from governmental authorities, it is hoped that these institutions will in due course reach the level of other renowned autonomous research centres in the country.

The third category of social science research includes the degree-granting institutions like Colleges or Universities. But many of the Colleges and Universities have not provided an environment conducive to research due mainly to reasons like strikes, factional struggle and ideological struggles perpetrated by political parties or groups. Other inherent weaknesses of these institutions range from influence of older traditions in research, red tapism in getting timely financial assistance and leave for research scholars. Financial procedures for spending research fund are so cumbersome that they constitute yet another source of irritants to scholars who invariably left for other autonomous research centres.

There are two more categories of social science research centres which exist elsewhere in India excepting in North-East India. These are : (i) Private consultative firms that conduct research under contract from private or public sector firms and government departments, and (ii) the scientific and engineering institutions that have attached social science cells or departments. The various State Governments of the North-Eastern region used to depend on these types of firms for arriving at policy decision-making for the setting up of industries or development projects.

Myron Weiner has studied 28 highly selected case studies to show the stages of development of policy research in India. From these case studies we may have a general understanding of the nature of applied research particularly in the tribal areas. For example, in Project Number 2, the National Council of Applied Economic Research (New Delhi) and the Institute of Applied Man-Power Research (New Delhi) examined the employment potential in selected tribal areas. While the National Council for Applied Economic Research contended that the use of tractors and the mechanisation of agriculture generated secondary employment, the Institute of Applied Man-Power Research found that there was manpower shortage in some skilled categories of industries located in the tribal areas as the tribals were not qualified for the posts requiring skills. The result was that there was heavy influx of migrants to capture those posts thereby creating high unemployment rate among local tribals. Applied research would indicate that there was need for training facilities which were then inadequate in the tribal areas, so the local tribals could be absorbed in those posts where skill was required. But the Home Ministry denied the Institute of Applied Man-Power Research the permission to publish the results as findings were "sensitive". The Industries and Labour Departments of North Eastern States and Union Territories would not be far lagging behind the Home Ministry in shelving such results as too sensitive for publication or for application in planning, development and administration.

Again, take Project Number 3 which deals with the delivery of services to tribal areas. This project was conducted by the Institute of Management (Ahmedabad). It aimed at studying the utilisation of expenditures for rural development in a predominantly tribal district of Gujarat. The finding was that 80 percent of the investment was spent for salaries of employees while a meagre 20 percent only was actually spent for developmental activities. The result was that there was little development inspite of multi-crore rupee investment. The Rural Development Department of the Government of Gujarat which had sponsored the Research Programme vehemently disagreed with the findings and had been refused to release the study of publication, leave alone the application of results of such research studies. Whether the governmental authorities of the seven units of North East India would venture to invest money on such research projects is a big question mark.

Next, in Project Number 6, the Operation Research Group (Baroda) conducted research on distribution and use of electricity in rural India. The finding of the study was that the State Electricity Boards applied the same procedures for production, promotion and distribution of electricity for both the rural and urban areas. The result was that such similar procedures for submission of application forms and payment of bills would hit the poeple of the rural areas as they have to cover a longer distance to reach the nearest office of the Electricity Board. It was further found that the income of the people of the rural areas, unlike of those urban areas, fluctuated from month to month. It only revealed that the State Electricity Boards were more interested in production rather than in promotion and distribution of electric power. This is more true in the case of the State Electricity Boards in North Eastern region where the majority of its people are in the rural areas and tribal in character. But what these respective State Electricity Boards would do for the convenience of the tribal and rural people of the region ? Are they ready to apply the results of such research findings to ameliorate the conditions of the very people whom they are to serve ?

Similarly, Project Number 18 also made a study of project developments in the tribal areas. The study was conducted by one of the Tribal Research Institutes for the Home Ministry relating to applied studies that might assist the Government for project developments in tribal areas. The study revealed that the concerned tribal area contained land-holdings which were comparatively large with low density of population and lack of resources for a change from shifting to intensive cultivation. Yet another study revealed that the Home Ministry rejected a proposal from a certain State Government for irrigation projects in a tribal area where the bulk of tribals did not own land and would only marginally benefit from the proposed schemes. How far the State Governments of North East India would risk investing in tribal research when the Home Ministry or any otherCentral Ministry could outright reject tribal development projects submitted by the former ?

Finally, we may also refer to Project Number 21 which dealt with the relationship between a particular policy or proposed policy and a policy objective or set of objectives. This particular project examined the relationship between the medium of instruction and school dropout rates among the tribal communities. The project was conducted by the State Institute of Education, Maharashtra. The finding of the project was quite significant. Tribal children learned more rapidly when early teaching was given in their tribal mother tongue rather than in Marathi, the regional language. Consequently, the drop-out rates also declined. But before applying the results of such research, an innocent question was raised in the State Assembly about the reversion of the language policy. Immediately, the Chief Minister of Maharashtra terminated the project as it was "Creating misunderstanding". Again we ask, whether in similar situations, the Chief Ministers of North Eastern States would readily depart from the path chalked out by the Chief Minister of Maharashtra? This question is raised because it comes before the question of applying the results of research studies in planning, development and administration in North East India.

The above are some of the cases to show that it was very difficult elsewhere in the country to apply the results of research studies in planning, development and administration. It becomes much more difficult in the case of North East India in view of the fact of lack of research facilities in the region. But since the craze for social policy research is also gaining ground in the country it is only right and proper to consider the following facts.

Public policy, as has been pointed out by Myron Weiner, is made within the framework of a certain political process, Once a public policy is made it is implemented by bureaucrats within the framework of an administrative apparatus having its own narrow political process. This narrow political process of the administrative world at times functions independently and at other times interacts with the broader political process of a given political unit. It is here that a question has been raised whether social scientists, researchers and investigators can fit in with these processes.

So far as the interaction between the social scientists and the bureaucrats is concerned, there has always been a general complaint by the former that research studies are rarely utilised by policy makers. On the other hand, some bureaucrats have politely replied that what they lack is not additional knowledge but additional fund. Other less sophisticated bureaucrats have even bluntly pointed out that social scientists lack experience and as such the results of their findings are not practical in approach and, therefore, cannot be utilised.

The real cause for this state of affairs appears to lie not in the mutual distrust between the academics and the bureaucrats but in the government control over the dissemination of research. Bureaucrats would definitely require and depend on proper research to support their project planning and evaluation but are, at the same time, afraid of critical findings. Therefore, more often than not, bureaucrats depend on research from their own government research units rather than on research units from outside. This has been the general experience in North East India. The end result is that the government has a firm control over such research and in majority of cases refused to apply the results of research findings. Even when a research project is entrusted to units outside the government, the government takes great care to see that "Political risks" be reduced if not altogether eliminated by withholding permission for publication of the results of research findings which tend to be or are "critical" of the government. But there is one pertinent question that bureaucrats and the government have failed to give a satisfactory reply : By restricting the publication of the results of the government sponsored research findings that are either "Critical" or "sensitive" does it mean that the respective State Governments deny the elected representatives and the members of the general public the right of access to studies funded with tax-payers' money ?

What is more serious is that the social scientists are mostly confined to data collection and seldom engaged in policy research. An attempt has been made recently to conduct policy research only in matters relating to economy, management and public administration. Even here as in other fields of social sciences, social scientists have yet to raise querries about some fundamental questions like : Why does a particular policy fail ? What are the alternatives to it ? What are the cost and benefits of such alternatives ? This type of policy research will help generate further fundamental questions on some doubtful but operational concepts like; decentralisation, integrated rural-development, non-formal need based education, semi-feudalism and pilot projects. In social science research one fundamental question will lead to another. The next question then is whether we are aware of comparative public policy research when we try to imitate : China's foot-doctors, Singapore's Housing Programmes, Israel's Land Reclamation and Afforestation Programmes, Taiwan's Family Planning Programmes, or Cuba's Adult Literacy Programmes. After all, every policy made in these countries is based on the context of their social, economic and political conditions. This may be said of North East India also.

We may not have for North East India a model of any plans, projects and programmes from any region of India unless we take into consideration the social, economic and political context of the North Eastern Region. Most of the present day ills in the North Eastern Region are due to sloppy, if not faulty, planning based on wrong analysis and interpretation of data and wrong comparative application of experiments conducted elsewhere in India without the bureaucrats and the government ever willing to accept the brutal facts behind those data and experiments.

Thus it is too premature to expect all concerned in North East India to apply the results of research findings in planning, development and administration in the absence of adequate research facilities in the region. We cannot also always depend on outside research agencies as the process is time consuming and the results of which may become outdated by the time we make an attempt to apply their research findings. At the same time, we are not ready, in North East India, with participatory research either.

It is at this juncture that the region is fortunate in having an agency like the North Eastern Council, which may assume the role of a co-ordinating agency for social scientists, bureaucrats and the government to meet and put their heads together in solving the varied problems of the region. Without entering into a controversy over the role of the North Eastern Council in its advisory functions in matters relating to development and security of the region, at least in the field of policy research it may be expected of its role of a neutral body acting as a cushion against any possible mutual pin-pricks from the world of the academics, the bureaucrats and the government. Through the North Eastern Council we hope to start applying the results of policy research findings in the field of planning, development and administration which had been hitherto neglected by the academics, the bureaucrats and the government due mainly to a communication gap among themselves. Now, let the North Eastern Council bridge the gap by providing adequate research facilities, training facilities, and facilities for publication of policy research findings, and advices to governmental authorities of the region to apply the results of policy research findings with liberal financial assistance from the North Eastern Council.

In addition to the North Eastern Council, we have also other institutions like the North Eastern Hill University, the North Eastern Regional Centre of the Indian Council for Social Science Research, the North East India Council for Social Science Research and other autonomous research agencies in the region which could cater to the needs of the governments of the various units of the region. As a matter of fact a number of research projects had been entrusted to these agencies by Central Ministries like the Directorate of Science and Technology, the Department of Ecology, and even by the U.N. agencies. There is no reason why the State Governments of the region should fight shy of the research facilities offered by these research institutions to enable them to apply results of general and tribal research in planning, development and administration. It is encouraging to see that recently the Government of Meghalaya have entrusted research studies in Integrated Rural Development Programmes to the Department of Economics of the North Eastern Hill University. It is a very good begining indeed. Now, we are waiting only for the application of research findings to set the trend in North East India.

REFERENCES

FREEMAN, H.E. ; C.C. SHERWOOD., 1968. *Social Research and Social Policy*, New Delhi : Prentice-Hall Inc.

WEINER, MYRON., 1979. Social Science Research and Public Policy in India, *Economic and Political Weekly*, XIV, 37-38 : pp. 1579-1587. and pp 1622-1628, 15th and 22nd September, 1979.

3

The Emerging Ethnographic Profiles of the Eastern Himalayas : Notes on Some Tribes of Arunachal Pradesh

S.N. RATHA

I

Arunachal Pradesh, situated on the eastern flanks of the Himalayan range east of Bhutan and north of the Brahmaputra Valley comprising evergreen tropical forests, large river beds, as well as snow-crowned mountains varying in height from 4000 to 23000 ft., cradles the habitations of a large number of tribes of mutually unintelligible languages and distinct ways of life. The climate of the region varies from below freezing point in the winter to over 80° F in summer.

The State covers an area of 83,578 square kilometres and as per 1991 counting, had a population of 8,58,007. This work out to be approximately 10 persons per square kilometres. There are eleven districts in Arunachal Pradesh : Tawang, East Kameng, West Kameng, Upper Subansiri, Lower Subansiri, West Siang, East Siang, Lohit, Dibang Valley, Tirap and Changlang. The administrative and ethnic boundaries do not necessarily coincide, but most tribes are contained within the limits of one district.

II

Ethnographically Arunachal remained one of the least known areas of the world until the early fifties of the present century. The earlier records (Dalton 1872, Lorrain 1910, Dunbar 1915, Cumming 1921, William 1944) are mostly incomplete and superficial. The region was exposed to systematic scientific enquiry with the publication of Professor Haimendorf's ethnographic notes on the tribes of the Subansiri region and *Exploitation in the Eastern Himalayas*' in 1947. Since then there is a steady flow of literature, though our knowledge of Arunachal ethnography is still far from complete. The pioneering works of Elwin (1958a, 1958b, 1959a, 1959b) and those of Haimendorf (1962, 1980, 1982) throw considerable light on the tribal life of the region. Detail information on individual tribes come from the works of Shukla (1959), Sharma (1961), Singh (1962), Srivastava (1962, 1973), Roy (1966), Dutta (1969, 1978), Bhattacharjee (1975), Pandey (1978), Kumar (1978, 1979), Deuri (1982). The Assam Sahitya Sabha brought out a hand book on tribes of Assam, Nagaland and Arunachal Pradesh containing notes on the Aka, Adi, Dafla, Mishing, Nocte, Wanchu, Tangsa, Khampti, Mishimi, Singpho, Apatani, Hill Miri, Tagin, Sherdukpen, Monpa, and some other tribes of Siang and Kameng districts (Bhattacharya, 1962). To these can be added the three volumes of District Gazetteers (Dutta Chowdhury, 1979, 1980, 1981).

The major tribal communities are the Monpas, Sherdukpens, Akas, Khowas, Mijis, Bangnis and Sulungs of Tawang, East and West Kameng Districts; the Nishis, Apatanis, Hill Miris, Tagins and Na of Upper and Lower Subansiri Districts; the Adi groups, Membas and Khambas of East and West Siang Districts; the Mishmi groups, Khamptis, Singphos, Meyors or Zakhrings of Lohit and Dibang Valley Districts and the Noctes, Wançhos, Tangsas and Lisus of Tirap and Changlang Districts. Apart from these, the tribal list of Arunachal Pradesh contains many other tribes with populations, sometimes less than a thousand persons.

There seems to exist a great deal of confusion in the nomenclature of the tribes of this area. A name used by members of a tribal groups for themselves may not be used by, or even known to, the members of another branch of the same tribe. The term Nishi by which so many of the tribesmen of the Subansiri District refer to themselves is not used by their fellow tribesmen in Kameng District, who call themselves as Tagin, whereas the Nishis themselves use the term Tagin to describe their northern neighbours in the Sipi Valley and the upper Subansiri valley (Haimendorf 1982 : 11).

III

AKA

Aka, a major tribe of the Kameng district known to itself as Hruso, meaning a man or a human being. The name Aka seems to have been derived from the Assamese term *Anka* (drawn) indicating intricate line drawings on the faces of the females of the tribe. The Tibetans call the Aka as *Ka-nog,* the Dafla as *Manga* or *Laeing,* Bangro and Miji as *Gannu.*

The Aka territory is bounded by that of the Miji on the north, of the Sherdukpen on the west, of the Dafla (Bangni) on the east, and Darrang district of Assam to the south.

The Akas live in elongated huts of 100-140 ft., built on piles about twenty of which form a village. The villages are built on hill tops. Linguistically they are closer to Adi and Dafla; and more closely to Miji with whom they intermarry.

The tribe is divided into two major divisions; *Kotsun* and *Kovatsun,* each of which is further divided into a number of groups of sub-clans. These sub-clans maintain a vertical hierarchy and the marriage is hypergamous. The highest sub-clans are *Khowsow* and *Jassesow*. The size of the house and the quantity of jewellery worn are indicative of the social status of the family. The wealth of family is measured by the number of *mithuns* it owns. A person of status is called *Nichleu-Nuggo* and each village is suppose to have one. At one time Akas owned slaves *(Khulo)* whose status was lower than the free man. An Aka married by his/her own choice. Matrilateral or a patrilateral cross cousins are preferred. The family is patrilocal in residence. The descent and inheritance are patrilineal. However, the mother's ornaments are inherited by the daughters.

The village is the unit of political organization. The village council, consisting of a chief (*Gaonburah),* his two assistants (*borah* and *gibba*) and the elder members of the village community, is know as the *mele*. The Aka society attaches considerable importance to the age and wealth of an individual. Woman chiefs are not uncommon among the Akas. A woman chief is referred to as *Nugum* (Rani or Queen). In early sixties the villages of Jamiri and Hushigaon had women chiefs. There is no fixed place for the meeting of the council. But it normally meets in front of the chief's house. All members of the village are expected to be present and participate in the council meetings and discussions. Every sixth or the seventh year inter-village meetings are organised "to promote cordiality and goodwill among the neighbouring villages".

The jurisdiction of the council extends from internal disputes in the house to the inter village feuds, "Cases of theft (which were in fact very rare), quarrels or fights, elopement and adultery, murder and vengeance as well as sorcery and witchcraft all within its province" (Elwin 1965 : 72).

Aka economy resolves round slash and burn cultivation. The primary agricultural implements are the hoe and the *dao*. Rice and maize are stapple foods.

The Aka religion is a combination of belief drawn from Buddhism, Hinduism and indigenous beliefs. The Akas, living close to Sherdukpens, display the prayer flags and the wheels like the Tibetan Buddhists and during festivities pay homage to the Buddha. Some Akas name their supreme god as Haridev. In some villages temples are built in his honour. The foundation for the temple is, however, laid according to the indigenous method by sacrificing a cock.

The indigenous Aka pantheon contains a hierarchy of gods and spirits. The higher gods are identified with the sky, the mountains, the earth and the water respectively. The supreme god is called *Tcharo* or *Pu mu-sogo*. He is the benign ruler of men and animals. The sun is believed to be a goddess and the moon a god and are propitiated with sacrifices.

The earthquakes are caused by the mischievous mole cricket borrowing into the earth and telling the god supporting the earth (*Phumbadege*) that all people on earth have died. The god shakes the earth to see if, this is true. Hence the Akas shout, "we are alive" when an earthquake is felt.

The Akas burry their dead with the head to the north and face to the west; the knees are bound to the chest and the hands placed just below the chin. The dead body is taken out through a side door and never through the front door. Most personal belongings which includes a *dao* (a big chopping knife) of the deceased are buried with the body. The grave is floored with wooden planks and mats on which the body is laid. The body is then covered by earth. A dome of split bamboos with small cotton flags on four sides is made to the north of the grave where a post with an arm is erected. A basket of meat, beer, etc., is hung from the arm and is kept for ten days. The Akas believe that the dead go under the earth and proceed west wards until they come to the place where the sun and the moon set. From there they ascend to heaven. Children dying at birth and those dying unnatural death directly go to heaven.

ADI

The Assamese used the blanket term of Abor (meaning wildmen) for virtually all the hillmen of the Siang district. This term is currently replaced by the term Adi and includes a large number of tribes or sections thereof. These are Pailibo, Milan, Tagin, Gallong, Ashing, Minyong, Shimong, Karko, Bori, Bokar, Pasi, Pangi and the Padam. Most of them prefix the term Adi to their tribal name. Thus, Minyongs refer to themselves as Adi Minyong and the Gallongs as Adi Gallong, etc.

The Adi villages are perched on the southern slope of the outer range of the Himalayas roughly between the Dibang and Subansiri rivers. Within the hills the habitations are spread along the Dihong valley and its off-shoots the valleys of Yamne and Siyoun.

The Adis follow patrilineal descent and inheritance and are patrilocal in residence. The clans are exogamous and the sub-tribe intermarry. Though the tribe does not seem to recognize class distinction within it, Haimendorf suspects some traces of class division (Haimendorf 1982 : 17). The main economic activity is centred around slash and burn cultivation.

The Adi religious belief revolves around the conception of a supreme double deity. He is *Donyi-Polo*. The Adis believe that there existed a vaccum (*Keyum*) before this creation and out of the vaccum was born *Sedi,* the creator of the universe. He is the supreme authority of truth, peace, purity, love and justice, equality and wisdom. He became perceptible through *Donyi* (sun) and *Polo* (moon).

DAFLA (Nishi)

A major tribe of Arunachal Pradesh, the Dafla are mostly found in Subansiri district. Like Abor, the term Dafla was used to describe the majority of hillmen of the western part of the present Subansiri district and the adjoining areas of Kameng district. The term has a derogatory connotation meaning a barbarian. The Dafla themselves want to be called Nishi or Nishang (Ni = man). The Daflas of Kameng district refer to themselves as Bangni. The Kameng Daflas refer to their eastern counterparts as Tagin or Tagin Bangni. The Mijis call the Dafla as Gazi. Haimendorf suggests that the Hill Miris and Daflas 'merge and overlap' and together they may be designated as Nishi (Haimendorf 1982 : 10).

The Daflas avoid river banks and build their huts on piles on hill slopes. A Dafla dwelling which is self contained and autonomous houses 10-12 nuclear families. A settlement contains 3 to 30 dwellings. A Dafla dwelling or a cluster of dwelling is called *namping* though in the Kameng area a cluster is referred to by a separate term-*hawan,* meaning a village. But the concept of a village or village organization does not seem to have well developed among them.

The Daflas are patrilinealin descent and inheritance and patrilocal in residence. The Clans are exogamous and exogamy is very strictly enforced. The Daflas place much value upon alliance by matrimony. They have developed an institution of ceremonial friendship called *nin-asa*.

In the past the Daflas too owned slaves who were primarily war captives. The children of such slaves automatically became members of the master's clan and were treated as free-man. In course of time they merged in the master's community.

The Daflas are shifting cultivators and animal breeders. They raise rice, maize and millet in their *jhum* fields.

In the Dafla religion the sun is the patron deity and is conceived as the great mother (*Ane Duini*). She is benevolent, keeps constant vigil and bestows all necessaries of life. But she is rarely worshipped but remember with respect and gratitude. Most religious activities of the Dafla centres around *Ui*, a very much feared willy spirit. They also worship the ancestral ghosts (*Orum*) who hover around homestead and cause harm if dissatisfied.

There are three classes of priests who combine in them magico-religious as well as medical expertise. Among them the *But Nube* is the general medicine man, the *Nigik Nube* is a minor medicine man and *Nyoki Nube* is the practitioner of black magic.

SHERDUKPEN

The Sherdukpen is primarily a localized tribe of the Kameng district found in two villages : Rupa (*Thongthui*) and Jigaon-Shergaon (*Senthui*) drained by a stream which originates in Bhutan. The Rupa people call themselves as *Thongji* or *Thongi* whereas Jigaon-Shergaon people are known as *Senji*. The tribe, however, does not object to the term Sherdukpen used by the outsiders.

The tribe is divided into two classes each of which consists of several exogamous patrilineal clans. The upper class is known as *Thong* and comprises the clans of *Thungdok, Thungshi, Thungo, Krime, Mosubi, Wangdza, Klengtung* and *Lamaguru*. The later originated from a man who on his return from Tibet after study called himself *Lamaguru*. The Thungdok cannot intermarry with *Klengtung* and a *Thungo* cannot marry a *Lamaguru*. All other clans in the class intermarry. The lower class referred to as *tsao* or *tsaw* has within it the clans of *Megedzi Shindzadzi, Dingla, Mondozi* and *Midzidzi*. In the past, each class was endogamous. Though, at present, class exclusiveness in marriage is not strictly followed, inter class marriages are frowned upon.

The Sherdukpens are primarily traders and played the role of middle men between the plains of Assam and the hills beyond. In Assam they sell chillies. oil seeds, and radishes and buy rice and cloth. They sell ponies to Monpas of Towang and maintain a cattle trade with Bhutan.

The Sherdukpens consider themselves as Budhists and seem to be strongly influenced by Tibetan Buddhism. At Rupa there is a large and well appointed *gompa* in which the usual Buddhistic rites are performed. Haimendorf observes that in 1980 all Lamas were from Tibet and no Sherdukpen was being trained for taking up to Lamaism in any of the *gompas* of Kameng district (Haimendorf 1982 : 174).

Buddhism appears to be of recent introduction and an older indigenous religion centering the worship of *khik* seems to be much more deeply rooted in Sherdukpen tradition. The main rite in honour of *Khik* can only be performed at Rupa on a site outside the village. The feast known as *Khiksaba* is celebrated in November or December and lasts of seven days. Without performing this feast and giving offerings to *Khik,* Sherdukpen may not pertake of the grain from the new harvest.

The priests conducting the rites of the *Khiksaba* are Sherdukpens and are called *Khikzizi* (Zizi=Priest). They are invariably of the *Megedzi* and the *Dingla* clans, both of which belong to the lower class but traditionally furnish the priests for the cult of the *Khik.* The villages of Rupa decide who should be trained as *Khikzizi,* while it seems that they take no interest in the training of Sherdukpen youths as *Lamas.* Apart from these priests of *Khik* there are also Sherdukpen Shamans. These are called *ranmat* (*ibid* : 174-175).

There are also other local deities and each village has its own presiding deity to look after its welfare. Male spirit known as *Sinpus* and their female counterparts *Sinumus* are feared as harmful beings. The priests (*Zizis*) drawn from both *Thong* and *Tsao* sections of the communities are initiated to the profession after a series of visions; and are ritually married to their tutelary spirits.

APA TANI

The Apa Tani is a small but very important tribe of Arunachal Pradesh. They inhabit a large valley situated at an altitude of 1,500 metres and surounded by thickly wooded mountains rising to heights of more than 2400 metres.

The Apa Tanis live in compact well ordered and disciplined villages of a few hundred households. The Apa Tani settlements with their terraced fields stand in complete contrast of their shifting-cultivator neighbours. They "have transformed their valley into an intensely cultivated oasis in the wilderness of sparcely inhabited hills".

The Apa Tanis are divided into two distinct status groups-the *guth* (the upper class or the aristocrat) and the *guchi* (the lower class or the commoners); and the mobility across class is not allowed. In the past, the *guchi* class contained slaves as well as free born commoners.After their emancipation around 1960, the former slaves too have, the same status as the free born *guchis*.

The Apa Tanis are not only good farmers and irrigation experts, they are also skilful traders. They are most actively engaged in economic activities. They produce high class cloth, iron implements and a salty substance gained from vegetable ash (*Khar*) for trade. *Daos* and knives of Apa Tani manufacture are very much in demand in the area. They go on long trading expeditions. Apa Tani women are seentravelling to neighbouring villages with basket loads of material for trade. The Apa Tanis purchase pigs, *mithans,* dogs, fowls, Tibetan beads, small prayer bells (*mege*), fibre rain coats, fibre rain hats, plaited cane and grass belts, etc.

The Apa Tanis believe in the existence of a world beyond known as *Neli* peopled by deities, spirits and the departed Apa Tanis. All such supernatural beings are called by the generic term *ui*. To the Apa Tani all *uis* seem to have equal importance.

A class of gods known as *Tigo-ui* is connected with happiness and prosperity and worshipped at wedding ceremonies, etc. The *Guniyam ui* (or *Chiching ui*) are connected with unfortunate events and worshipped to ward-off illness, etc. *Yalu ui* are gods of disputes and war and are propitiated on the eve of raids, criminal cases, etc. Llarge groupof goods known as *Hilo* (or *Yulo*) - *ui* living in forests, hills, sky and near but not inside the village. *Niri-Korlang* resides in the sky and provides protection against hailstorms; *Tagung ui* also dwells in the sky and guards against thunderstorms and excessive rain; *Augura ui* is believed to protect the Apa Tani from diseases when they visit the plains of Assam. These gods, together know as *Korlang ui* are worshipped annually by a priest representing the entire village or even two neighbouring villages..The gods connected with wars and raids have almost become obsolete with the stopping of such activities. The sex and the future qualities of a child still to be born are believed to be the handiwork of some unspecified *ui*. All those who die a natural death go to *Neli* where they meet their relatives who predeceased them. Life in *Neli* is believed to be similar to life on earth where people work, grow crops and ultimately die and go to another land of the dead. Though *Neli* is believed to be under earth, it is considered to be a pleasant place. Those who die of accidents or such other unnatural events go to what is known as *Talimoko* situated in the sky. These departed ancestors from both *Neli* and *Telimoko* are believed to frequent the earth at times but their visitations are not welcome. The souls which have gone to *Neli* are known as *Yalo* and those to *Telimoko* as *Igi*. To satisfy an angry *Yalo* a rite known as *ayo-asi-mendu* is performed. A rite known as *ropi* is performed to prevent the *igi* of a slain man or woman from returning to earth.

Though on occasions an Apa Tani directly address himself to the gods, a priest (*nyibu*) is required to act as a mediator between men and gods. Entry into the profession is marked by careful selection and apprenticeship (*Buo*) to an experienced *nyibu*. The Apa Tanis have not come under any appreciable influence either from Buddhism or from Hinduism or from Christianity.

MONPA

The main population of the Monpa inhabit the high altitudes of the western part of Kameng adjoining Bhutan. Culturally they are akin to the people of the eastern most Bhutan.

The Monpa settlements, particularly in high altitudes differ from those of most other populations of Arunachal Pradesh. Unlike the wood and bamboo structures of the Adis, Apa Tani and the Nishi, the Monpa houses are of permanent nature and are built largely of stone.

The Monpas are divided into a number of classes of different status. In this division one notices some regional variation. Members of higher classes do not share a drinking cup with members of lower classes, but there is no ban on interdining.Class endogamy had been strictly followed in the past which is very much coaxed now, though there is/was no restriction in having matrimonial alliance with a non-Monpa of high status (Haimendorf 1982 : 159).

The Monpas mostly live in nuclear families. The practice of fraternal polyandry is noticed, though not extensively, among the Monpa. A Monpa divides his property in his life-time among his sons keeping a share to himself, giving somewhat a larger share to his eldest son and dividing rest equally among his other sons.

The Monpa economy combined in itself agriculture as the primary base with considerable importance attached to animal husbandry, trade and commerce. Most farmers of the Dirang circle grow rice on irrigated fields, maize, millet, wheat and barley. On higher slopes they mainly grow wheat, barley and potato. Though most part of the Monpa land is under permanent village, they also practice slash and burn cultivation on a smaller scale compared to other tribes of the region.

Monpas use large and heavy ploughs and cross-breeds between *mithun* and Indian cattle. These animals are large and very strong. Two men are needed for ploughing. One man manoeuvres theploughand the other walks between the ploughing bullocks which are kept far apart by a long yoke, and take care to see that the shaft remains fastened to the yoke. In agricultural expertise the Monpas are only next to the Apa Tanis.

The Monpa system of land tenure differs substantially from most other tribes of Arunachal Pradesh. The major territorial unit is called *tso* and each *tso* contains several villages. A unit smaller than a *tso* called *mang* which is coterminus with a single village, is seen comprised within some but by no means all *tso*. Both *tso* and *mang* contain communal land, known separately as *tso-sa* and *mang-sa*.

In the past the territory contained in a *tso* was administered by an elected headman known as *tsoba*. He was expected to control and maintain all Buddhistic Shrines and to ensure the performance of all ceremonies. At present the head of a *tso* who is informally elected for a period of three years by all the villagers comprising it is called *tsorgen*. He is supported by a council of village elders. With the exception of major crimes like murder, his authority extends over most civil and criminal cases. Men elected as *tsorgen* belong to one of the higher classes. Individual villages also have a council in which each household is represented by one member.In recent years the government have appointed village headman (*Gaonbura*) in most Monpa villages.

The Monpas are Mahayana Buddhist. Monastries and nunneries are focal point of religious life. The great monastery of Tawang modelled in respect on the monasteries of Tibet, represents one of the most prominent institutions of the Gelugpa sect south of the Himalayan main range .... it is fully operational and novices continue to be recruited from most villages of the Tawang sub division (Haimendorf 1982 : 164).

The orthodox scriptural Buddhism, however, has not been able to completely submerge the indigenous faith of the Monpas. The local deities continue to be worshipped. The practices, connected with their worship are referred to as *Bon*. Close to many Monpa villages one notices a sanctuary consisting of several flat stones where rites in honour of these deities are performed. The priests of these cults are called *bun* in the Tawang region and *phramin* in Dirang area. These priests have no relation with the *lamas* or the *Gompas*. They worship the local deities with animal sacrifices and also offer eggs, meat, fish, rice and beer to various spirits and local gods (*ibid* : 170)

There are also shamans known as *Yu-min* who are subject to possession by gods and spirits and who, while on trance, can read the future of man. Both men and women can become *Yu-min* but the function cannot be combined with that of a *lama*. Undoubtedly the *Bon* cult represents an archaic belief system.

WANCHU AND NOCTE

A dominant tribe of the Tirap district, the Wanchu society is organised under great chiefs, each controlling a number of villages. The tribe is divided into three hierarchical classes. The hereditory chiefs known as *Wangham* constitute the highest class. The commoners are known as *Wangpen*. In between are those who are the descendants of the *Wangham* men married to *Wangpen* women. This class is known as *Wangsa*. *Wangpen* women are never allowed to marry *Wangpen* men, though in case of non availability of boys of their own class they may be married into the *Wangsa* class. The Wanchu classes resembles those of their neighbouring Noctes. Their unmarried boys and girls live in unisexual dormitories known as *Morungs*.

The Wanchus are *Jhum* cultivators and own their *Jhum* land individually which they can sell or purchase. In the past they were very skilful head hunters. The last incident was reported in 1956 from the Niauchha village. In olden days a boy could be married only after he came out successful from a head-hunting expedition.

The Wanchu religious belief centres around a high god living in the sky who is kind and benevolent. They believe that there are a large number of malevolent spirits who live on the earth invisible to the human eye. Like the Assamese *Bihu,* The Wanchus perform agricultural rituals three times a year.

An important tribe of Tirap, the Nocte, at one time, like the Wanchus were skilful head hunters; and like the Wanchu, the Nocte society is also organised around great chiefs. They live in long established houses, build *morungs* for boys and girls. The society is divided into three classes like those of the Wanchus. The Nocte are very much influenced by the Assamese Vaishnavism.

IV

Through the description of these randomly selected communities, we have tried to present an overall picture óf the society, economy and religion of the people of Arunanchal Pradesh.

The economy presents variations in wide range. We have the Sulungs of Subansiri subsisting in almost completely on food gathering and hunting and minimal slash and burn cultivation, and the extremely skilful farmers like the Apa Tani, representing two extremities of a pre-industrial economy. But a major area of Arunachal Pradesh is under the *jhum* cultivation. Tribes like the Nishi, have combined agriculture with animal husbandry, whereas the Hill Miris subsist primarily on trade as middle men between the plains on one side and the hills on the other.

The religious beliefs in Arunachal Pradesh present a colourful spectrum. "The great majority of the tribal societies of Arunachal Pradesh", writes Haimendorf (1982 : 146), "share a world view and a social atmosphere that have remained outside the oribit of the great historic civilizations of south Asia". However, two parts of the state namely the Kameng (undivided) district on the west and the Tirap district on the east came under external cultural and ethnic influence. Kameng came under the Buddhistic influence from Bhutan and Tibet; whereas Tirap came under the Vaishnava influence from Assam and Buddhistic influence from Burma.

Inspite of these influences there runs across Arunachal, a general belief in a supreme God who is just benevolent and good. There are also a host of demons and evil spirits who prey upon mankind and to whose propitiation most of the attention of the people and their priests are devoted. These beliefs have found their way to motivate the believer to carve elaborate wooden images of all kinds of super natural entities. Religion through the wooden iconography in Arunachal Pradesh presents an interesting area of study.

REFERENCES

BARUA, T.K. M.,1960. *The Idu Mishimis*, Shillong : North East Frontier Agency Administration.

BHATTACHARYA, P.C., 1962. *Ashomar Janajati* (Tribes of Assam). Gauhati : Assam Sahitya Sabha.

BHATTACHARJEE, T.K., 1975. *The Tangams*, Shillong : Research Department, Arunachal Pradesh.

BOWER, U.G., 1953. *The Hidden Land;* London :

CUMMINGS, R.C.R 1921. *Census of India, Assam,* Part I, Appendix B.P. XIII.

DALTON E.T., 1872. *Descriptive Ethnology of Bengal,* Calcutta : Government Printing Press.

DEURI, R.K., 1982. *The Sulungs,* Shillong : Directorate of Research, Arunachal Pradesh.

DUFF, B., 1972. *Report on the Miri Country and the Operations of the Miri Mission,* Simla.

DUTTA, P. C., 1969. *The Tangsas,* Shillong: Directorate of Information and Public Relations, NEFA.

DUTTA, P.C., 1978. *The Noctes,* Shillong : Directorate of Research, Arunachal Pradesh.

DUTTA CHOWDHURY, S., 1979. *Lohit District Gazetteer,* Shillong : Government of Arunachal Pradesh.

DUTTA CHOWDHURY, S., 1980. *Tirap District Gazetteers,* Shillong : Government of Arunachal Pradesh.

DUTTA CHOWDHURY, S., 1981. *Subansiri District Gazetteers,* Shillong : Government of Arunachal Pradesh.

DUNBAR, G., 1915. *Abors and Gallongs,* Calcutta : Memoirs of Asiatic Society of Bengal.

ELWIN, V., 1958a. *Myths of the North East Frontier of India,* Shillong : Directorate of Information and Public Relations, N.E.F.A. Administration.

ELWIN, V., 1958b. *Democracy in N.E.F.A.,* Shillong : Directorate of Information and Public Relations, NEFA Administration.

ELWIN, V., 1959a. *A Philosophy for N.E.F.A.,* Shillong : Directorate of Information and Public Relations, N.E.F.A. Administration.

ELWIN, V., 1959b. *India's North East Frontier in Nineteenth Century,* London : Oxford University Press.

FURER HAIMENDORF, C. von, 1947. *Ethnographic Notes on the Tribes of Subansiri Region,* Shillong.

FURER HAIMENDORF, C. von, 1947. *Exploration in the Eastern Himalayas,* Diaries of travel in the Subansiri Region 1944 and 1945, Shillong.

FURER HAIMENDORF, C. von, 1949. Anthropology and Administration in the Tribal Areas of the North East Frontier, *Eastern Anthropologist* 3 : 37-49.

FURER HAIMENDORF, C. von, 1962. *The Apatanis and their Neighbours,* London : Routledge and Kegan Poul.

FURER HAIMENDORF, C. von, 1980. *A Himalayan Tribe : From Cattle to Cash,* Delhi and Berkley.

FURER HAIMENDORF, C. von,1982. *Highlanders of Arunachal Pradesh,* New Delhi : Vikas Publishing Corporation.

KUMAR, K., 1978. *The Boris*, Shillong : Directorate of Research, Arunachal Pradesh.

KUMAR, K., 1979. *The Pailibos*, Shillong : Directorate of Research, Arunachal Pradesh.

LORRAIN, T.K. 1910. *Dictionary of the Abor-Miri Language*, Shillong

LUTHRA, P.N.,. 1971. *Constitutional and Administrative Growth of NEFA* Shillong : Directorate of Information and Public Relations.

PANDEY, B.B., 1978. *The Hill Miris*, Shillong : Directorate of Research, Arunachal Pradesh.

ROY, S., 1966. *Aspects of Padam-Minyong Culture*, Shillong : North East Frontier Agency Administration.

SHARMA, R.R.P., 1961. *The Sherdukpens*, Shillong : Research Department, NEFA Administration.

SHUKLA, B. K., 1959. *The Daflas of the Subansiri Region*, Shillong : Research Department, NEFA Administration.

SIMONS, F.J., 1963. 'A Ceremonial Ox of India : The Mithan', In *Nature, Culture and History*, Madison.

SINGH, R., 1962. *The Akas*, Shillong : Research Department, NEFA Administration.

SRIVASTAVA, L.R.N., 1962. *The Gallongs*, Shillong : Research Department, N.E.F.A. Administration.

SRIVASTAVA, L.R.N., 1973. *Among the Wanchus*, Shillong : Directorate of Research, Arunachal Pradesh.

STONOR, C.R., 1957. Notes on religion and ritual among the Dafla tribe of the Assam Himalayas, *Anthropos*, 52 : 1-23.

WILLIAMS. R.F., 1944. *Tour Diaries of the Assistant Political Officer*, Pashighat, November 1940-April 1944, Shillong.

4

Society and Culture Among the Tribes of Arunachal Pradesh : Tradition and Change

JAYANTA SARKAR

Arunachal Pradesh, home land of about 28 major tribes has an area of 83,578 sq. km. and is bounded by Bhutan, Tibet and China, Burma and Brahmaputra Valley of Assam in the west, north, north-east, east and south respectively. Many of the tribes are divided into a number of sub-tribes. Out of 6,31,839 population of the State, the Scheduled Tribes numbered 4,41,167 (Census, 1981). The State of Arunachal Pradesh now has eleven districts namely Tawang, West Kameng, East Kameng, Upper Subansiri, Lower Subansiri, West Siang, East Siang, Lohit, Dibang Valley, Tirap and Changlang.

The present paper gives a brief descriptive account of the traditional aspects of the society and culture of some major tribes. The significant changes that have come in the tribal societies have also been highlighted.

Migration

In the absence of any document, the exact routes through which these tribes have entered to this region are still obscure in most of the cases. However, two possible routes are believed to be responsible for the influx into the different parts of this difficult terrain.

The Tai group of people such as Khamtis, Phakes, Shyam entered in this place of their present concentration through different passes across the Patkai range. They were followed by the Singphos from the Kachin State of Burma. Probably the Tangsas have also entered through this route. The other routes were several northern passes of Bhutan and Tibet through which the tribes have entered in present Kameng, Subansiri and Siang districts.

Economy : Agriculture

The tribes living in the higher altitude in general, practice shifting cultivation, commonly known as *Jhum* cultivation in north-eastern region, with the exception of the Apatanis of Upper Subansiri district who have a well planned irrigation system for their age old terrace cultivation. The Monpas living south of Sela know the use of plough which is slightly different than those used in Assam plains. The Sherdukpen also use primitive type of plough. The Nas of Subansiri also knew the use of plough but in their present place of concentration, the terrain does not permit ploughing, so they have adopted terrace cultivation. All these three tribes also practise *Jhum* cultivation along with the plough and terrace cultivation.

Table 1 gives a picture of the agricultural practices of the tribes living in the high hills and foot hills. The table shows the tribes who have primitive hunting, gathering and different ways of agricultural practices as their main livelihood.

The Apatani land, a vast plateau in higher altitude, might have inspired them to take up the terrace cultivation. The Monpas and Sherdukpens practice a mixed type of agriculture comprising of both shifting and permanent cultivation according to the situation of different plots of lands.

Table 1

Name of the tribes and their main livelihood

Category of Livelihood	*Name of Tribes*
Hunting and Gathering	Sulung
Shifting Cultivation	Aka, Ashing, Bangni, Bangro, Bokar, Gallong, Nishi, Miniyong, Hill Miri, Memba, Idu Mishmi, Kaman Mishmi, Taraon Mishmi, Nocte, Tangsa, Wancho
Both Shifting and Terrace Cultivation	Nishi, Padam, Singpho
Terrace Cultivation	Apatani
Both Shifting and Plough Cultivation	Monpa, Sherdukpen
Plough Cultivation	Khamti

Khamtis are the only tribe in Arunachal Pradesh who practise only the plough cultivation. The system they brought alongwith them from Irawaddy valley and have been continuing with the support of very good system of irrigation. Their plough is different than that used in the Brahmaputra valley.

The land among the high hill tribes, as already mentioned, in general is owned by the clan which a clan member gets for cultivation purpose. Though the Wanchos have a Chief system even then he is not the owner of the entire land.

Among the Adis, the village has its own agricultural land called *patat* which is controlled by the *Kebang* (village council). Each *patat* has different plots owned by the different clans. The *patat* alloted to a clan is divided into smaller plots of different sizes for distributing amongst its members and these are called *ariks*.

The agricultural land among the Khamtis is owned by the *ChaoFa*, the Chief of the village. He allots the lands to the others who want to live in the village.

Economy : Trade

Trade was one of the main sources of livelihood for the tribes inhabiting the high hills near the international border and some passes. On account of such strategic location the Kaman Mishmi, Maras (Tagins), Nas and certain section of the Tangsas became good traders. The Kaman Mishmis used to exchange their *bih* (poison), *gathewan* (an adoriferous root), *manjeet* (madder) and *teethah* (a bitter root, greatly esteemed for its medical qualities) for yak, brass pipe, gongs and copper vessels. The Mishmis used to visit Sadiya once in every year during November-March. They would bring their own products as well as the things obtained from others and bartered these with cows, buffaloes, salt and coloured beads. The tribes like the Maras and the Nas monopolised the trade in certain areas of Upper Subansiri district. (Sarkar, 1987).

In the foot hills, the Khamtis proved themselves as very good traders. They used to bring their surplus products at Sadiya and in exchange used to take salt, clothes, etc. (Sarkar, *ibid.*)

Social Organisation

All the tribes of Arunachal Pradesh practise clan exogamy. Their rule of residence is patrilocal. No tribe is fully practising village exogamy or village endogamy. However, taking the frequencies of marriages into consideration the Wanchos can be classified as the only tribe who follow the village endogamy. Only the people belonging to Chief's 'class' strictly follow the village exogamy for their marriage with the girls of similar status, otherwise spouses are taken from the same village by the different classes (Sarkar 1987a). The members of the Chief's clans of the Khamti in general take their wives from the other such clans living within or outside the village.

The Khamtis, Singphos, Monpas can broadly be classified as the tribes practising monogamy, whereas the Mishmis, Tangsas, Wanchos, Noctes, Nishis and others prefer to have more than one wife. On the basis of obtaining the mates the whole Arunachal tribes can broadly be divided into two categories. The tribes like the Khamtis, Singphos, Tangsas, Kaman Mishmis, Sulungs have a special system in which one particluar lineage avoids direct exchange of bride. (Sarkar, *ibid.*)

This system has framed a prescribed marriage in which the MBD (mother's brother's daughter) are always prescribed and preferred. The Adis, Nishis practise both MBD and FSZ (father's sister's son) marriage. The Wancho, marriage system can not be included in any of these categories. Among the Wancho, marriage takes place within four classes namely the *Wangham* (Chief), the *Wangsa, Wangsu* and *Wangpen* (commoner). The *Wangham* can marry a *Wangpan* girl only from the village. The marriage between *Wangsa, Wangpan* and *Wangsu* is permitted and practised. With certain variation among the Wanchos, the childern of other tribes adopt the clan names of their father. Among the Wanchos, when a *Wangham* marries a *Wangpan* girl the children neither belong to the *Wangham* nor to the *Wangpan* instead they form a separate class called *Wangsa* (Sarkar, 1987).

The elder brother's widows are generally married by the younger brothers among all the tribes. The Kaman Mishmis, the Hill Miris and the Tagins follow a system of marriage which is a special characteristic of those tribes. In these societies after the death of father one can keep the stepmothers as wives and enjoy normal conjugal life.

The wives amongst the tribes of Arunachal Pradesh are considered as the asset of the family as they do all the domestic as well as agricultural activities. On account of this the presence of the females in the family is very much essential, which perhaps has lead to the adoption of giving very high bride price for bringing a female as wife.

As a high bride price is required to get a wife the presence of more than one wife automatically shows a person's richness which gives him a higher economic as well as social status in their society.

Among all the tribes of this region the Gallongs have a special type of marriage which has been described as 'Fraternal polyandry' (Sarkar, 1973). The Wancho and Nocte girls immediately after their marriage do not go to live in their husband's residence. The girl pays occasional visits to her husbands' residence but lives with her natal family till she is pregnant. During pregnancy she remains with her own family members but goes to the husbands' house before delivery. After delivery she permanently stays with her husband.

Among the Padams and Miniyongs also the girls generally do not go to stay with the husband in the latters' residence after marriage. Only after the delivery of a child usually they go to the husband's residence along with the new born baby.

The Monpas consider the birth of a child in wife's residence or in the maternal uncle's house as inauspicious. So the child is to be born in the house of its father.

Social Stratification

The Sherdukpen society is mainly divided into two classes the *Thongs* and *Chhaos*. *Thongs* enjoy a higher social status. The Miji society has two classes namely the *Nyubbu* and *Nyullu*, which are further sub-divided into various stratas. *Nyubbu* enjoys a higher social status in their society (Roy Burman, 1971).

The Apatani society has two broad divisions, the upper class called *Mite* or *Guth* and the lower class known as *Mura* or *Guchi*. The *Mite* or *Guth* is the class of rich people while the *Mura* or *Guchi* consists of the large body of commoners which at one time used to include slaves. A *Mite* can be downgraded as a *Mura* as the result of some lapse, but once he becomes a *Mura* he can never regain his original status. These two classes are endogamous and interchange of position is restricted by the social norms (Haimendorf, 1962).

The Tagin society is stratified into four distinct classes namely the *nibu* (priest), *nite* (rich), *open* (the poor) and *nyira* (slave). The *nibu* enjoy the highest status in the society as they know the traditional myths and can control the spirits. Next comes the *nite* in the social hierarchy, they are the rich people having *mithuns* (bos frontalis), other domestic animals, Tibetan *daos*, gongs, beads, etc. The third comes the *open*, the poor and the last position in the social hierarchy is held by the *nyira* or slaves.

These classifications are not rigid. If one learns the mythology and lore he becomes a priest and can enter into the *nibu* class. Similarly, the *nite* can get a wife from the *open* class (Choudhury, 1982).

The Khamti society is mainly classified into the Royal class and the commoners. In between the Royal class and the commoners come the class of the rich people who mostly belong to the minister's clans. The Singphos are also classified into the Chief and the commoners, though such distinction is not very much apparent in the society as among the Khamtis.

The society among the Noctes is actually divided into two broad classes. The Chief and his descendants form a separate class called *Lowangjat* and the commoners are termed as *Sanajat*. Such differences can be observed during the social functions. Similarly, as has been mentioned, the Wancho society is stratified into four classes namely the *Wangham, Wangsa, Wangsu* and *Wangpan*. These differences also become very much prominent during the social functions. (Dutta, 1978)

Bachelor's dormitory

The Adis (except the Gallongs), Wanchos and Noctes have bachelor's dormitory in each village for the males. The boys of different age groups stay in these dormitories and learn the social and biological norms of their respective societies. Each dormitory has different groups of boys which are classified mainly on the basis of age. The members of the Wancho and Nocte dormitories (*morung*) help the villagers in their agricultural activities as well as in some other occasions where the involvement of more persons is essential. These *morungs* also help the Chief in proper control of the village. Each *morung* has its own area within the village. These dormitories had a vital role in head hunting and inter village feuds which was in vogue amongst these tribes in past. Among these two tribes there may be more than one *morung* in a village but the Adi villages have only one bachelor's dormitory (*moshup)*. The members of the Adi *moshups* are known as *Moshup Ko,* consisting of young unmarried boys. Each group has a specific function to do (Sarkar, 1987; 1990).

Disposal of death

Through out Arunachal Pradesh, with certain exceptions here and there,the dead body is buried by the tribes. Among the Monpas and Khamtis the dead body of the rich people is cremated, in other cases it is buried. The Akas, Sherdukpens, Sulungs, Tagins, Apatanis, Nishis, Adis, Mishmis in general bury the dead bodies. The Tangsas cremate the dead bodies just by the side of the deceased's house. The Wanchos neither bury nor cremate the dead bodies, instead they keep the corpse on a platform in the graveyard called *Gukn* near the house till the bodies get decomposed. Then from the decomposed body the head is separated and kept in a specific place under a stone or earth.

Political organisation

The tribes of Arunachal Pradesh have mainly three types of political organisations. These are the Chieftenship, the democratic village councils and other forms.

Chieftenship : The Khamtis have their own traditional political organisation called *Mukchup* with a clear charter about the nature of the work to be performed by each official . The head of the political organisation is the *ChaoFa* who controls the village and the other members are : (i) *ChaoFaKen* or *Chaofa Mao*, (ii) *Chao Moong*, (iii) *ChaoHootem*, (iv) *ChaoHooHoo*, (v) *ChaoHooson*, (vi) *Chao Moo*, and (vii) *Tengso,* the messenger. The *ChaoFa* in consultation with his ministers and other officials gives his judgment as per the *Thamasat,* in which the Khamti customery laws are recorded. The judgment given by the *ChaoFa* is final. Though the Singpho Chief theoretically has control over the villages, the disputes are settled by the village elders. The Chief has no responsibility in this regard. It is the village elders who actually deal with all sorts of disputes (Sarkar, 1987).

The Nocte has a strong political organisation called *Ngothun*. The members come from the different sections of the tribe who in most cases are the elderly persons of the sections. The council is presided over by the Chief called *Lowong*. The council has several officials with specific functions to do. The officials are *nongba, ramba* and *tamba* and the members are called either *noktang* or *kampa*. *Ngongba* acts as a minister to the Chief who consults him in all cases. *Tamba* is a special messenger to the Chief. On consultation with the ministers, elderly persons, the Chief takes the decision (Dutta, 1978).

The political organisation of the Wanchos is also well developed. Each village has a traditional council called *Wanchu-Wancha*. The council, like the Noctes, comprises of several officials with special functions. The *morungs* play important role in the political organisation of the Wanchos. Disputes and other conflicts are generally solved by the *morungs* of the villages. If the problem can not be solved by the *morungs* it is referred to the chief *(Sompa)* who in consultation with the officials, elderly members of the village and also with the leaders of the *morungs* takes the decision. The decision taken by the Chief is considered as final (Sarkar, 1987).

Democratic Organisation : The Monpa political organisation can be considered as well developed democratic system existing in Arunachal Pradesh. Each Monpa village elects one representative for a single big village or for a group of hamlets. The representative called *tsorgens* is responsible for the administrative and judiciary problems of the village. The *tsorgens* are elected for a period of three years. He can be removed also before the term is completed on the ground of inefficiency, etc. by the General body. He is supposed to supervise also the religious ceremonies alongwith the welfare activities to be performed for the villagers. The *tsorgen* has his representatives called *tsobla* in each village or hamlet who are also elected. Apart from *tsobla* he gets a number of messengers known as *gomins* (Elwin, 1965).

The Adi political organisation is known as *Kebang* and it is famous throughout Arunachal Pradesh for its nature. The *Kebang* is the judicio-administrative organisation of an Adi village. The influential and experienced persons as well as impartial persons of the village are elected as the members of *Kebang*. The election of these members are done in a meeting of all the elderly members of the families. The head of the *Kebang* is known as *Kebang Abu* or *Meeloom*. The members are called *Kebang Ami*. A *Kebang* virtually controls all the activities of the village. The members are elected by the villagers after regular intervals. The *Kebang* gives full opportunity to the accused to defend his own argument. After hearing from both the sides the *Kebang Abu* gives the judgment which is generally considered as final. If any body challenges the judgment, the *Kebang Ami* or *Meeloom* from other villages are called and the case is decided again (Sarkar, 1987).

The political organisation of the Sherdukpens, Akas and Apatanis are also to some extent democratic but these are not so well organised as those of Monpas and Adis. Each Sherdukpen village has a council, called *Jung*. The members are usually taken from the village elders and are selected by the villagers.

The Aka village council called *Melley* also gets members in the similar way. The Apatanis have an almost similar type of village council with less control over the village than those of *Kebang* and *Jung*. These are known as *Buliang*. For each clan there is a *buliang* and the discussion is held on a place inhabited by that clan called *Lapang*.

Almost all the other tribes have their own village councils which are mainly formed by the village elders. The disputes are settled by them within the village.

Other forms of Political Organisations : The Kaman and Tarao Mishmis and also to some extent the Tagins can be considered as more weak in political organisation. Practically they do not have any village council. An old man who is respected by the villagers due to his personal influence or ability to negotiate with the supernatural power is generally approached to settle down the disputes.

The village councils, whether controlled by the Chiefs or by the village elders in a democratic way, are not only judicial organisations but also perform as the main administrative organisations of the village and are supposed to direct all the activities of the village according to their traditional law and customs.

Religion

On the basis of religious belief the tribes of Arunachal Pradesh can broadly be divided into two groups; the Buddhist and those who believe in benevolent and malevolent spirits.

The Buddhist tribes of Western Arunachal Pradesh, living mainly in the high hills of Kameng and a few in Subansiri and Siang districts, profess the Tibetan Buddhism (*Mahayana)* where as the Khamtis living in the foot hills of Lohit district follow *Hinayana* Buddhism.

In the Monpa villages a *gompa* is the most sacred place where the Buddha images and the holy books are kept. One or more officiating Lamas are attached to a *gompa.*

The religion of the Sherdukpens is a co-existence of Buddhism and traditional belief. They worship Lord Buddha and side by side follow the traditional shamanistic practices which also play an important role in their life. They believe in witchcrafts and evil spirits and to control these they seek the help of the traditional priests called *Jijis.* The Membas, Khambas and Nas living in high hills of Siang districts and Subansiri districts are also Buddhist by religion.

Almost each Khamti and Singpho village has a monastry, locally known as *Bapuchang.* The monks of various grades such as the *Mahasthabir, Sthabir, Bhikku, Shramaneya* are attached to these monastries. The sacred books are also kept in these monastries. For the Khamtis the monastry is also an important place of learning where the boys learn their own script along with Pali.

The Singphos who are living in the close proximity of the Khamtis have greatly been influenced by them and quite a large number of them have accepted *Hinayana* Buddhism, though side by side they practise their traditional religious performances like the Sherdukpens (Sarkar, 1987).

Though Christian missionaries are not allowed to enter inside Arunachal Pradesh, a few Adis and Tangsas have embraced Christianity. Similarly, the Akas of Kameng and the Noctes of Tirap districts have been influenced by the Vaishnavism and a good many of them have accepted Vaishnavism as their religion.

All the other tribes believe in various spirits. The traditional priests of the respective tribes play a major role in pleasing or controlling these spirits through the sacrifice of *mithun,* cow, pig, fowl, etc.

Changes

These tribes of Arunachal Pradesh, with a few exceptions such as the Khamtis, Akas and Noctes practically had no frequent contact besides the tribes, with the outsiders till the introduction of Administration in this region. Though the first administrative centre inside the territory was established in 1912 at Pasighat under an Assistant Political Officer, the administration actually started entering into the interior of this region only between the years 1953 to 1955. Even then the tribals started coming in frequent contact with the people of Brahmaputra valley only after 1962 when the communication facilities started developing rapidly.

The most notable change have come in economic sphere of their life.Two types of changes have been observed. Those who are living adjacent to the international border became directly effected due to the sealing of border. The traders of local products and especially those tribes who were working as 'middle men' are facing the economic hardship as the barter of these local products with the people living beyond the border have stopped.

The Arunachal Administration is trying to tackle this problem. A number of co-operative stores have come-up in the remote administrative centres such as Taksing, Anini, Pongchau, Wakka etc., to supply the essential cereals to the local people at subsidised rates.

The administration has also taken up programmes in which the tribes of this State are being encouraged to take up wet cultivation wherever the terrain permits. This wet cultivation has attracted a number of tribes like the Singphos, a few Mishmis, Adis and Nishis and the Tangsas. They are coming down from the hills and trying to establish their villages in the foot hills where the flat lands favourable for wet cultivation are available. Use of the plough and bullocks for cultivation which was unknown a few years ago could get a place amongst the Adis, Singphos and Tangsas. These tribes employ the outsiders; mainly the Nepalese and people from Bihar, to cultivate their lands, These outsiders come during agricultural season and clear the jungle, cultivate it with plough for about two years and only after that the owner of the land gets a share of the crops.

Some of these tribes, living in the foot hills, under the encouragement of Arunachal Administration have started undertaking timber and some other businesses like construction of Government quarters, roads, etc.

A number of tribes as has been mentioned, were keeping slaves capturing the latter from the neighbouring tribes. Arunachal Pradesh administration banned the slavery system which has compelled the Sulungs who were slaves to the neighbouring Nishi and Tagins, to start cultivation of their own.

Educational facilities along with the nutritional help to the school going childern have also been extended to almost all the remote areas. The percentage of literacy in whole of Arunachal Pradesh as per 1981 Census has risen to 20.95 as against 7.13 of 1961 and 11.29 of 1971 Census. In 1947 there were only two primary schools in the foot hills adjacent to Assam, now one University, three degree Colleges, one Regional Institute of Science and Technology have come up. Number of educational institutes have gone up to 1558.

The Panchayati Raj in Arunachal Pradesh was introduced in 1967. The tribes having different forms of village councils have shown the adjustability with this new system. In the villages, both the traditional and new types of councils exist. They hardly come into direct conflict as in most of the cases the new Panchayat members take the opinion of the leaders of the traditional council before taking any vital decision.

Such rapid development in all over Arunachal Pradesh has two fold reactions. A group of people, specially the younger generation who have come in contact with the outsiders have started disliking some of their traditional customs like tattooing, insertion of nose plugs, polygamous marriage, bride price, slaughtering of animals, etc. On the other hand, some elites have started revitalising those cultural elements which are considered good for strengthening their cultural identity.

REFERENCES

CHOWDHURY, J.N., 1982. *Arunachal Panorama*, Shillong : directorate of Research, Government of Arunachal Pradesh.

DUTTA, P., 1978. *The Nocles*, Shillong : Directorate of Research, Government of Arunachal Pradesh.

ELWIN, V., 1965. *Democracy in N.E.F.A.* Shillong : Directorate of Research, Government of Arunachal Pradesh.

FURER HAIMENDORF C. von, 1962. *The Apatanis and their Neighbours*, London : Routledge and Kegan Paul.

PAI, M. B. 1981. *Census of India*. Delhi, Series 25, Part-II A and Part-II B.

ROY BURMAN, B.K., 1971. *Rupa : A Sherdukpen Village in Arunachal Pradesh*, Monograph Number 1, Census of India, New Delhi

SARKAR, J.K., 1987. *Society, Culture and Ecological Adaptation Among Three Tribes of Arunachal Pradesh*, Calcutta : Anthropological Survey of India.

SARKAR, J.K., 1987a. Marriage System in North-East India', In *Marriage in India* (Tribes, Muslim and Anglo Indians) Edited by B.B. Goswami, D. Danda and J.K. Sarkar, Calcutta : Anthropological Survey of India.

SARKAR, J.K., 1990. Po : A Socio-Political Institution of Wancho', In : *Social and Political Institutions of the Hill People of North-East India*, Edited by J.K. Sarkar and B. Datta Ray, Calcutta : Anthropological Survey of India.

SARKAR, N., 1973. The So-Called Polyandry Among the Gallongs, *Man In India*, 53, 2

5

World View of the Lisu : A Little Known Ethnic Group of Arunachal Pradesh

ASIM MAITRA

The way a people react to, and treat and perceive natural and supernatural phenomena, social and cultural events, relationship within themselves and outside, and disease and injury, reflects a manifestation of their concepts of different aspects of life, which for lack of a more precise term, is often referred to as 'World View'. This is somewhat a nebulous concept. However, this concept has been used in anthropological literature, and studied systematically since after the second World War. In essence, world view is a set of inferences or assumptions that the people derive or make about their own world and the world around them as well as other people. It is that more essential, basic and effective part of cultural or social tradition which provides the people the answer to what is worth doing and why. Such assumptions or inferences do not always reflect the reality, they are not, on the whole, illogical, but they are very often deducted from inadequate information, and not based upon scientific generalisations. From this point of view, the concept of world view may broadly be classified into two categories-the scientific and the existential which are self explanatory. Existential world view is mainly based on presumptions and unscientific generalisations. The world views of the so called backward or preliterate communities of the world are more or less existential in nature, whereas the world views of the so called advanced or highly educated communities of the world are more scientific in nature. But, both the types or categories of the world view are primarily meant for the survival of the human beings or societies.

The concept of world view has been variously defined and analysed by the scholars. Mehra (1977) and Adhikary (1984) reviewed critically the definitions given by different scholars. In the context of the present study, I feel it imperative, to quote some of the relevant definitions, as background.

'Mental apprehension of reality' is the world view of a community, says Sol Tax (1941) which he evolved from his study among the Guatemalan; he differentiated world view from social relations. Redfield (1952) defines world view as "the way a man, in a particular society, sees himself in relation to all else". He refined this definition in his subsequent studies (1953, 1955, 1956 and 1971) and says that world view involves "both secular and sacred spheres of life and activities, and includes both stated and unstated conceptions of the people towards everything as it comes to them". He further opines "World view is the insider's total vision and conception of everything". Forde (1954) says that "World view is expressed not only in belief system, but is also derivable from customs, rituals and actions, and there is a close relationship between the belief and the context in which they arise". Influenced by Redfield (1952) Mandelbaum (1961), while studying the Kota, uses the concept in three levels of relationships-"Man to man, man to nature and man to supernatural". To Geertz (1968) world view is the "cognitive, existential aspects of a given culture". He differentiates it from ethos which is an evaluative element of a culture. Alan Dandes (1968) looks for world view "in any aspects of the cultural material-in kinship, in child rearing, in politics or in economy, which is often implicit rather than explicit". He points out folklore as the most important source for the study of world view. World view is a combination of three systems-cognitive, attitude and action says Mendelson (1968). He treats the cognitive system with the level of scientific world view, the attitude system with any world view, and the action systems with behavioural observation. He considers philosophy a part of world view and gives religion a prominent place in the study of world view.

Jones (1972) tries to reconcile the different approaches to world view and affirms that at the level of common denominator it includes beliefs. In her book-"National Symbol" (1973), Douglas says that cosmology and world view are same, and tries to assert the relationship between the cosmology and the social form. To Kearney (1975) world view is synonymous with cognitive anthropology but he makes a distinction between world view and the practices of cognitive anthropology, viz., ethno-cience and ethnosemantics, According to Vaughan (1977) "World View" is more accurately a matrix which channels and encompasses the totality or cultural experiences, it implies that societies organise natural and supernatural phenomena into integrated meaningful system what might be called philosophic system". It is evident from the content analysis of the definitions given by different scholars from abroad that the world view of a community is actually embeded in almost all aspects of their life. Let us now look at the definitions of world view given by Indian scholars.

In India, the study on world view is very meagre. Foremost among the Indians who have devoted their genius to the concept of world view and its analysis is Prof. S. Sinha, Prof. N. K. Bose also tried to define it from his experience and information generated from tribal India. Mehra (1977) made an endeavour to project the world view of Indian tribes out of the published anthropological literature. It is Adhikary (1984) who for the first time in India made a systematic study on world view based upon intensive field work of the Birhor, a nomadic hunting and gathering community of Orissa in relation to their society. Mahapatra (1984) also wrote a theoretical article on "World View, Meta-philosophy and Nature". So far the author is aware, this is perhaps all about the work on world view in Indian Anthropology. Sinha (1958) defines world view in terms of "man's conceptualisation of and relation with nature, other men and the supernatural phenomena". He (1984) sees it as a "dynamic process of rationalisation and conceptualisation for creating a meaningful world of living". Ghosh (1968) defines world view as a way of looking at things''. To him, world view is a mental disposition. It is transmitted from one generation to another and is conditioned by culture, language and religion. He deals with the sociolinguistic aspects, ethnocentricism and the emotional aspects of Mishmi life in terms of dominant underlying motivations. According to Bose (1971) "world view springs from the inner self, through new knowledge, and faith in past history. It is a wave of traditon, of current experience, and of hopes and fears regarding the future". He says that world view is linked with social change. Mehra (1977) says "there is either a defined area of social life which can be termed world view or that world view is to be abstracted from observation of social life". He is of the opinion that world view cannot be studied by the observation of behaviour alone. Adhikary (1984) applied successfully the conceptual framework of world view as a tool or technique to study the social reality, and the social and cultural dynamics of the Birhor community. Mahapatra (1984) tries to conceptualise world view on "three planes-the sensory, the extrasensory and the moral". In his opinion, one must take into account the space and time dimension to study world view. In the sensory plane, he includes the juxtaposition of the self and the other, the external world, animals, plants, men and women, material objects and so on as space dimension; and the historic past, present and future as time dimension. In the extra-sensory plane, space dimension is concerned with the supernatural beings, spirits, powers, heaven and hell, etc.; and the time dimension subsumes the mythical past, *continuous future* (transmigration of soul, etc.) *discontinuous future* (unredeemed souls, etc.) or *cumulative future* (concept of karma, etc.) and so on. The differentiation of good and bad, their gradation and combinations, the ideal, virtuous and upright man, etc. are the subject matter in the moral plane. In conceptualising this world view, it seems, Mahapatra is inspired and guided by the Hindu philosophy of life which, to my mind, may evoke problem in its application to the communities outside Hindu fold. However, he suggests to incorporate both the thinker and the man of world to get integrated world view of a people.

In studying the world view of the Lisu, who are located mainly at the present Vijaynagar circle (Daodi) in Miao sub-division in the Tirap district of Arunachal Pradesh; their main concentration is in a village called Gandhigram; I follow the lead given by Adhikari (1984) though the omitted the Birhor concept of health and the beliefs associated with it; a vital aspect of their world view, i.e., the manner in which they react to, and treat disease and injury in relation to their society.

The Universe

The Liso do not have a specific term for the universe. but they do have their own idea or belief about the origin and structure of the Universe. The structure or outline (*nemahi)* of the universe, was created by a spider like creature referred as *ngema* later on, it was filled with earth by a creature known as *jephu*. Then two girls named *Agama* endowed with supernatural power, created the hills, the mountain, the rivers, the forest, and so on. The Lisu divide their universe into four parts. They are *Hiwo,* the sky; *Minay,* the earth; *Amisu*, the world beyond the sky where the souls of the deceased live; and *Obulus,* the world below the earth-where ant like man, designated as *Afudu,* live. As regards the world above the sky or beneath the earth, the Lisu can say nothing about its shape, or nature. To the Lisu, the structure of the universe is just like the net of a spider. But it is solid in nature. This origin and structure of the universe is known to a few old men and women only, and there is no other notions on the universe.

Concept of time

The Lisu are mostly guided by some prominent natural and environmental phenomena for their day to day activities. When the cock crows at dawn, they get up from sleep and start domestic work, when they see sun rise, finish their morning meals. When the birds, and hens return to their nest, the Lisu stop chore. Therefore, the Lisu concept of time may be term 'ecological' following Evan-Pritchard's (1940) terminology which he coined while working among the Nuer. The Lisu have crystalised idea of time as they have developed their own almanac referred as *Ekhosodu,* i.e. Annual calender of months and days. The calendar is given on page 72.

Ekhosodu
(Lisu Calendar)

No.	*Thinyi* or *Ingne* *(Name of the day)*	*English Meaning*
1.	Tholanyi	War day
2.	Lunyi	Evil spirit day
3.	Funyi	Snake day
4.	Konyi	Horse day
5.	Yonyi	Sheep day
6.	Menyi	Monkey day
7.	Ganyi	Hen day
8.	Nanyi	Dog day
9.	Wenyi	Pig day
10.	Haynyi	Mouse day
11.	Anyinyi	Cow day
12.	Danyi	Tiger day

The Lisu calendar is lunar-as they count their month from moon (*hephu*) rising to moon rising. The Lisu month is know as *iha*. When the moon is first visible that is counted as the 3rd or 4th day of the month. The Lisu week consists of twelve days, and the name of the day and the year (*vikho*) is same. They could not clearly explain to me how the calendar is read out. But they can very well say what is the day to day as per calendar; which day is good or bad, in which year there will be more rain or draught. A year is counted a new after twelve years. The period from morning (*nene*) to evening (*Kukhu*) is considered one day, i.e., *thinyi*. The period is called *moolu* when the sun (*mimi*) stands over their head. According to Lisu belief, sun is moving round the earth; night (*rishi*) occurs when the sun goes under the earth, and when it comes out day begins. The Lisu say the cock (*agafew*) crows thrice at night. When it crows for the first time, it indicates midnight (*sarhoa-tishi*), and the last time crowing of cock indicates dawn. When the birds (*ngea*), cock and hens (*gana*) begin to return to nest, the Lisu understand evening is approaching. The Lisu divide the year into two seasons-*mucho* (winter) and *manu* (summer or rainy). When the grass begins to dry, leaves of some trees begin to fall down and when a flower called *muchosiwe* blossoms, the Lisu understand the approaching of winter. Summer season is indicated by the growing of new leaves and grasses, and when the birds give birth to new offsprings, and by rain (*mahe*). It is also indicated by the blossoming of flower named-*monusiwe*.

The Lisu calculate the age of a person by counting the number of times the paddy crops harvested in the *jhum* (shifting) field. For example, the age of a child is considered three if the paddy crop is harvested thrice after his or her birth. When the stature of a child reaches the waist of an adult male or female, then only the Lisu parents start counting the age of their children. This is due to prevalence of high rate of infant mortality.

Supernatural Deities

The Lisu do not consider every natural phenomenon animated. But they do attribute natural phenomena as an act of supernatural deities which are not many in the Lisu community. Each deity has a definite area of activities in nature. The Lisu propitiate and offer sacrifices to these deities. These supernatural deities are believed to play significant role in their life. The Lisu have the concept of supreme being or Almighty, designated as *Wusa*. *Wusa* is their supreme deity. He is all powerful, can see and know every details of the things happening in the world, and everything done by the Lisu. *Wusa* is generally thought to be benevolent and does not interfere in the domain of other deities. The Lisu concept of *Wusa* does not fully connote the general notion of god, in that they do not worship *Wusa*, and can not utter the name of *Wusa* on every occasion. The Lisu remember *Wusa* when they apprehend sudden danger in life like falling from the tree or high hill, facing a tiger or a snake and so on. It brings misfortune to the person who calls for *Wusa* without any real cause, the Lisu believe. *Phula* is the popular deity. The Lisu place all their grievances and difficulties to *Phula*, who controls all the evil spirits commonly known as *ni*. *Phula* always does good to the Lisu. He is believed to help all the honest people. To appease *Phula*, pig, goat and white cocks, are sacrificed by the Lisu. *Phula* lives in *yihango*

Lo is regarded as the presiding deity over the flood (*azeyzilla*), storm (*loha*), earthquake, and rain. To stop the natural calamities the Lisu propitiate this deity by sacrificing animals (goat and pig). *Lo* can take any shape of a man or animal or bird. *Mamugolo* is the presiding deity of thunder (*mogu*) and meteor (*nebichi*). He lives in the sky, and does not do any harm to the Lisu, of all these benevolent deities, the Lisu maintain a close relationship with the *Phula*. The Lisu have the concept of only one female deity known as *Nima,* the deity of forest.

Concept of Disease and Evil Spirits

The Lisu have their own theory of disease and therapy which is based on causes and symptoms. Accordingly, the diseases suffered by them are classified into five categories-*nina, nimana, nabidina, nadudu* and the fifth category is the disease whose causes are unknown to them. *Nina* is the disease caused by the wrath of evil spirit. *Nimana*, is the stomach troubles caused by the eating of forbidden things (fruits, leaves, stems and so on) mistakenly. *Nabidina,* is caused by the germs, and the *nadudu* is the diseases caused by physical injuries. It has been observed that most of the diseases suffered by Lisu are attributed to the wrath of evil spirits commonly named *ni*. The Lisu believe that the *ni* originated along with them from the same mythical gourd or pumpkin. The Lisu got the physical shape of human beings whereas the *ni* did not. That is why the *ni* are jealous, and always remain angry with the Lisu, and try to trap them in difficulties. *Ni* have no fixed shape, they can assume any shape of man or animals, they desire. Each *ni* has got specific name, and place to reside, and each *ni* is responsible for a particular disease. The *ni* live in river, lake, cave, trees, stone, road and so on. *Ni* can be seen by a *nifa,* a person expert in dealing with *ni*. *Ni* punish the Lisu by inflicting different types of diseases only, and the Lisu live in constant fear of *ni*. Musi *ni, Sizi ni*, Macha *ni* and Yodosi, are the names of different *ni*.

View of Soul

The concept of soul is firmly rooted in the Lisu community. They even consider that *ni,* the evil spirit, is nothing but a form of soul. According to their belief, a Lisu male has got nine souls, and a Lisu female has seven souls. The common term for the soul is *choba*. Soul is a life or living matter possessed by man or woman.

Out of nine or seven souls, two souls are vital for each man and woman. One is named *Ha*, and the other called *Mamisu*. From birth to death *Ha* remains with human body, when it leaves the body, man or woman dies. When *Mamisu* leaves the body, human beings sleep. There is a constant fight going on between *Mamisu* and *ni* as per their belief, the Lisu see dreams because of *Mamisu*. Each soul is tied by a rope called *logu* with god - *Phula*. A man has nine such ropes and woman has seven. All the members of a Lisu family are tied together by a big rope with god-*Phula*. When a small rope of a member is disconnected by the evil act of *ni* from *Phula*, the member concerned falls sick and it is the foremost duty of the *nifa* to repair the rope and thereby to cure the sick person. After the death of a person, where the soul *Ha* goes, the Lisu have no idea; but *Mamisu* goes to reside in the *Mamisumi*, the land of soul above sky. Sometimes *Mamisu* comes back in the shape of a ghost called *nibu* to disturb the *Lisu*, and to ask for his or her belongings. *Nibu* does not do any harm to the Lisu. The Lisu feel the presence of a *nibu* by the peculiar sound that sometimes comes out from a grave-yard or a dirty place. The Lisu, then bury the belongings and *Nibu* disappears. The Lisu do not have the idea of ancestral spirits and ancestor worship, as they could not provide any data on this aspect of life.

Knowledge of Forest Ecology

The Lisu cannot conceive their life without forest. *Simami* is the term used for the forest. They can easily move or negotiate with the difficult hills, terrains and forests. Forest provides them fire-wood, timbers, fodder, crops, vegetables, games for hunting and so on. Forest is also the place of romance, they love to remain in the forest from early morning to evening. This is proved by the fact that during the day, no active or adult members of a Lisu family can be found in the village. Few invalid olds and few children try to break the silence of the day in a Lisu village. They are well aware of the ins and corners of the forest and the hills around their habitation, and they have coined their own terms to describe them. The whole range of hills around them is termed *Mugaphiko, ko* means hills. On the north, there are hills namely : *Gasako,* ten days are required to climb it, here lay the ruins of different types of planes of second World War; *Ziyawudoko,* requires seven days; *Thawasse* needs five days, and *Huanushiduko* needs three days foot march from their village. On the east, stand *Soluma, Wachi,* and *Sewpuko* hills. All these hills are snow-clad.

The forests around them abounds in wild animals, and birds, and medicinal plants and herbs. The Lisu are expert hunters, and they eat all types of animal except horse (*ama*), cat (*aruya*), snake (*nifu*) and frog (*opa*). The Lisu have a fictious relationship with the tiger (*leme*) and boastly say that they are never attacked by a tiger. The tiger simply looks at them and goes away. Not a single incident of death from the attack of tiger is reported in the community. But they face frequent attacks of bear. It is said that bears attack invariably on their faces. Surprisingly, I found four cases of face injuries caused by bears during my field work. There is an interesting story to explain as to why bears always attack a Lisu on the face. Bears generally live in the part of the forest where big trees are available. The Lisu fell these trees by their sharp axe for timber and firewood. Bears notice them and think over it. Bears say in their mind, "We are having big teeth, but cannot fell a single tree, and how these people are doing that, their teeth might bigger and stronger than us; let us see them". The Lisu smile and say "in order to see our teeth bears attack us on the face". For hunting wild animals, the Lisu hunters remain in the forest for months together. They have identified trees, plants and herbs, which are used as food during simultaneous failure of crops.

Phenomena of Birth

The birth of a child is considered by the Lisu as the gift of the god-*Phula* who creates new soul (*choha*) according to his wishes and sends it in the womb of a woman. To get this gift of *Phula,* cohabitation and sexual intercourse is a must for the husband and wife. To the Lisu, mere sexual intercourse by a couple does not lead to the birth of a baby; the couple must get the blessing of *Phula.* They argue that there are some married couples having regular sexual relation but fail to produce a baby. Because, they are devoid of the blessings of *Phula*. The term-*soluma* is used for a barren lady and *solufa* is used for an impotent man. Barrenness, abortion, and still birth are explained as an evil act of the spirit named-Si *ni* who to punish the couple concerned destroys the embryo of a baby (*janemay*). The Lisu do not believe in rebirth, and do not like to restrict child birth as it goes against the will of *Phula*.

View of Marriage

The Lisu term for the marriage is *chozadi,* it is an old term and the new term marriage for the Christian Lisu is *lephecha*. The Lisu consider them or all human beings, like birds and animals, a part of nature. They see birds and animals to live in pair and to produce offsprings. A Lisu or a man should marry and produce children to preserve and to continue the generation which is a part of nature. They do not regard age as a factor for an effective and happy marriage. A junior boy can easily marry a senior girl. The Lisu prefer to remain as husband and wife till death. That is why a Lisu widow or a widower does not find any difficulty for re-marriage.

View on Women

The Lisu treat woman as an equal natural partner in life, though the Lisu women have no right of inheritance of immovable property, no say in the decision-making process and religious affairs. They are equal in the sense that there is no clear cut sex-wise division of labour in the present Lisu society. Lisu women equally participate with men in all types of indoor and outdoor activities. It is not that women will always cook food, men also prepare food. Majority of the husbands consider the position of their wives equal in the Lisu society, but some wives treat their husbands as superior. Lisu women are in-charge of all household goods. Without their permission Lisu husbands cannot dispose any article. Entire responsibility of managing a household lies mostly with the women. A dominant view is that Lisu women are considered intrinsically innocent. They can not do any harm to their husbands and the society as a whole. It is the men who misguide women, provoke them to do mischiefs. That is why to settle a dispute only men are held guilty and get punishment accordingly.

Tales, Songs and Dance

Tales of the Lisu are characterised by the narration of an orphan boy, i.e., *Jachi mami*. A good number of tales are composed with the hero as an orphan. The major part of every kind of tale is occupied by the deeds of supernatural deities, specially, the deity-

Lo. Almost in all the stories, the boy falls in love with a rich beautiful girl of *Lo*. They marry and become rich by the blessings of *Lo*. These tales reflect the intimate relationship between the Lisu and the supernatural deities. Life of a Lisu is inseparable from supernatural forces. It also reflects their poverty and the craving for wealth.

The Lisu have a slight different conception of songs. No doubt, they sing song for recreation and entertainment. But Lisu song implies competition-no competition, no song. That is they sing songs always in a competitive manner. They sing songs sitting face to face in two groups. One group finishes, the other group begins, it is just like conversation, there little tune in their songs. It is marked by the absence of musical voice. In the traditional society, a Lisu never sings songs alone, if anybody does, it means he or she is in deep sorrow, in a pensive mood. Depending on the age of the singers, the Lisu songs termed *mogua* are classified into two categories-*Moguabu* and *oyii*. *Moguabu* are the group of songs sung by the old men and women, and the *oyii* songs are voiced by young men and women, boys and girls including childern. Marriage ceremony, house constructing and harvesting are the three occasions for songs.

The Lisu term for dance is *wakhi*. The performing art of the Lisu is of two types-*wakhikhi* is a group dance performed by the Lisu irrespective of age and sex. *Cheyngo* is generally a competitive dance, here the dancers form two groups. It can be performed also in a non-competitive way. For instance, to welcome and to receive the dignitaries, *cheyngo* is performed by old women and men. Like song, the Lisu do not have the conception of dance performed by single person. Occasions for dance and song are same.

Folk materials (tales, song, dance, etc.) indicate the social personality of the Lisu which is more expressive of happiness and honesty than unhappiness, melancholy and dishonesty. They are good and brave fighters, and never lose a face to face battle. They aspire to become rich and desire to achieve high status.

Concept of Work (Mi)

By work the Lisu mean the things or activities done to sustain life. They survive on food grains, fruits, etc. which are grown in the earth or field; plants and trees draw their substenance from the earth. Therefore, it is of paramount importance for survival, they think, to know the method of agriculture, or the technique of cultivating the land. Agriculture, both settled and shifting type, poultry, piggery and collection of firewood are the major works of the Lisu. The Lisu love to work hard, and want others to do so. Throughout the year, from early morning to dusk they work incessantly. From November to March is the period when the intensity of work lessens. During this period, the Lisu become busy in arranging marriage for daughters and sons. It is a rarity to see a Lisu sitting idle and indulging; in gossiping. Idleness is thought to be the cause of poverty. Hence, they consider idlemen the enemies of the society. Even very old men and women are found working in the vegetable garden or preparing food for pigs, though they are greatly respected. They want to die working. Every Lisu is a potential labour force irrespective of sex and age. Exchange of labour is a feature of their economic life. The Lisu highly value economic independence and cooperation. For instance, during peak agricultural season if the members of a family are unable to work due to illness, others will come and cultivate their land. The Lisu hardly engage labourers on the basis of payment cash or kind.

The Headman

The headman of the Lisu village is designated as *Chowu*. *Chowu* is viewed as a god-gifted man. All the powers for social control, maintenance of peace, law and order are delegated to *chowu*. He is a keeper of the Lisu society. *Chowu* acts as an administrator or magistrate, a judge, an advocate, a leader and a great soldier of the Lisu. In short, *Chowu* is a secular head. His main function is to give impartial judgment in every case. He is required to exercise the vested authority in the maintenance of right, in punishing the wrong doers, and rewarding the righteous and brave people. *Chowu* is selected by the will of the Lisu following trial and error method. He is above the will of the people. If a *chowu* is found incapable of dispensing justice to his people, he is immediately eliminated from the post. A Lisu to be selected as *chowu* should be intelligent, courageous and physically strong. The Lisu say, the man should have presence of mind, sharp memory, imaginative power, sufficient knowledge of the traditional rules and customs and the ability to understand the *swakush* (psychology) of the mob. The Lisu believe that a man to be designated as *chowu* is born by the blessing of god-*Phula* with all these noble qualities.

Phenomenon of Death (Sochi)

According to Lisu philosophy, god-*Phula* gives life, and *ni* takes it away. Life is termed *choba*. *Choba* of a Lisu is made up of two souls mainly-*Ha* and *Mamisu*. When *Ha* leaves a body, a Lisu dies. After the death of a person; the soul-*Mamisu* goes to *Mamisumi;* where the soul-*Ha* goes, the Lisu have no definite idea. Some say it mixes with air. The Lisu believe that death brings complete cessation of life. Once left, a soul cannot re-enter into human body. All kinds of deaths are attributed to the evil acts of *ni*. Death due to old age, snake-bite, the attack of bear, falling from tree, diseases, pregnancy and so on, in all these cases *ni* are held responsible. Some think that death is natural phenomenon, it cannot be prevented. Death due to pregnancy is considered very harmful. Souls of such women cannot reach *Mamisumi* it turns into a ghost called-*niha* or *nibu*. Then she gives all sorts of troubles to the Lisu. To avoid that harmful situation, the Lisu take the unborn baby out of mother's womb and bury it separately. By this act of separate burial souls of both the mother and baby reach *Mamisumi* and the birth of ghost is avoided.

Aspiration

Thought of old age and future generation termed *zu* occupies a prominent place in the life of a Lisu. In fact, the whole gamut of Lisu life revolves around this thought. Burden of old age importunes them again and again. They do not like to live to the age of invalid. Before reaching that last stage of life, death is welcomed. In other words, an old Lisu man or woman prefers to die when he or she still has the capability to do a little bit of household activities. At old age, they expect help and care from any son, preferably the youngest son called *zadi*. They becomes more happy if they get care from their daughters. In order to achieve this goal of life, they do not like to restrict birth, on the contrary, they prefer to produce as many children as they can. The logic behind this attitude is that at least one of the children will surely look after the old parents. Death is joyful to the Lisu when they die leaving behind sufficient stock of food grains and a large number of children, grand children and great grand children. It gives them great pleasure to see that his or her generation will continue after death, and they will find no difficulty in maintaining life. An old Lisu becomes more happy to see the coffin and the site of burial before death. Death becomes painful to the old Lisu when they die for want of food, when there is no one to look after them. It is customary for the Lisu to narrate the different experiences of life to sons or daughters, and relatives before death.

Knowledge of Hindu Society

The Lisu have a very poor knowledge about Hindu or Indian society. Knowledge on the Hindu society is mostly derived from the economic interaction with the Nepali ex-army men who have been given permanent settlement near the locality of the Lisu, since 1964, by the government of India. At the initial stage, the pattern of interaction between the Lisu and the Nepali settlers was one of cooperation and reciprocal. At present, it is one of conflict and competition. The Nepali settlers are arranged in hierarchical order which is followed rigidly. Ethnic composition of the Nepali settlers is as follows : Brahmin (priestly class), Chhetri (warrior class), Pradhan (business class), Mugar (agriculturist), Rai (agriculturist), Limboo (agriculturist), Gurung (agriculturist), Tamang (agriculturist), Kami (blacksmith), Sonar (goldsmith), Domai (tailor), Sarki (cobbler), and Bhujal (palanquin bearer). In the new ecological and social setting, none of these castes follows their traditional callings, they are all, irrespective of high or low statuses, engaged in agriculture.

Views of the Lisu on the Hindu society as reflected through their contact with the Nepali settlers may be summarised as follows

(i) Hindu Society is divided into different groups. No unity or cooperation exists between the groups. The Lisu are not aware of the hierarchical order prevailing in the Hindu society.

(ii) They prefer to lead on individualistic mode of life, without bothering the difficulties and comforts of others.

(iii) They are mostly corrupt and dishonest people.

(iv) Sex rules are not rigidly maintained in the Hindu society, besides husbands, their women sleep with many other men.

(v) Hindus are not labourious, and they are heavily addicted to alcoholic drinks.

(vi) They cannot explain why they are called Hindu.

It is interesting to note that the Lisu look at other people or societies in contrast to the good qualities or characters of their own people or society. According to their own evaluation these qualities of the Lisu are : the rigidity of sex rules, tremendous amount of unity and cooperation, maintenance of strict secrecy, and laboriousness. The Nepali also take these characters of the Lisu for granted. The term-*Kalafa* is used to refer Hindus or Indians. The Lisu say, this is the term actually used by the Burmese for Indians. They have borrowed it from the Burmese. *Dimpha* and *Chonepha* are the two Lisu terms used .to designate Hindus or Indians. *Dimpha* means outsider, and *Chonepha* means black people. For the British and American people, the Lisu use the term-*whaphupha*, which mean white people. *Thoubufa* and *Xichafa* are two terms used by the Lisu to designate my position in their society. *Thoubufa* is male person who writes about their culture and society in general fashion ; and *Xichafa* is again a male person who throughly investigates and interpretate the rules, customs. norms and behaviour of the Lisu for their good. These two words very often floated to my ears while I was moving in or around the Lisu village with my interpreter and informants for collecting information.

It is obvious from the description that the Lisu confront many visible and invisible things in the natural and supernatural domains, in their ecological and social circumstances, and by creating a meaningful way, they maintain a kind of intimate relation with them. The human world of the Lisu, the natural and supernatural domains, the habitat and ecological setting, and their neighbours are linked together to form a meaningful world of living for the Lisu.

REFERENCES

ADHIKARY, A.K., 1984. *Society and World View of the Birhor*, Calcutta Anthropo logical Survey of India.

BOSE, N.K. 1971 *Tribal Life in India*. New Delhi : National Book Trust.

DOUGLAS, M., 1973. *Natural Symbols : Explorations in Cosmology*. Penguin Books.

DUNDES, A., 1968. *Every Man His Way : Rreadings in Cultural Anthropology* New Jersy : Prentice-Hall Inc.

DUNDES, A., 1971. Folk Ideas Units of World View. *Journal of American Folklore*, 84, 331 : 93-103.

EVANS-PRITCHARD, E.E., 1940. *The Nuer*, Oxford : The Clavendon Press.

FORDE, D., 1954. *African Worlds*. London : International African Institute.

GEERTZ, C., 1968.'Ethos, World View and the Analysis of Sacred Symbols', In *Every Man His Way: Readings in Cultural Anthropology*, Edited by Alan Dundes. New Jersey : Prentice Hall Inc.

GHOSH, S. K., 1968. The Mishmi World View, *Man In India*. 48, 4 : 327-336.

JONES, W.T., 1972. World Views : Their Nature and Function, *Current Anthropology* 13,1 : 79-109.

KEARNEY, M., 1975. 'World View Theory and Study', In *Annual Review of Anthropology*, Edited by B.J. Siegal *et. al.* Volume 4 : 247-270.

MAHAPATRA, L.K., 1984. World View, Meta-Philosophy and Nature, *Journal of Indian A nthropological Society*, 19,3 : 264-268.

MANDELBAUM, D.G., 1961. 'The World and the World View of the Kota', In : *Village India*, Edited by Mckim Marriot, page 228-260, Bombay : Asia Publishing House.

MEHRA, J.D., 1977.'The World View of Indian Tribes'. In *Tribal Heritage of India*, Edited by S.C. Dube. page 58-84, New Delhi : Vikash Publishing House Pvt. Ltd.

MENDELSON, E.M., 1968. 'World View', In : *International Encyclopedia of the Social Science*, Edited by D.L. Sills. Volume 16; The Macmillan Company and the Free Press.

REDFIELD, R., 1953. *The Primitive World and Its Transformation*, Ithaca : Cornell University Press.

REDFIELD, R.,1955. *The Little Community : View Points for the Study of a Human Whole*, Chicago : University of Chicago Press.

REDFIELD, R., 1956. *Peasant Society and Culture : An Anthropological Approach to Civilization*, Chicago : University of Chicago Press.

REDFIELD, R., 1971. *The Little Community and Peasant Society and Culture*. Chicago : The University of Chicago Press.

SINHA, S., 1958. Tribal Cultures of Peninsular India as a Dimension of Little Tradition in the Study of Indian Civilization : A Preliminary Statement, *Journal of American Folklore* 71 : 504-518.

TAX, SOL., 1941. World View and Social Relations in Guatemala, *American Anthropologist*, 43 : 27-42.

VAUGHAN, J.H., 1977. 'An African World View', In : *Conformity and Conflict : Reading in Cultural Anthropology*, Edited by J.P. Spardly and D.W. Mccurdy, Little Brown and Company.

6

The Institution of Chieftainship Among the Noctes and Wanchos of Arunachal Pradesh

PARUL CH. DUTTA

Tirap is one of the districts of the Arunachal Pradesh bordering on Myanmar (Burma). It is the home of a number of tribes belonging broadly to the Indo-Mongoloid group. Noctes and Wanchos are two amongst these tribes who inhabit the middle and the western portion of the district respectively. They were once reputed for head-hunting, but with increase of all round security and economic stability they had since settled down to peaceful ways of life, taking keen interest in various development schemes for their own welfare. They are two distinct groups of people from the points of view of culture, customs, religion and language.

Lowang and *Wangham* are current terms of the Noctes and the Wanchos respectively meaning the chief of a village. The age old institutions of chieftainship amongst them point to centralized authorities entrusted with the maintenance of law and order of the village, nay of the entire community. They have a strong system of local self-government. In each village community of the Noctes and Wanchos, the chief is the ultimate controlling authority of the village for all social, political, administrative and religious purposes.

As to the genesis of the institution, nothing can be said very definitely. It is known from a study of anthropology that no primitive society is without a system of social and political control, either symbolized by the institution of chieftainship, hereditary or elective council of elders, individual leadership by virtue of wealth, energy and initiative, and so on. But the actual form of such authority is, perhaps, in the ultimate analysis, determined by the external and internal circumstances of the particular primitive society. It will, therefore need a thorough investigation into the past history of circumstances of the Noctes and the Wanchos in order to form an idea of the origin of chieftainship among them. In all probability, they might have carried the institution along with them during their migration to their present home.

There is a story current among the Noctes about their real or mythical first chief. His name is given as *Khunbao*, who was a very talented and powerful person. He was reputed to have crossed through the Hukong valley of Myanmar with some of his followers and attendants and came over the Patkoi Hills to a place called *Sajuok,* near the present Laptang village which is situated at a distance of about 8 km. from the District Headquarters, Khonsa towards north-west. In reaching *Sajuok,* he had to traverse a very difficult route. The inhabitants of the area already settled there acknowledged him as their chief. The present chiefs of Namsang, Borduria and Laptang are said to be descendants from *Khunbao,* the first chief. It is to be mentioned that all the Nocte villages are still under the centralized control of these chiefs, claiming their origin from the traditional first chief, *Khunbao*.

The Wanchos also have a similar story to tell. According to their tradition only five families first migrated to their present home at a time beyond the reckoning of their memory. They established the village-called Wanu-still in existence. Of the five families, the *Ralong Ham Jan* family was the most powerful, and they were first acknowledged as rulers of the Wanchos. Then came the *Wangham's* family claiming precedence over others and tried to establish their title to the chieftainship. A convention was arranged with the members of the *Ralong Ham Jan* family and the decision went in favour of the *Wangham* family's claim. Since then the tradition referred back to this family as the original chiefs of the Wanchos.

The office of the chief is now hereditary and the eldest son only succeeds his father after his death. Among the Wanchos and the Noctes the chief's families form a separate class by themselves recognised as superior to others. The system of chieftainship therefore, has great effect on the social composition of the Wanchos. It is class-ridden society, recognizing a privileged and an under-privileged class.

The Nocte society is composed of two distinct classes *Lowang Jat* and *Sanajat*. The Chief (*Lowang*) and his descendants form the *Lowang Jat* and the commoners are called *Sanajat*. Outwardly the difference between these two classes is not very obvious or conspicuous-but the fact remains that the former considers the later as inferior by birth and normally engage them as labourers. The *Sanajat* is also called *Pansa Jat* in the upper Nocte area. There are a number of clans or lineage groups under these two classes. The clans of the *Lowang* class are collectively called *Ngopu* while *Sanajat* clans are grouped under three collective names, i.e., *Khosia, Bangsia* and *Basia*. In Laju area, the Chief's clans are called *Kepi* and the commoner's *Tangmo*. Besides regulation of marriage, the distinction that exists between the two classes manifests itself in various other social privileges and behaviour. To cite an example, when the *Kepi* group kills a buffalo, the head never goes to the share of the *Tangmos*. In fests and other social festivals, the members of the two groups will never mix up and sit together. The chief's family can claim a bride from the commoner's clans barring few but never the other way round.

The Wancho society is also conspicuously divided into distinct classes. Although there is no tradition or folklore defining the privileges of the classes yet it can be said safely that the obvious class divisions evolved originally from their political institutions. There are four classes among the Wanchos-each class depending on the foundation of clan and sub-clan unity, and organised hierarchically. The highest of these classes is the *Wanghams,* claiming relations with the chiefs. The members of this class enjoy special honour and privileges in life. Their position is pivotal and the society seemingly revolve around it. In the lowest rung of the ladder are the *Wangpans*-the commonalty. Between these two are the *Wangsas* and *Wangsus*-two classes sprung up from matrimonial alliances between *Wanghams* and *Wangpans.* A *Wangsa* has his origin in the union of a *Wangham* man and *Wangpan* woman, and is regarded only next to a *Wangham* is social standing. The *Wangsas* on the other hand are the children of matrimonial alliances between *Wangsa* fathers and *Wangpan* mothers. They occupy the third strata in the social classification, i.e., they are in between the *Wangsas* and the *Wangpans.* The *Wangsas* and the *Wangsus* are not eligible for the office of the *Wanghams* since they are of mixed blood-compounded of royal and commoners heritage. They however are allowed to participate in important social functions, and sometimes given important portfolios such as looking after the chief's *morung.*

Here, an obvious question arises as to who becomes the chief ? As the chief is the head of the village and holds the highest position in the society, only a *Wangham* of pure blood is entitled to become the chief. It is because of this underlying principle a *Wangham* chief particularly is supposed to marry a *Wangsia*-the daughter of another *Wangham* born of *Wangham* wife. A *Wangham* can marry more than one *Wangsia* and the eldest son, born of any of the *Wangsias,* can become the chief. In case there is no son-then the post will go to the nearest kin of the deceased chief, preferably to the eldest son of the deceased chief's brother. He also must be son born out of a *Wangsia.*

It is therefore, evident that the Wancho chiefs are under obligations of continuing the pure blood line-by marrying only in the

Wangham's family. Social distinction between these classes as it has already been pointed out is very clearly marked in every sphere of their life. For example, the *Wangpans* are not allowed to take meal, sitting in the same row with the *Wanghams.* They cannot marry a girl from *Wangham* family. The *Wanghams, Wangsas* and *Wangsus* practically form the core of the village aristocracy. For the purpose of marriage, the *Wangham, Wangsa* and *Wangsu*- constitute one class, the royal class called the *Wang Jan* and the *Wangpans* forms the other class. At Wakka, these two classes are known as *Gangsa* and *Pansa.*

The chiefs in both Wancho and Nocte societies enjoy, as it goes without saying, the most privileged positions. They are the head of the village and in fact the controlling authorities. In the social set-up they derive maximum benefits from all points of view. As for example, when the whole village go for hunting and fishing expedition, the largest share of meat of fish falls to the chief. The whole village help in the cultivation of his field. The chief's house is built by the co-operative labour of the entire village.

Though it is trute that the chiefs enjoy privileged positions in society, they are primarily responsible for the security and well being of the whole community under their charge. They are accordingly expected always to act in most responsible manner making their contributions to the all round prosperity of the society. It is no wonder that the life of the community and many festivals among the Noctes and Wanchos move around the chief and his family. On all ceremonious occasions, it is the chief who leads. When a chief dies, the whole community becomes concerned. In other words, it becomes a state occasion as in the case of leaders and heads of modern states with the difference that here the ceremony and rites connected with the occasion are traditionally determined and assume a semi-religious character.

Functions and Powers of the Chief

The chief is called *Lowang* among Noctes and *Wangham* by the Wanchos. He is the head of the village as well as the council of elders subservient to him and functions as its Chairman. He holds the final decision on any affairs, social, political, administrative and religious. But of course, he is supposed to take council with other members of the village council. The chief guides the political life of the village, arbitrates in disputes and decides cases, civil or criminal in nature within the village and also organises developmental activities. The villagers are not free to move their own, when a matter concerns the whole village without the expressed sanction of the chief. In bygone days it was the chief who decided about head-hunting expedition.

The chief had the right and power to dispense punishments to offenders, found guilty of committing murder or theft. He however usually consults the village council as a form of propriety. As it has already been noticed, the chief is not only the judicial head but also the prime executive head of the community as a whole. It is his responsibility primarily to ensure that no quarrel or dispute is allowed to assume serious perpetration, threatening the peace of the community life. He was the defender of his village against outside attack, when in ancient time, a state of general insecurity prevailed.

As the head of the village, the chief's order binds everybody in principle. In practice, however, village council has a role of corrective influence on the chief and guides him along the right path.

The Village Council

The council of village elders is called *Ngothun, Ngongthun* or *Ngongthit* in Nocte and *Wangchu-Wangcha* in Wancho. The council, both among the Noctes and Wanchos, is an well organized institution. The chief is always the chairman of this organization by right. The system of administration of justice and management of village affairs is quite democratic in the sense that the chief do not rule arbitrarily but act on the advice and counsel of the village elders. Thus, the chiefs are not autocratic rulers. There are a number of members who are called differently and each member has different duties and responsibilities.

The Nocte *Ngothun* has the following members :

Ngongba : He is popularly called *Handiqui* (an Assamese term). He acts as assistant to the chief and has the privilege of private discussions with him. He enjoys a good position in the village, performs rituals, and organises festivals.

Ramba : An important member of the council. He acts as a sort of public liaison. It is his duty to keep the villagers informed of any important happening in the village such as holding of *Ngongthun*, heralding of festive occasions and likewise. He also acts as a priest.

Tanba : *Tanba* (or *Kamba* or *Tanti*) is the messenger of the chief. He acts as an envoy of the chief in other villages.

Besides the above mentioned officials, there are a number of old persons who are also members of the council. They are called *Noktang*, and selected one from each clan, on the basis of their knowledge of tradition and customs. Their function is mostly negative and limited only to pointing out any lapse or mistake in procedure. On the positive side they guide the proceedings of the council along traditionally approved conventions.

In Laju area, there is another official called *Nyamtai*, whose duty is to work as a middle man or arbitrator for disputes at the instance of the *Ngongthun*, and the *Lowang* in particular.

The members of the Wancho village council are called *Wangcho*, *Wangcha*, *Ngopa* and *Wangcham* respectively.

Wangcho and the *Wangcha* are collectively called *Khonsai*, and they act as ministers. The chief usually consults them in every important matter before giving a final decision.

The *Wangcham* acts as messenger of the chief and the council, and represents the chief in other villages.

The *Ngopa* functions as the counterpart of *Ramba* of the Nocte council.

In conclusion, it may be said that chieftainship which is an age old institution among the two tribes under discussion, is continuing till today, even after introduction of Panchayat Raj Regulation (1967),with marginal changes in form and strength. The people are tradition bound and they have due regards and respect for their traditional system. The traditional village councils are not finding a strong rivalry in the statutory Panchayat system.

7

The Pattern of Kinship and Friendship Terminology of the Apatanis of Arunachal Pradesh

D.K. DUARAH

I

Kinship has been called the core of social organisation of a society. Firth (1936) describes kinship as "the rod on which one leans through out life, the regulator of behaviours in innumerable situations". Kinship plays an important part in the socio-cultural aspect and socio-economic affairs of all human societies. It may also be called as a constituant of human culture and social grouping. The major groupings are consanguinal kin and affinal kin. In human societies, these social groupings are bounded with specific functions, rites and obligations towards each kin relationship, to perform or to abide by in their normal course of life as well as in accidental affairs.

The Apatanis inhabit the picturesque valley around Ziro, the head quarters of the Lower Subansiri district. They are expert agriculturist and practise wet rice cultivation with indigenous method of irrigation. Their village settlement is of permanent type. The houses are constructed in systematic manner. The nuclear family is most common. In marriage, clan exogamy and tribe endogamy is general rule and have no preferential type. Their religious belief and practices may be called as animistic. The society is governed by a council called *Bulliang*.

The kinship system of the Apatani is characterised by preponderance of classificatory terms although there are some distinctive terms too. From the kinship terminologies of the Apatanis, it is apparent that there are extensive use of the same term for kins of different generations and even for both consanguineous and affinal kins; especially in terms of address. Another special feature is use for some terms after the name of different segments of an animal for a particular set of kin groups.

In the present context, the kinship system is used to include, in a limited sense, the kinship terminology, both the terms of address and reference use by each sex. The kinship terms were collected through unstructured interview and non participant observation. The genealogical tables were collected from respondents belonging to both the sexes.

II

Analysis of the genealogical tables (Table 1, 2, and 3) revealed that there are some terms which are used extensively both to address and reference; but the terms of reference are distinctly and specially applied compared to that of the terms of address. The number of terms used in address are fewer than that of the reference. Another speciality is that the terms used to address male and female individual even in primary relatives, is different in some relationships.

In primary kin relatives, the terms for father-*Abba*, mother-*Ane* or *Ama*, elder brother-*Atte* and elder sister-*Atta* in male speaking, and *Ani* for elder sister in female speaking. These terms are used both to address and reference. While younger brother, younger sister, son, daughter are addressed more commonly by their personal name and distinctive terms are used in refering them. The refering terms in case younger brother, younger sister is often used to address also. The terms of reference of own children is *Ohho* and the distinguished term for son and daughter is *Milaba* and *Niim* respectively. In refering younger brother and younger sister by male, the term use is *Annu* and *Barmi* respectively, where as the female use the term *Baro* and *Annu* for them. So, it appears that term for younger brother and younger sister is different for male and female speaking. The term of reference for husband and wife is *Milo* and *Mihi,* but while addressing they use their respective name and often use nick name.

The term *Ato* is used to address father's father, mother's father and all the grand fathers of parents in ascending generations in cognetic relationship; which also extended to affinal side, i.e., to address wife's father, husband's father and all such kins of their ascending generations. Hence, the term *Ato* includes the persons such as-Fa Fa, Fa Fa Fa, Mo Fa, Mo Fa Fa, Wi Fa, Wi Fa Fa, Hu Fa, Hu Fa Fa. Similarly *Ayo* is used to address-Fa Mo, Mo Mo, Wi Mo Mo, Hu Mo, Hu Fa Mo, Mo Mo Mo. In referring these kins, *Ato* and *Ayo* stands only for consanguinal kins; but for affinal kins-Wi Fa, Hu Fa, Wi Mo, Hu Mo and such other relatives, the word *Bo* is suffixed with the parent term. The term *Ato-Bo* is further extended to refer Hu e Br, Wi e Br, Wi y Br, and *Ayo-Bo* to Hu e Br Wi, Wi e Br Wi, Wi y Br Wi; while in addressing *Ato* stands only for Hu e Br, *Ayo* and often by name for Wi e Br Wi. Hu e Br Wi is addressed as *Atta* and Wi e Br and Wi y Br are addressed by their respective name. It is revealed that sons and wives in affinal relations occupies the same status and enjoy the respect and behaviour from their son-in-law as deserved by the parents, i.e., Wi Fa, Wi Mo, Hu Fa, Hu Mo. The terms *Ato-Bo* and *Ayo-Bo* are also used to refer elderly persons contemporary to their real parent-in-laws of that clan as well as the village.

Atte-the addressing as well as referring term of elder brother in primary relationship, is extended to address F a e Br, Fa y Br. The same term often by suffixing the personal name is used to address the elderly persons of their contemporary age of the clan as well as of village and community.

The term *Annu* is used primarily for younger brother, in male speaking is also used to refer brother's sons (nephew) by both the sex. In practice their personal names are used to call them. In this respect the term *Baro* used for younger brother in female speaking is not implied. But in affinal side of female speaking, the term *Annu* includes to refer Hu y Br, Hu y Si, e Br Da, y Br Da, Fa e Br Da, Fa y Br Da, Fa e Si Da, Fa y Si Da. *Annu-Abang* is a term commonly used to refer brothers elder and younger in age of ego's kins and community.

Atta, a term used to address elder sister by male in ego's generations, is used as well as to address Fa e Si, Fa y Si, Mo y Si, and in affinal side to Hu e Br Wi, Hu e Si, and Wi e Si, by the both male and female individuals. In referring the affinal relations *Atta-Bo* stands for Hu e Si, Wi e Si and *Ayo-Bo* for Hu e Br Wi only.

The term *Barmi* is used by a man to refer to his younger sister. It is also extended to cover a wide range of female kins of a man who are younger to him and belong to his generation or the descending generation. In male speaking, use of the term *Barmi* is open; while in female speaking, it is restricted in cognetic side and open in affinal side. So in referring the term *Bari* covers (in male speaking)-e Br Da, y Br Da, Wi y Si, Fa e Br Da, Fa y Br Da, Fa e Si Da, Fa y Si Da, Wi e Br Da, Wi y Br Da, Wi y Si Da; and in female speaking-Hu e Si Da, Hu y Si Da. The personal names of all these kin are used to address them.

To designate the maternal uncles (Mo Br), the term *Akku* is used, both to address and refer. The same term is further extended to their sons, but they are referred with the term *Akku-Bo*. This signifies that not only the maternal uncle, but also their sons enjoy the same status and honour from the addresse and equally possess the same obligations towards the nephews Ohho-Bo after the death of their father. The clan members contemporary to the Mo Brs are also termed as *Akku*. While mother's brother's daughters are address with either by *Atta* or by personal name basing on their age by speaker; and referred them with a common term *Annu Ami* alongwith mother's sister's children, for whom their names are used to address.

Achi is used to address the relatives such as elder brother's wife, father's brother's wife, mother's brother's wife, and mother's brother's sons's wife. In referring the relatives, except father's brother's wife, where the term *Ann* or *Attemi* is used ; the same term *Achi* stands for all.

Nyahi is a term of reference used to denote daughters-in-law such as y Br Wi, So Wi Hu y Br Wi, father's brother's son's wife, husband's father's brother's son's wife. All of them are addressed with their personal name except son's wife, where the term *Amii* is used.

The term *Mabbo* is used to refer one's own son-in-law and also it includes e Si Hu, y Si Hu, Fa e Si Hu, Fa y Si Hu, Hu e Si Hu, Hu y Si Hu, Fa e Br Da Hu, Fa y Br Da Hu, Hu Fa e Br Da Hu, Hu Fa y Br Da Hu. The addressing term of all these relatives is either by their own name or by *Aou* and after prefixing *Aou* with the name. The term of reference for Da Hu Fa and Da Hu Mo is *Dun Mabbo* while So Wi Fa and So Wi Mo is *Ajing-Bo*. The term *Ajing-Bo* is also used to in referring mother's sister's husband, wifes sister's sons. The term of addressing for them is by their personal name.

The term *Ohho* is used to designate ego's own children irrespective of sex and age in primary relative which is also used to refer in female speaking to husband's brother's children and husband's father's brother's sons. By suffixing the term *Bo*-it refers to e Si So, y Si So, e Si Da, Fa e Si So, Fa y Si So, Hu y Si So. Similarly the term *Ohho-asi* refer to So So, So Da, Da So, Da Da, Fa Br So So, Fa y Br So, Hu Fa e Br Da, Hu Fa y Br Da. It appears that *Bo* is suffixed by the maternal uncles to refer their nephew while *Asi* is suffixed to refer the children of the first descending generation.

The Apatani society permits polygamous type of marriage, though in practice it is less in number, the kinship terminology for such step relationship are, such as, *Ane* - an addressing term of the step mother, the reference of which is *Anchi*. The children of step mother are addressed with their personal names and also with the same terminology as used in their own brothers and sisters. The term of reference for the first wife children is *Nit-Ohho* and second wife's children is *Nichi-Ohho*. The distinction of sex is made later by suffixing *Milabo* and *Niim* with *Niim* and *Nichi*.

III

Apart from the individual terms discussed above for each categories of relationship, there are some collective compound terms which are used to designate a large number of relatives (*Nyan*) of different generations. The term *Milabo-nyan* is used for the father's mother's brother's and *Niim-nyan* for all the mother's affinal kins. Another collective term is *Barm-atang* which covered the sisters and their families. Using of these compound terms indicates that these groups of relatives possess same type of obligation towards the speaker and in turn deserve similar honour and respect.

Similarly, all the affinal kins of a male, viz. the father-in-law, his brothers and their sons; though designate with a common term *Ato-Bo,* amongst them only four persons are selected at the time of marriage; the first one is termed as *Dirang,* second one as *Lache,* and the rest two as *Arhimichu* or *Poniyo*. All the four persons are collectively referred as *Ari,* as they are entitled to receive the bride price (*Ari*) from the groom. The bride price is shared among them proportionately as per their status. In return they have the obligation to pay a reciprocal amount of paddy among other items as presentation to the bride. One interesting feature is that, the bride's father may or may not be any one of these four persons, but it must be confined within the lineage group of the bride. After marriage, the relationships are counted only at the time of festivals and individually organised social and ritual functions, wherein the son-in-law (*Mabbo*) has to pay and honour them with their due share. Similarly, the *Ari* group also possess some sort of obligations towards them in natural calamities and other social events.

Like the *Ato-Bo,* among the maternal uncles (*Akku)* of an individual, irrespective of sex; only two persons are selected who are addressed as *Koro* and *kabo*. Both of them commonly termed as *Ali,* as they are entitled to get one fore limb (*Ali*) each, of the sacrificed animals like cow, *mithun* in rituals and festivals. These persons are also must be within the same lineage of the mother. Out of all the mother's brother's, only these two persons, *Koro* and *Kobo,* have the obligation towards that particular nephew and not by all. In this way, for all the nephews, the *Ali* personals are selected. Hence, for a couple the total number of *Ali* personals are four, two from each side. Once such relationship established, it continues throughout the life and even after their death; as these relationships are inherited by one of the sons of the *Koro* and *Kobo;* and hence the relationship continues.

The kinship term used to designate maternal uncles of father and mother of an individual is *Gyasi;* as they are entitled to get as honour in rites and ceremonies the ribs (*Gyasi*) of sacrificed animals. Similarly, the maternal uncles of grand parents, i.e., of second ascending generation is expressed with the term *Leopani* and their next ascending generation with *Kuting*. The term *Kuting* covers all the maternal uncles above this generation of a couple. The ceremonial gifts for *Leopani* and *Kuting* personnels is a piece of bacon or pork, the size of which vary depending upon the nature of relation. The constituent persons in *Gyasi, Leopani* and *Kuting* relationships are 2, 4 and 4 respectively for an individual from both father's and mother's side. The marital relationship from *Leopani* onwards is permitted by the society and hence often new relationship is developed. These persons also possess obligation towards the addressee or speaker, specially in natural calamities.

IV

In addition to the relationship counted in consanguinal and affinal side; the Apatanis establish relations in the form of friendship tie, the service and help rendered by them is similar to that of kins and often more than that, specially at the time of natural calamities. The term use to express these friends is *Buinee*, a popular term in the Apatani society. The persons considered for developing such relationship are generally outside the clan with whom no kin relationship is counted. The friendship ties once established, it continues generation after generation unless there happens major dead lock. Usually, the sons either by dividing among themselves or any one generally the eldest son inherit all the *Buinee* of their father. A fresh establishment of *Buinee* can only developed during the celebration of *Mloko* or *Myoko* festival. The females can also establish such friendship ties, but not counted within the term *Buinee*. This relationship is often be called as ceremonial friendship of *Buinee-Ajina,* as the first establishment of this friendship took place during the *Mloko* or *Myoko* festival and have to renew in each annual celebration. The right and obligation of *Buinee* is of reciprocal nature.

From the foregoing discussion it is apparent that the Apatani people use extensively the same term to various kin relatives of different generations, both in cognatic and affinal side. Each kin relatives deserves specific respect and behaviour from the speaker and some of these relatives also possess prescribed obligation towards the addressee. Some of the kinship terminologies are inherited by the sons along with the obligation even after the death of their father. Prevalence of collective terms, viz. *Ari, Ali, Gyasi, Leopani* and *Kutings* above all the friendship the expressed by the term *Buinee* are some of the interesting features of the Apatani kinship systems.

Table 1
Apatani Kinship Terminologies

	Congnatic				Affinal			
	Female kin		Male Kin		Female kin		Male Kin	
Second ascending generation	Mo Mo	- Ayo	Mo Fa	- Ato				
	Fa Mo	- Ayo	Fa Fa	- Ato				
	Mo Mo Mo	- Ayo	Mo Fa Fa	- Ato				
First ascending generation	Mo	- Ane	Fa	- Abba	Wi Mo	- Ayo-bo	Fa e Si Hu	- Mabbo
	Mo e Si	- Atta	Fa e Br	- Atte	Hu Mo	- Ayo-bo	Fa y Si Hu	- Mabbo
	Mo y Si	- Atta	Fa y Br	- Atte	Fa e Br Wi	- Achi	Mo e Si Hu	-Aningbo
	Fa e Si	- Atta	Mo e Br	- Akku	Fa Y Br Wi	- Achi	Mo y Si Hu	- Ajingbo
	Fa y Si	- Atta	Mo y Br	- Akku	Mo e Br Wi	- Achi		
					Mo e Br Wi	- Achi		
Ego's generation	e Si	- Atta	e Br	- Atte	Wi	- Mihi	Hu	- Milo
	y Si (M.S)	- Barmi	y Br (M.S)	- Annu	e Br Wi	- Achi	e Si Hu	- Mabbo
	Y Si (W.S)	- Annu	y Br (W.S)	- Baro	y Br Wi	- Nyahi	y Si Hu	- Mabbo
					Wi y Si	- Barmi	Hu y Br	- Annu
					Wi e Si	- Atta	Wi y Br	- Ato-bo
					Wi e Br Wi	- Ayobo	Wi e Si Hu	- Barbo-Libo
					Hu y Si	- Annu	Hu e Br	- Ato-bo
					Hu e Si	- Atta	Hu e Si Hu	- Ato-Mabbo
					So Wi Mo	- Ajingbo	Hu y Si Hu	- Mabbo

							Da Hu Fa	Dun-Mabbo
							So Wi Fa	Ajingbo
							Wi y Br	Ato-bo
							Da Hu Mo	Dun Mabbo
First	e Br Da (M.S)	Barmi	e Br So	Annu	So Wi	Nyahi	Da Hu	Mabbo
	y Br Da (M.S)	Barmi	y Br So	Annu	Wi e Si Da	Barmi	Wi e Si So	Ohho-bo
descending	e Si Da	Ohhobo	e Si So	Ohhobo	Wi y Si Da	Barmi	Wi y Br So	Ajingbo
generation	y Si Da	Ohhobo	y Si So	Ohhobo	Wi e Br Da	Barmi	Wi e Br So	Ato-bo
	Da	Ohho (nime)	So	Ohho	Wi y Br Da	Barmi	Wi y Br So	Ato-bo
	e Br Da (W.S)	Annu		Milo-bo	Hu e Si Da	Barmi	Hu e Si so	Ohho-bo
	y Br Da (W.S)	Annu			Hu y Si Da	Barmi	Hu y Si So	Ohho-bo
					Hu e Br Da	Ohho	Hu e Br So	Ohho
					Hu y Br Da	Ohho	Hu y Br So	Ohho
Second descending	So Da	Ohho-asi	So So	Ohho-asi				
	Da Da	Ohho-asi	Da So	Ohho-asi				

Table 2
Range of Application : Terms of Address

Terms of address	*English equivalent*	*Denotative term*	*Relative denotes*	*Classificatory terms*	*Relative classed*
Abba	Father	Abba	Fa		
Ane	Mother	Ane	Mo		
Ato	Grand father/ Mother-in-law			Ato	Fa Fa, Mo Fa, Wi Fa, Hu Fa, Hu e Br, Hu Fa Fa, Wi Fa Fa, Fa, Fa. Fa, Mo Fa Fa.
Ayo	Grand mother/ Mother-in-law			Ayo	Fa Mo, Mo Mo, Wi Mo, Hu Mo, Wi e Br Wi, Hu Mo Mo, Wi Fa Mo, Mo Fa Mo.
Atte	Elder brother/Uncle			Atte	e Br, Fa e Br, Fa y Br.
Annu	Younger brother/Nephew			Annu	y Br (M.S.), e Br So, y Br So.
Baro	Younger brother	Baro	y Br (W.S)		y Br (W.S)
Atta	Elder sister/Aunt			Atta	e Si (M.S), Fa e Si, Fa y Si, Hu e Si, Hu e Br Wi, Mo y Br Da, Mo e Br Da, Mo e Si, Mo y Si.
Ami	Elder sister	Ami	e Si (W.S)		e Si (W.S)
Barmi	Younger sister			Barmi	y Si (M.S)
Akku	Maternal uncle			Akku	Mo e Br, Mo y Br, Mo e Br So, Mo y So.
Achi	Aunt/Sister-in-law			Achi	e Br Wi, Fa e Br Wi, Fa y Br Wi, Mo e Br Wi, Mo y Br Wi, Mo e Br So Wi, Mo y Br So Wi,
Ammi	Daughter-in-law	Ammi	So Wi		
Aou	Son-in-law			Aou	Da Hu, e Si Hu, y Si Hu, Fa e Si Hu, Fa y Si Hu.

Table 3
Range of application : Terms of reference

Terms of reference	*English equivalent*	*Denotative term*	*Relatives denotes*	*Classificatory terms*	*Relative classed*
Abba	Father	Abba	Fa		
Ane	Mother	Ane	Mo		
Miloba	Son	Miloba	So		
Nime	Daughter	Nime	Da		
Ato	Grand-father			Ato	Fa Fa, Mo Fa, Fa Fa Fa, Mo Fa Fa.
Ayo	Grand-mother			Ayo	Fa Mo, Mo Mo, Fa Fa Mo, Mo Mo Mo.
Ato-bo	Father-in-law			Ato-bo	Wi Fa, Wi e Br, Wi y Br, Wi e Br So, Hu Fa, Hu Fa Fa, Wi Fa Fa, Hu e Br, Hu y Br.
Ayo-bo	Mother-in-law			Ayo-bo	Wi Mo, Wi e Br Wi, Wi y Br Wi, Hu Mo, Hu e Br Wi, Hu Fa Mo, Wi Fa Mo, Wi Fa e Br So Wi, Wi Fa y Br So Wi.
Atte	Elder Brother/ Paternal Uncle			Atte	e Br, Fa e Br, Fa y Br.
Atta	Elder sister Aunt			Atta	e Si (M.S), Fa e Si, Fa y Si, Mo e Si, Mo y Si.
Annu	Younger Brother/ Younger sister (W.S.)/Nephew			Annu	Y (Br (M.S.), y Si (W.S.), e Br So, y Br So, e Br Da (W.S.)

(Contd.)

Terms of reference	*English equivalent*	*Denotative term*	*Relative denotes*	*Classificatory terms*	*Relative classed*
					Y, Br Da (W.S), Fa e Br Da (W.S) Fa y Br Da (W.S), Fa e Si Da (W.S) Fa y Si Da (W.S), Hu y Si.
Barmi	younger sister (M.S)/ Younger sister-in-law/ Niece			Barmi	y Si, e Br Da, y Br Da, Wi y Si, Fa e Br Da, Fa y Br Da, Fa e Si Da Fa y Si Da, Wi e Br Da, Wi y Br Da, Wi e Si Da, Wi y Br Da, Hu e Si Da Hu y Si Da.
Ami	Elder Sister(W.S)	Ami	E Si (W.S)		
Baro	Youger brother (W.S.)	Baro	y Br (W.S)		
Atta-bo	Sister in law			Atta-bo	Wi e Si, Hu e Si.
Akku	Maternal uncle			Akku	Mo e Br, Mo y Br.
Akku-bo	Maternal uncle's son			Akku-bo	Mo e Br So, Mo y Br So.
Achi	Elder Sister-in-law/Aunt			Achi	e Br Wi, Mo e Br Wi, Mo y Br Wi, Mo e Br So Wi, Mo y Br So Wi.
Ohho	Children	Ohho	Children	Ohho	Hu e Br So, Hu y Br So, Hu Fa e Br So Hu Fa y Br So, Own children.
Ohho-bo	Children-in-law			Ohho-bo	e Si So, y Si So, e Si Da, y Si Da, Fa e Si So, Fa y Si So Hu e Si So, Hu y Si So.

Ohho-asi	Grand son			Ohho-asi	So So, So Da, Da So Da Da, Fa e Br So So, Fa y Br So So, Hu fa e Br Da, Hu Fa y Br Da.
Mabbo	Son-in-law			Mabbo	e Si Hu, y Si Hum Da Hu, Fa e Si Hu, Fa Y Si Hu, Hu e Si Hu, Fa Y Si Hu, Fa e Br Da Hu, Fa y Br Da Hu, Hu Fa e Br Da Hu, Hu Fa y Br Da Hu.
Dun-Mabbo	Daughters	Dun-Mabbo	Da Hu Fa, Da Hu Mo.		
Ajingbo				Ajingbo	Mo e Si Hu, Mo y Si Hu, Wi e Si So, So Wi Fa, So Wi Mo, Wi y Si So.
Nyahi	Daughter-in law			Nyahi	y Br Wi, So Wi, Hu y Br Wi, Fa e Br So Wi, Fa y Br So Wi, Hu Fa e Br So Wi, Hu Fa y Br So Wi.
Milo	Husband	Milo	Husband		
Mihi	Wife	Mihi	Wife		
Annu Ami				Annu Ami	Mo e Br Da, Mo y Br Da, Mo e Si So, Mo y Si So, Mo e Si Da, Mo Si Da.
Annu Abang				Annu Abang	Fa e Br So, Fa y Br So.
Ann/Attemi		Ann/Attemi	Fa e Br Wi Fa y Br Wi		

8

Indigenous Health Practices Among the Idu Mishmi of Arunachal Pradesh

S.S. DATTA CHAUDHURY
G.C. GHOSH

Indigenous health practices refer to the measures relating to preventive health care, diseases and its curatives which are being used by the people as medical therapy. The urge to lead a life free from disease and ailments was perhaps developed through the severe experiences of sufferings. This impulse had possibly compelled the human society to exploit the abounding nature for remedial measure. The disease and its remedial measures thus have a direct relation with the biotic and physical environment in which the population is nurtured. Therefore, the disease pattern and its specialised curative knowledge may be distinct for a particular location or even

Reproduced by the permission of the authority of the Journal *Human Science*, Vol. 33, No. 1, 1984 pp 24-34.

for a region. India being a vast country having varied ecological niche provides a unique opportunity to study this aspect in terms of its peculiarity and variety.

This specialised knowledge earned through hard experiences of trial and error method is threatened to disappear with rapid growth and innovation of medical sciences. The advancement of medical science and its application for the betterment and maintenance of human society is most welcome though there should be serious effort to explore the areas of indigenous health practices in order to record and examine the various methods which are still in practice among our people particularly of rural origin. This will not only help us to know one of our most important cultural heritage but also promises to give new dimension in the field of pharmaceutical research.

It is gratifying to record that this particular aspect of Indian culture has found place in some of the monumental works of earlier ethnographers. Though it was not attempted as it is proposed presently, the importance of tribal medicine and the like could draw the attention of Dunbar (1915), Boding (1925), Redcliffe Brown (1948), Shukla (1959), Srivastava (1962), Vidyarthi (1963), Saikia (1964), Roy (1925), Mittal (1978), Sinha (1979), Pulu (1979), Mathur (1982) and others. These apart, there are a number of studies particularly on the curative aspect of local vegetations which are being used by our rural population (Jowle 1961, Jain (1968). Studies of folk medicine in Indian context by Kourennoff and George (1970), Jaggi (1975), Morley and Wallis (1978) and others have added a new dimension to this scientific enquiries. While these studies of the ethnographers, natural scientists, and social scientists, are of immense value and deserve high appreciation of special merit, still there is need to probe this aspect of Indian culture particularly of rural origin through systematic scientific endeavours.

With this aim in view a study was undertaken among the Idu Mishmi of Arunachal Pradesh. Unlike other parts of India, Arunachal Pradesh has experienced the development of rapid communication system relatively late and hence it is reasonably expected that most of the elements of indigenous health practices of the Idu Mishmi will remain undisturbed.

The Idu Mishmi are primarily concentrated in newly formed Dibang Valley district of Arunachal Pradesh which was previously under the administrative control of Lohit district authority.

The data for the present study was collected in the year 1981-82 from three villages, namely, Koronu, Enjens and Old Koronu which come under the Riang Sub-division of Dibang Valley district. The information on the indigenous health practices was gathered from the people having specialised knowledge on the subject and preferably from those persons who were consulted by the villagers in case of any disease or ailments. The data were collected on schedules specially designed for the purpose and sometimes through direct observation method. The medical records preserved at Riang Hospital were consulted to understand the prevalence of disease in the area. Available vegetations which are used by the people as curative were also collected and preserved for further study.

The Idu Mishmi possess Mongoloid type of physical characteristics having yellow to light brown skin colour, presence of epicanthic fold, broad chin, flat nose and wide nostrils. Dalton (1872) also concluded "...their features are in fact of a coarse Mongoloid type".

The Idu are easily distinguishable from their neighbouring communities by virtue of their peculiar fashion of hair dressing. Both male and female shave a portion of frontal hair almost in a similar way and brush it back to form a tussel.

PREVENTIVE HEALTH CARE

Sanitation

The concept of health and hygiene among the Idu is not of very high order. The villages are devoid of any specific dumping place for refused material. The drainage system is extremely poor and every house drains out its waste at the rear portion. Houses are designed to have a particular place to be used as latrine and the latrine is cleaned through natural process. But in few cases improved system of sanitation was observed which indicates the impact of external influence.

Cleanliness

The Idu Mishmi of older generation and the female in general are not accustomed to take regular bath. This is partly due to insufficiency of water and colder climate and largely due to their cultural habits. The female during their menstruating period take bath and clean their garments regularly. The use of soap is seldom met with. In earlier times they are reported to clean their body and garments with the help of soapnut (sapindus trifoliatus) locally known as *Alambra*. Washing of hands and feet before taking meal is not in their practice. The use of water after nature's call is seldom reported and sometimes they use leaves for such purpose.

Food Habits

The food stuff both of animal and vegetative origin are cut to pieces and boiled in water adding a little common salt and chilley. In earlier times they used to use copper vessels as container which is now replaced by aluminium pots readily purchased from the local market. Earthen pots are also not uncommon. They generally use bamboo tubes to collect and store water. Now-a-days plastic or iron container is becoming very popular.

The food items of the Idu include cereals, animal proteins, vegetables and alcoholic drinks prepared out of rice. Milk is not consumed by the Idu. They take almost all kinds of animal protein except '*hulla*'(hullack) and domesticated cat. The excess meat and fish are preserved by smoking process for future consumption. The Idu female do not take the meat of *mithun*, buffallo and pork. But young girl of non-pubetal age and old lady having four to five issues consume these forbidden food. The most common vegetables they consume are arum *(So-na)*, sweet potato (*Geja*) and gourd *(Cekapu)*. Drinks are prepared locally by fermenting rice. Sometimes drinks are also prepared out of millet. The catalytic agent which are used for fermentation is known as '*pae*'. In the days of scarcity they are totally dependent on forest products.

Midwifery

In Idu society the job of midwifery is generally attended by the experienced relatives. There is no such specific person to perform the job. In some cases the *'Bamni'* is called for who cut the umbilical cord without touching the mother. Before doing so the *Bamni* chants some incantation over a cup of water and gives it to the prospective mother to drink so as to save her from all kinds of sufferings. The umbilical cord is cut with the help of bamboo split.

Disposal of Dead

In the event of death of an individual his or her relatives are informed and the dead body is kept on the plank of the house till their arrival. Then they call for the *Bamni* who performs the ritual before it is taken to graveyard. The graveyards are located outside the residential area. The grave pit is usually 8 ft. in length, 4 ft. in breadth and 3 ft. in depth and is dug out by the village boys. The pit is walled by bamboo splits and covered by leaves to give it a hut like shape. The deadbody is placed inside the pit along with some of the deseased's belonging including animals like chicken and pig. The burial rituals are performed according to financial condition of the concerned family.

In case of suicide they place the head of the deadbody in southern direction and observe pollution for five days. In case of homicide, the deadbody is placed in somewhat angular position and no pollution is observed. In the event of a child death within six days of birth, the body is not buried. It is wrapped in a new cloth and is kept on a high tree within a basket in nearby forest.

Termination of Pregnancy

The concept of small family for better life and prosperity is not well accepted by the Idu society as they always prefer to have larger number of issues for economic reasons. But the need for termination of pregnancy was always felt particularly in case of conception of unmarried women. At the early stage of conception, as they believe, the termination of pregnancy may be affected by jumping from a high place. It is also reported that the extract of a particular plant called *Apatama** is generally used for this purpose.

---

*Specimen could not be collected for identification

Prevalence of Disease in Dibang Valley

There is a spatial variation in the nature and variety of diseases much depending upon the bio-social environment in which the population live in.

It is, therefore, necessary to have an idea of deseases of different variety prevailing in the study area. With that aim in view the medical records of Riang Hospital was consulted to have a glimpse of the situation which has been furnished in Table 1.

Diagnosis of Disease

There is no medicine man in the Idu society. Diseases and other ailments are treated by knowledgeable persons either of the family or of the village. Diagnosis of disease is done through experience on the basis of symptoms, such as aversion towards food,

Table 1

Prevalent Types of Diseases Among the Idu of Dibang Valley as per Medical Records of Riang Hospital

Sl. No.	*English Terminology*	*Local Terminology*
1.	Arthritis	Ruha-Chi (na)
2.	Boil	Malu
3.	Chicken pox	Anusu
4.	Cold	Drongo
5.	Conjunctivitis	Elombrasi
6.	Cough	Masu
7.	Diarrhoea	Khreha-Bru
8.	Dysentery	Ya-Ya
9.	Exzema	Akuthu
10.	Fever	Ngi
11.	Fracture	Duba
12	Goitre	Kaneko

13.	Headache	Ikuji
14.	Influenza	Manu-ngi
15.	Leprosy	Tidi
16.	Malaria	Ango
17.	Muscular pain	Thoyu
18.	Measles	A-I-Bu
19.	Otitis Media	Akona-Ma-Akubraloga
20.	Ring worm	Taruge
21.	Scabies	Maso
22.	Trachoma	Elombra-Ma-Akubraloga
23.	Wound	Yagu

body pain, body temperature, colour of the stool and urine, cough, headache, etc. After the diagnosis medicines either of vegetative or of animal origin are administered. The quality of medicine, its timing, duration and frequency vary according to the severity of the disease.

Disease and Curatives

Information on the disease and its curatives was collected from the knowledgeable persons who are regularly consulted by the villagers. Information thus obtained was verified from the persons who had suffered earlier or were suffering at the time of enquiry. The data include the description of disease with local name, its symptoms and curatives of vegetative and animal origin. The information on the preparation of the curatives was also collected whenever available. In some cases, diseases are treated only by magico religious practices which have been described separately.

Allergy *(Bru)* : Appearance of rash on body due to intake of some particular food item. As a curative paste made out of leaves of zanthoxylum alatum, Roxb (*Athana*) is applied.

Asthma *(Ethri)* : This is diagnosed on the basis of acute respiratory trouble and is treated with the curative of animal origin only. The extract of gall bladder of bear (*Ahu Imu*) with tea is taken to get relief. There is no restriction of diet.

Berbituary : In such case a paste is prepared out of the bark and leave of Arisaema tortosum. Schott *(Bikimbo)* and is administered to the patient.

Body pain (*Thra*) : In case of muscular pain in the body, leaves of Thea sinensis, Linn (*Ajikhima*) or Dischidia bengalensis. Colbs (*Ahu-n-La*) of Euryleferox salisb (*Thratame*) or Lindera melastomacea, Benth (*Tayuna*) are boiled in water and are drunk. Sometimes bears fat (*Ahu-so*) is also used to massage the body.

Boil *(Malu)* : It is identified on the basis on inflamation on the skin surface occasionally with pain and pass. The extract of leaves of Gymura crepidioides, Benth *(Jarimuna)* and paste prepared out of the bark of *Anuko** plant are applied on the affected area.

Cough and cold *(Masu* and *Drango)* : These are diagnosed on the symptoms of cough, sneezing and running nose. The leaves of the Lindera melastomacea, Benth *(Tayuna)* is boiled in hot water and the extract is prescribed to drink.

Conjunctivitis *(Elombrasi)* : The symptom of this disease is redish sclera with burning or itching sensation. A few drops of breast milk is applied as a curative.

Cut or wound : In such case the extract of the leaves of Mukania scandens, Linn *(Eroena)* or Ageratum conyzedis *(Enupuna)* or Gymura crepioides, Benth *(Jarimuna)* or Justica gendarussa, Lumf *(Na-Adu-Tama-Na)* is applied on the affected parts.

Diarrhoea *(Khera-Bru)* : This is diagnosed on the basis of loose motion and stomach pain. As curative the extract of rhizome of Coptis tita *(Ero-ng)* or stem of Calocacia affinis, Schoff *(Arthombo)* or seeds of Myrobalan *(Konkalari)* or leaves of Arisaema tortuosum, Schott *(Bikimbo)* or fruits of Canabis sativa, Linn *(Kanupi)* is prescribed to drink. Sometimes the extract of gall bladder of bear *(Ahu-Imu)* with a cup of water is drunk. The stomach of porcupine *(Aso-Ya-Pu)* and the intestine of monkey *(Amesu Ambra)* are also taken sometimes. In such case the prescribed diet is rice and rice beer *(Yo)*.

Dysentery *(Ya-Ya)* and Blood Dysentery *(Ya-A)* : The dysentery is diagnosed on the basis of loose motion with undigested food stuff. When this symptom is accompanied by blood, it is identified as blood dysentery. The curatives are similar to those of Diarrhoea.

---

*Specimen could not be collected for identification

Epistaxis : This is diagnosed on the symptoms of bleeding through the nose. As curatives, the fumes of burning leaves of Drymaria cordeta, Willd *(Ach-Ya-Na)* or Calocasia affinis. Scott *(Arthombo)* are inhaled. The ashes of burning leaves are also applied on the occipital region of the patient.

Fever *(Ngi)* : This is diagnosed on the symptoms of high temperature, pain in body and aversion to food. The extract of rhizome of Coptis tita *(Ero-ng)* with hot water is drunk like tea. Sometimes paste prepared out of the leaves of Paederia foetida, Linn *(Arkhumuru)* is smeared on the body.

Fracture : Paste prepared out of the leaves of Justica gendarussa, Lumf *(Na-Adu-Tama-Na)* or Pothos cathcartis, Schott *(Anuruchina)* is applied on the broken parts.

Infection after delivery : In such case the *Paa,* the catalytic agent used for the preparation of rice beer, is administered. The *Paa* with a glass of water is taken to get rid of the infection.

Leprosy *(Cidigilya)* : This is generally identified on the basis of decaying of fingers and toes. In such cases, the paste prepared out of the stem of Calocacia affinis, Schott *(Arthombo)* is applied on the affected part.

Malaria *(Ango)* : This is diagnosed on the symptoms of discontinuous temperature with shivering accompanied by yellow coloured urine and body pain. It is treated with the extract of rhizome of Coptistita *(Ero)* and also with the paste of leaves and roots of Trichasanthes wallichiana Ser, Hight *(Eda-Ru)*. The paste is smeared on the body. Sometimes they take the powder of *Kasturi (Ala-Pi)* as a curative.

Rheumatism *(Tanaga)* : This is diagnosed on the symptoms of pain in back bone and waist. As curative they apply bear's fat *(Ahu-So)* or *Kasturi (Ala-Pi)* or Tiger's fat *(Amra-So)* or Hornbill's fat *(Pandra-So)* on the affected region.

Ringworm *(Masupru or Taruge)* : This is identified on the symptom of circular shaped skin rash. As a curative the paste prepared out of the leaves of Drymaria cordeta, wild *(Arh-Ya-Na)* is applied on the infected parts.

Scabies *(Masu)* : This is diagnosed on the symptoms of skin irruption with iching sensation. In such case the paste prepared out of the fruits of Stephania hernandifolia, Walp *(Arthokapu-Na)* is applied on the infected part.

Snake bite : In case of snake bite, at first a knot is given on the long parts of the victim's head hair. Then the upper and lower portions of the punctured areas are tied up with the bunch of victim's head hair. Leaves of *Amasi Anjata** are chewed and the paste is applied on the punctured area.

Tape worm : In such case mixture of wild lemon with opium is taken as drink.

Tooth ache *(Ta-Na)* : In such case the seed of Solanum Khasianum var, Chatterjinam *(Cetaka)* is burnt and the smoke is inhaled. Sometimes diluted snake venom is applied after testing its strength on the Calocasia affinis, Schott *(Arthombo)*.

Tuberculosis *(Te-Beli)* : This is diagnosed when fresh blood comes with sputum accompanied by cough. In such case the extract of leaves of Stephania hernandifolia, Walp *(Arthokapu-Na)* is taken with water for seven consecutive days. There is no restriction of diet.

Magico-religious Curatives

These apart, there are other ailments, such as Goitre *(Kaneka)*, Trachoma *Elombra-Ma-Akubra-Loga)*, Otitismedia *(Ako-Na-Ma-Buga)*, Gangrine i*(Bathuta)*, Chicken pox *(Anusu)*, Measles *(A-I-Ba)*, Irregular menstruations, Impotency, Insanity, veneral disease, etc. for which the Idu people have no specific medicine. In such cases they call for *Bamni (Egu)*, the priest who is considered to have some magical power to cure these diseases.

---

*Specimen could not be collected for identification

Unlike other tribal societies, the Idu society does not have any medicine man to attend the patient. Instead, this role is performed by the *Bamni*, their priest, who also acquires the knowledge of curing diseases through supernatural power either from *Bamni* or in the dreams. A *Bamni* is supposed to have the power of curing a variety of ailments depending upon his experiences. The social position of the *Bamni* is somewhat higher and it is directly related to his expertise. The payment for such services is given in kinds and it depends upon the financial position of the clients.

There are four different methods which are usually observed by the *Bamni* in curing a disease, particularly in case for which there is no local medicine or the local medicine proved ineffective. These methods are:

(a) *Doo*, (b) *Annungo,* (c) *Ayii*, and (d) *Amresa.*

Doo : In this case the *Bamni* chews a small piece of *Ali (ng) ta** and then brings it out on his palm. Thereafter he puffs in all direction to find out the reason of sufferings. In some cases *Bamni* sucks the blood or the sputum of the affected persons to identify the evil spirits. The evil spirit is thus being identified, the *Bamni* keeps the patients segregated from other members and offers him a piece of *Ali (ng) ta* for his consumption. The patient is also advised not to speak while taking the *Ali (ng) ta.*

Annungo : This ritual is performed if the patients gets some what relief after the performance of *Doo*. In this case the *Bamni* holds a Dao in his right hand and shows his right palm towards the window and spells out some incantation for a period of about half an hour. During this process the *Bamni* request the evil spirits not to cause any harm to the patient. While doing so the *Bamni* offers a small piece of *Ali (ng) ta* to the patient and directs him do the same as it was done in the process of *Doo*.

Ayii : This ritual is performed when the patient feels better observing the ritual of *Annungo*. To satisfy the evil spirit this ritual

---

*Specimen could not be collected for identification

is arranged by the patient which is conducted by the *Bamni*. In such case a hen is sacrificed in the name of evil spirit and the patient is offered a piece of *Ali (ng) ta* to chew during the performance. The ceremony is performed during the night and it takes about 6-8 hours.

Amresa : This is the last ceremony observed by the patient, so as to get relief from the ailments finally. In such case two hens and one pig are sacrificed to satisfy the evil spirit.

Seasonal Variation of Disease

Diseases have positive relationship with the climatic condition and thus there exists some seasonal variation. The Idu people broadly conceive three seasons in their region, i.e., summer, rainy and winter. In the area of the present study the diseases were found to vary according to seasons which are as follows :

Seasons	*Diseases*
Summer	Diarrhoea, Dysentery, Malaria, Fever, Body pain, Pains in joints, Chest pain.
Rainy	Skin disease, Chicken pox, Measles.
Winter	Headache, Cough, Cold, Asthma, Trachoma, Conjunctivitis, Ringworm.

Conclusion

The Idu Mishmi, like many other Indian tribes, practice indigenous methods of curing diseases along with availing of the advantages of medical facilities available in their area. In the present article an attempt has been made to record some of the items of health measures those are being practiced by the Idu Mishmi. Health measures both preventive as well as curative are deeply interwoven with the culture and biotic environment of human populations. The indigenous health practices of the Idu Mishmi have been discussed here along with their physical and cultural aspects, This indicates the profound knowledge of the Idu Mishmi with regard to their biotic surroundings. In dealing with the disease and curative we have tried to include the scientific term of curatives of vegetatives origin which may be useful for further pharmaceutical research.

Acknowledgements

The authors record their deep sense of gratitude to the Director, Anthropological Survey of India for providing necessary facilities to carry out this study. They are also thankful to Shri Sankar Das of Botanical Survey of India, Shillong for his ungrudging help and cooperation in identifying the botanical specimens collected and preserved during the field investigation by the first author.

REFERENCES

BARTHAKUR, K., 1971. *District Census Handbook*, Lohit district, Series 24, Part X.A.

BARUA, T.K.M., 1960. *The Idu Mishmis*, Advisor to the Govemor of Assam, Shillong.

BODDING, P.O., 1925. *Santal Medicine*, Memoir, Asiatic Society of Bengal 10 : 2.

CHOWDHURY, J.N., 1973. *Arunachal Panorama : A Study Profile*, Shillong.

DALTON, E.T., 1872. *Descriptive Ethnology of Bengal*, Calcutta : Firma K.L. Mukhopadhyaya.

DATTA CHAUDHURI, S., 1981. *District Gazetteer, Lohit District*. Government of Arunachal Pradesh, Shillong.

DATTA CHAUDHURI, S., 1982. *District Gazetteer, Tirap District*, Government of Arunachal Pradesh, Shillong.

DUNBAR, D.S.G., 1915. *Abors and Gallongs*, Memoir, Asiatic Society, Calcutta.

JAGGI, O.P., 1973. *Folk Medicine*, Atma Ram and Sons, Delhi.

JAIN, S.K., 1968. *Medicinal Plants*, National Book Trust, New Delhi.

JOWLE, M.A., 1961. *The Ethnobotany of Pre-Columbia Peru*, Aldine Pub. Co., Chicago.

KOURENNOFF, P.M. and GEORGE G.S., 1970. *Russian Folk Medicine*, London : W.A. Allen.

MATHUR, P.R.G., 1982. Anthropology of Tribal Medicine : Disease and Curing Techniques Among the Tribes of North Wynad (Kerala) *Man In India* 62, 3 : 295-312.

MITTAL, K., 1979. Primitive Medicine Versus Modern Medicine Among the Santal, *Journal of Social Research*, 22, 1 : 49-54.

MORLEY, P and WALLIS, R., 1978. *Culture and Curing : Anthropological Perspective on Traditional Medical Belief and Practices*, London : Peter Owen.

PULU, J., 1979. The Plants those are Used by the Idu of Lohit District for Medicinal Purpose, *Risarun*. 5,2, : 10-14.

REDCLIFFE-BROWN, A.R., 1948. *The Andaman Islanders*, Illinois: The Free Press.

ROY, S.C., 1925. *The Birhor : A Little Known Jungle Tribe of Chotqnagpur, Ranchi*, Man In India Office.

SAIKIA, P.D., 1964. *Studies in Dafla Social and Religious Life*, Department of Tribal Culture and Folklore Research, University of Gauhati.

SINHA,R. K., 1979. Disease and Disease Spirits Among the Pando Tribe, *Journal of Social Research*. 22, 1 : 89-96.

SRIVASTAVA, L.R.N. 1962. *The Gallongs*, Research Department Advisor's Secretariat Shillong.

SUKLA, B.R.K., 1959. *The Daflas of Subansiri Region*, North East Frontier Agency, Shillong.

VIDYARTHI, L.P., 1963. *The Maler : Study in Nature-man-spirit Complex of a Tribe in Bihar*, Bookland Private Limited; Calcutta.

9

The Sonowal Kachari : Some Aspects of their Social Life

KALYAN BARUAH

The Sonowal Kachari are a scheduled (Plain) tribe living within the geographical parimetres of Assam. Though there is no historical records, but like many other Kachari tribes, they nostalgically trace their ancestry from the Kachari kingdom established in the eleventh century A.D. at Dimapur. Some even contended that in the middle of the ninth century a strong Kachari Kingdom was established at Sadiya. After the advent of the Ahoms they shifted their kingdom to Dimapur in the thirteenth century (Saikia, 1981 : 8). Nevertheless the Sonowal Kacharis are the offshoot of the Tibeto-Burman Boro or Bodo group of people who are scattered in almost the entire north-eastern region of India. They branched out from the parent group and spread over to Sadiya of eastern Assam and contributed immensely in moulding synthetic Assamese culture. At present these tribesmen are mostly concentrated in the eastern part of Assam.

In this paper an attempt has been made to portray some component of the Sonowal Kachari social structure, viz., institution of marriage, kinship, clan and phratry.

Marriage

It is universally agreed that marriage is something more than institutionalized form of mating of opposite sexes. It is the fundamental way of making provisions for the economic need of the family. It's also concerned with division of labour, nursing, caring, protection, and education. Therefore, marriage to the anthropologist, is an institution which is responsible for moulding the primary unit of every human society. However, the form of marriage varies from culture to culture and from society to society.

The Sonowal Kachari usually select their mates from within the tribe. But sometimes mutual love leads to group exogamy. While selecting a mate in arrange marriage, clan exogamy is maintained. Though monogamy is the general rule but polygyny is permissible among the Sonowal. Among them, widow marriage is permissible and in such case the widow shares her second husband's house without performing any marriage rituals. Sometimes the village elders are invited to bless such couples. Bride price and dowry are not found among them. Though there is no social custom for divorce but quarrel between the couple may lead to separation. A divorcee can marry again without performing marriage ritual and customs.

The Sonowal Kachari arrange marriage ceremony in four traditional ways-i.e., (i) *nowa-dhowa* or *bor bia*, (ii) *hom-dia, bia,* (iii) *gandharba bia*, (iv) *churchuria* or *robha sarakai dia bia* (Sharma Thakur, 1972 : 33). The present investigation reveals that *hom dia bia,* a type of arranged marriage occurs rarely among the Sonowal. The *bor bia* or *nowa dhowa bia* is found among the wealthy Sonowals as huge expenditure is involved in it. It's also a type of arranged marriage which is observed with ardent zeal of the relatives and friends of the couple. In the *gandharba bia* or love marriage, the marriage rituals are not observed as because mutual love often leads to elopement. However, the *kolloh-ghuruka,* a custom connected with the *bor bia* is observed. The fourth category *churchuria bia* is another type of arranged marriage. This type is observed when people can not afford the expenditure and elaboration of the *bor bia*. In such type few elderly people are invited to bless the couple after declaring them as husband and wife.

Kinship

Genealogical histories of the Sonowal Kacharis are very shallow and even a middle aged man can hardly go beyond the second or third generation in reciting his ancestry. In terms of both depth and breadth knowledge of one's relative, it is generally confined to those kin with whom contact has been made.

Usually the people employ the term to designate their kinship universe by different terms. The concept 'family' may refer to all known kin to the effective kin network. Sometimes it may refer to fictive kinsmen as when a neighbour says, "he is like a family member". People also apply fictive kin terms to one another as an expression of solidarity and natural security, thus creating kinship obligation, among neighbours. 'Home' family refers exclusively to members of the household and '*sanch*' to the clan members.

The characteristic feature of the Sonowal Kachari kinship terminology is the paucity of the kinship terms. The use of the same term for persons of different generation and even for both consanguinous and affinal kinsmen are found among them. It has also been found that different terms are used to designate the same persons and sometimes same term is used to designate two different persons irrespective of even sexes. To distinguish sexes a suffix boy or girl is added to the term. Thus for example the term *bhotiza* is used to refer brother's son or daughter. But to distinguish the sex the term *lora* (boy), *suali* (girl) is added after the term *bhotiza*. The term *aboi* is used for ego's mother's mother, father's mother and also father's ceremonial friend who is always a male person. It is a term of reference as well as term of address.

Ceremonial Friendship

In addition to the consanguinous and affinal kinsmen among the Sonowals there is a practice of making friends ceremonially.

The ties of such friendship is very much akin to the kinship bond. Such ceremonial friendship never occurs between opposite sexes, and people are very choosy while selecting a friend. Generally selection of a friend is made from other than one's own clan with mutual consent. After selecting a person with whom friendship is to be made *diksha* (religious instruction) from a common *guru* is taken by both of them at the same time. As the Sonowals are Vaishnavite people therefore the pontiff of a *satra* (a Vaishnavite institution of Assam) gives *diksha* and make them his disciples and true Vaishnava. While taking *diksha,* the persons concerned sit close to each other holding hands and tell the *guru* about their intention of becoming friends. The *guru* declares them as friends in public and bless them. The male friends are called *hari-bhakat* and the females are called *dewo*. Informants Sri S. Hazarika and Sri L. Sonowal are *hari-bhakat*. Sri Hazarika said :

".....we call each other as *atoi* and my children call him *aboi*. My wife also calls him as *atoi*. We never call each other by name. The age is no barrier to establish such friendship and my *atoi* is younger than me."

The bond of such relationship is so strong that if for any reason one friend observes a period of *osowch* (pollution) the other person will observe the same.

Adoption

Among the Sonowal Kacharis adoption is prevalent and they consider adoption of an orphan of the nearest relative as a moral duty. But sometimes, to have psychological relief a couple without a male child adopt a boy from outside the community. Although adoption is permissible among the Sonowals but there is no special rites and rituals connected with adoption. But if the child is adopted immediately after birth with the umbilical cord, in such case a period of pollution is observed till the detachment of the cord and perform *sudhi sobah* for purification. From the present investigation it appears that the adopted child finds a very happy home and the child takes the surname of the foster father. As the child grows up the foster parents try to conceal the real identity of the child as far as possible and treat the child with utmost care and affection. An adopted male child inherits equal shares of property with the male children of his foster parents.

Phratry and Clan Organization

A clan is distinct from the family in many respects. Most common point of agreement between the two is that the clan, like the family strengthens the bonds of relationship among the members and recognises it through one of the parents side. Exogamy is an important characteristic of clan.

The Sonowal Kachari family is based on the integrative bond of kinship and this integration extends in two directions of their parents. But the descent is reckoned through one side. Though the bond of relationship also extends towards the mother's side, however, it is not as firm as father's side in depth and only at the time of marriage it is reckoned to avoid consanguinity.

Among the Sonowal Kachari, the *sanch* strengthens the bonds of relationship in a wider platform than the family and kinship network. A *sanch* is an unilateral descent group reckoned through the father's side which practice consanguinity and exogamy is the general rule of it. Every child regardless of sex is considered to be a member of father's *sanch*. Therefore it has become apparent that *sanch* is a patrilineal clan or 'gentes'. The distinctive feature of their clan's name is that it often ended with a suffix *'ari'* which is similar to that of the Bodo Kachari.

Four such *sanch* or clan constitute another bigger group called *khel* or *bangsa*. The present investigation reveals that the majority of the people can not remember their *bangsa* or *khel* identity and it is at the verge of extinction. The *bangsa* or *khel* members do not practice exogamy. It is not difficult to identify the *khel* or *bangsa* with that of a phratry. A phratry is a kin group in which served clans combine together and according to Lowie (1961 : 239) "Phratries may or may not be exogamous". Saikia (1981:26) reported fourteen *khel* or *bangsa* among the Sonowal Kacharis, viz. *Hagral, Madan,*

Dingial, Manikial, Bor Hajoal, Saru Hajoal, Muktal, Formal, Esmal, Kumral, Dhekial, Lathial, Dongral, and *Chetial*. However, the present investigation reveals three more *bangsas* or *khels* among the Sonowals, i.e., *Dhulial, Dekral* and *Ujani Kuchia*. Saikia (1981 : 7) opined that these *bangsas* or *khels* are units, based on occupation entrusted upon by the royal court of *Hallali Rajya,* the Sonowal Kachari kingdom, established in the year 830 A.D. at Sadiya.

At the time of the Burmese invasion of Assam (During 1816 to 1826 A.D.) to save the life, people fled to interior areas in panic fearing unbearable atrocities committed by the Burmese and took shelters in the interior areas together irrespective of their caste, tribe or community affiliation. Even after the Burmese left Assam, people once settled in the interior areas never went back to their original settlement site. In the process some Ahoms assimilated with the Sonowal Kachari socio-cultural fold. However, they could not adopt *sanch* and *bangsa* as because the members of such groups are bind together by a belief in common descent therefore among the Sonowals we still find the surname *Bailung* which is generally used by the Ahom priest along with *Choudang*, the henchman of the Ahom Court. They take their surnames as *sanch*. However, they do not have any *bangsa* or *khel* affiliation.

Summary

The present study reveals that the Sonowal Kachari constitute a distinctive identity in the Assamese cultural milieu. This can be ascertained by many social traits which are distinctive to the Sonowals only. For instance, unlike many other ethnic groups, the Sonowals have four ways of acquiring a mate. But at present only three ways i.e., *nowa dhowa* or *bor bia, gandharba bia* and *churchuria bia* or *robha sorakai dia bia* are reported. They consider adoption of an orphan of the nearest kin as a moral duty and sometimes adoption of a male child from outside the community also occurs. The genealogical history of these people are very shallow and the paucity of the kinship term is a special characteristic among them. Sometimes the same term is used to denote two different persons irrespective of even sexes. Besides the kin relations, these people establish relation of friendship ritually which is in it's effect very similar to the kinship ties, Although the Sonowal have Phratry but it has very little social significance and it is at the verge of extinction. There are some people of Ahom origin in the Sonowal Kachari social fold who do not have phratry affiliation and use their surnames as clans.

Thus we find that there are many distinguishing features in the social institutions among the Sonowal Kacharis which help to strengthen the bonds of group solidarity and have an impact on the national stability in the north-east India.

REFERENCES

LOWIE, H.R., 1950. *Social Organisation*, London : Routledge and Kegan Paul Ltd.

SHARMA THAKUR, G. C., 1972. *The Plain Tribes of Lakhimpur, Dibrugarh Sibsagar and Nowgong*, Guwahati : Tribal Research Institute, Assam.

SAIKIA, L. K., 1981. *Sonowal Kachari Sanskriti* (In Assamese Saikhowa; Assam.

10

Economy of the Karbis

B.K. MEDHI

The Karbis, popularly known as Mikirs, constitute one of the important tribes of Assam. The origin and the exact route of their migration to the present habitat is quite obscure. They are scattered over the districts of Kamrup, Darrang, Nagaon, Sibsagar and Karbi Anglong of Assam and Khasi hills of Meghalaya. They are mostly concentrated in the newly formed district, Karbi Anglong of Assam, which came into existence from Fabruary 1970 as Mikir hills and then changed the name to Karbi Anglong from October, 1976. They called themselves *Arleng,* the meaning of which is a 'slanting place near a hill' and thus denote the people living in the slopes of the hills. Though many scholars use the term *Arleng* as equivalent to the word 'man', actually the *Manit* or *Munit* is the proper term used by the Karbi to denote a person. The word *Arleng* is confined to the men of Karbi tribe only. Now-a-days, they identify themselves as Karbi, though the origin of the term is uncertain.

Agriculture

Agriculture is the primary base of economy of the Karbis. Most of them depend on slash and burn type of *jhumming*, though some of them have taken to permanent cultivation with plough and bullocks. A few people of Hamren area of the district of Karbi Anglong started terrace cultivation experimentally. In their *jhum* (*Ara*) field they cultivate mixed crop, i.e., different varieties of paddy, maize, ginger, mustard, sesam, turmeric, etc. in different divisions of a plot. Castor and cotton seeds are not sown in separate divisions, but sown together in almost all of the divisions. Among the vegetables, brinjal, chilly, tapioca, pumpkin, bottle gourd, ash gourd, arum, potato and different varieties of leafy vegetables are common in their *jhum* field.

Usually the entire village select a plot on a hill slope for *jhum* cultivation, where each of the family separately clears jungles according to their capacity. Selection of the *jhum* field is done through a meeting of the adult male members of the village. Before clearing the jungle, they perform a communal ritual, i.e., *Rit-arnam* to appease the god of the *jhum*. It will be relevant here to point out that, there are a good number of spirits, whom the Karbi relate with *jhum*. Among them *Rit-anglong, Hempi-anglong,* and *Rek-anglong* are remarkable, whom they propitiate in different times of the year.

It is pertinent to note here that, if a family shift its home from one village to another, the family lose the authority over *jhum* field of the existing village and gain another *jhum* plot in the new village. In a *jhum* field, they cultivate for two to three consecutive years and then it is abandoned for the growth of new vegetations. Such field could again be taken for cultivation after a period, which varies from three to six years or even more.

In the first year of cultivation, the jungle of the selected area is cleared in the months of January-February. In the clearing operation of the forest (*Rit*), both the males and the females participate. The jungle is then left dry till the end of February or the begining of March. After that, felled jungle is burnt into ashes, which is used as manure. Then the field is dug with hoes (*ko*) and seeds, roots and branches are soon broadcasted and planted. When the crops become ready for harvest, they cut, dig and carry them to their respective families. In the second and third year of cultivation, the plot is prepared by hoeing in the month of March and sowing and planting are started from the month of April.

Each family construct a temporary house (*rital*) in the field to be used for watch and care of the crops. The separated grains, roots fruits, etc. are measured with measuring baskets and brought to the village in carrying baskets. From the starting to the end of the cultivation, the females work equally with the males, sometimes even more in all the activities of cultivation.

In the past, the Karbi did not possess any kitchen garden or orchard. At present, most of them have started cultivation of various vegetables and fruit bearing trees. In the orchards, they grow plants of betel nuts, betel leaves, coconuts, various citrus fruits, jack fruits, pine apples, etc.

Other Economic Pursuits

The Karbis are habituated to collect a number of roots, shoots, tubers, leaves, fruits, etc. from the forests. Usually to compensate the niggardly products of *jhum* and especially during the period of crop failure, they have to depend mainly on collecting. Collecting is usually a feminine occupation, though the participation of men is not uncommon. It is a common scene to see a Karbi man to dig out white yam (*Dioscorea alata),* not only from the nearby forest, but also from the far away jungles, Women folk collect firewood from the *jhum* field as well as from the neighbouring jungles in a carrying basket. They collect edible objects from forests throughout the year.

Individual as well as collective hunting is a tradition among the Karbis. Hunting is solely a man's occupation. Bows (*thai*) and arrow (*thai-angsh*) and spears are the chief weapons employed. Dogs are trained to take part in hunting. Now-a-days, sometimes a Karbi possessing a gun sportingly practise individual hunting. But in old days, hunting, especially the collective hunting was very much cherished by them. Deer, bear, wild pigs, wild goats, rabbits, wild fowls, etc. were the main games. A number of traps and snares (*arhang*) were employed to kill different animals and birds. Even to this day, they kill small birds with the help of pellet-bow (*bopthali*) in their agricultural fields.

The Karbis believe that the deity *Than* is the owner of the forest. He moves throughout the jungle sitting on the back of a big-goat (*misung*). The deity *Than* is worshipped two times a year to attain the psychological permission for the use of forest products.

Fishing is another food gathering economy of the Karbis. They use fishing hooks, spears, different kind of nets and bamboo traps (*ru*) for fishing. They are acquainted with both automatic and manipulated types of nets and traps. Communal fishing is their pristine habit. They were traditionally aware of the method of poisoning fishes by means of a juice, extracted from indigenous plants, which they placed in water to stupefy the fish. The Karbis worship the deity *Murti* once in every year, who is the owner of water and seek his benediction during fishing expedition.

Animal husbandry and rearing of *eri* (Philosamiaricini) cocoons are two other economic pursuits of the Karbis. They mainly domesticate buffaloes, cows, pigs, goats, fowls, pigeons, ducks and dogs. Those who practised wet cultivation used bullocks as draught animals. Traditionally they were not accustomed to drink milk. In recent years, milk of cows, buffaloes and goats are given to ailing persons and used in preparation of tea or even drink by them. The goats, cows, and pigs supply them with meat. Hens and ducks provide them meat and eggs. Fowls, pigs, etc. are sacrificed in rituals to appease various deities and the eggs are used in divination by Karbi shamans.

Eri yarn are spun from the *eri* cocoons and are used to prepare warm *eri* cloth (*pe-inki*). They also sell *eri* cocoons and *eri* threads. District Karbi Anglong deserves applause for its highest production of *eri* cocoons in comparison to other districts of Assam. Hamren sub-division of that district is the biggest market of *eri* cocoons in North-East India. The Karbi rear *eri* pupa by feeding castor leaves, which they produce' in *jhum* fields.

Conclusion

The mild tempered and peace loving Karbi are uptill now very much dependent on nature for maintenance of their livelihood. Agriculture is their principal economy. Agriculture is not a mere way of maintaining the livelihood, but it is the way of life, which gives an expression to their socio-biological existence. The multifacet changes in modern times have driven some of them to the modern life and they stick to the various modern occupations. Still, the bulk of the Karbis depend on agriculture.

Jhum is the mainstay of the Karbis, which is a precarious cultivation, where the product is not certain. In *jhumming,* there are various disadvantages, yet they are compelled to depend on this type of cultivation. They have to shift their field frequently, because the fertility of the soil become insipid for the product of crops after the use of few years, sometimes even after the cultivation of the first year. In *jhum* cultivation, they use only human power exclusively.

Jhum cultivation always have small production and suffer a lean period in each and every year, when they have to solely depend on food collecting. In past, *jhum* fields were abandoned for ten to twenty years after the consecutive cultivation of two to three years. But due to the increase of population, now it is not possible to shift *jhum* field frequently. They are hardly able to leave a field for three to six years only. Decrease in the time span of the *jhum* cycle decreases the products of *jhumming*. Deforestation occurs in many areas, where now *jhum* cultivation becomes impossible. Moreover, government also demarcated large areas of the forest, previously used by them as sanctuary and gevernment forests, where they lost the right of cultivation.

In old days, the Karbis produced cotton and lac extensively in their *jhum* fields. But the gradually decreasing fertility of the *jhum* field discourage the Karbi cultivators from the cultivation of cotton. Plough cultivation has now-a-days become widespread among them. Ploughing and harrowing are the only two techniques to till and prepare the soil before sowing. It is notable that most of the Karbis do not possess land for wet cultivation. Some of them are in dearth of bullocks to harness the plough. Only a few cultivators have some knowledge of chemical fertilizers, crop rotation and other improved methods of cultivation. Their agricultural implements include plough, yoke, hoe, rake, sickle, axe, machete, weeders, etc. Most of the cultivators are poor and have no funds to invest in land. They have to borrow the required money from the money lenders. The borrowed money is usually spent for purchasing seeds, for paying the daily wages of the agricultural labourers, etc. A notable impinging factor that disturb the village economy is the defective marketing system. The cultivators do not get proper price for their products in the nearby weekly markets and due to the poor communication they cannot afford to send the products to the distant markets.

The pigs and the fowls are found in almost every family. These are domesticated for family consumption as well as for sale. The animals and the birds domesticated by them have a significant contribution in socio-economic and religious life.

During the year of crop failure and in lean period, the Karbis have to depend partially on collecting. Hunting now-a-days is practised more for sport than the primary desire to supplement the supply of food. They are expert in fishing. There is a Karbi proverb, the meaning of which is as follows 'Use poison (to stupefy fishes) according to the size of the pool, cork according to the bottle's mouth and use medicine according to the nature of the wound'. They relish dry fish very much, which they acquire from fishing in the nearby water sources or from the market.

The economic life of the Karbis intermingle with their magico-religious beliefs and practices. Every year, they worship a good number of demons and deities, who according to their belief have command on agriculture, hunting, fishing, domestication, birth, death, and in all socio-economic persuits of their life. To appease them, the Karbis arrange innumerable rituals in each and every year. They offer rice, rice-beer, vegetables, etc. and sacrifice fowls, pigs, etc. to appease them.

The Karbis consume large quantity of rice-beer in their day to day life, for which huge amount of rice is required. The mortuary rite of the forefathers, i.e., *Chomangkan* is the greatest ritual of the Karbis, which is believed to be diffused from the culture of the neighbouring Khasi tribe. In this ritual, they annually have to sacrifice a large number of animals and use huge quantity of rice, rice-beer, vegetables, etc.

Bordoloi (1972 : 13) rightly points out "Economically the Mikirs are very backward and most of them are povertystricken. During the lean month of the year, many families remain half-starved and sometimes they live on fruit of the jungles and wild roots. Their economic condition is further aggravated by the fact that a considerable portion of paddy is used by them for brewing beer. As their method of cultivation are still crude, their yield per acre is much less. Because of their poverty, they fall into the hands of the unscrupulous village money lenders".

REFERENCES

BARKATAKI, S., 1972. *Asamar Janajati*, New Delhi : National Book Trust.

BARKATAKI, S., 1981. *Assam at a Glance*, Guwahati : Bani Prakash.

BORDOLOI, B.N., 1972. *District Hand Book : United Mikir and North Cachar Hills*, Guwahati : Tribal Research Institute, Assam.

STACK, E. and LYALL C., 1908. *The Mikirs*, London : David Nutt.

TERON, L., 1974. *Karbi Janagosthi*, Jorhat : Assam Sahitya Sabha.

11

Management of Land and Forests in the Hill Areas of Assam-Retrospective and Perspective and Traditional Land-Man Relations in the Zeme Naga Society of North Cachar Hills

B.N. BORDOLOI

When we speak of the hill areas of present Assam, we refer to only two districts, namely, the Karbi Anglong and the North Cachar Hills. Both the districts are under the Sixth Schedule of the Constitution of India. Management of land and forests in these two districts has its own peculiarity prior to commencement of the Constitution, and even after the commencement of the Constitution some of these basic peculiarities have been still remaining in their modified forms. However, the management of land and forests between the hill areas and plains of Assam had more differences than alikeness due to the peculiar topographical situations, the life style of the people including their customary laws, administrative system and so on.

In this paper, first I propose to deal with the subject in respect of management of land and forests in the areas covered by the present district of Karbi Anglong and North Cachar Hills prior to the commencement of the Indian Constitution. Next, I propose to deal with the changes brought about by the Karbi Anglong and North Cachar Hills District Council in respect of the above subject since the operation of the provisions of the Sixth Schedule of the Constitution of India till now and the consequent impact. In the last part of this paper, I propose to highlight a specific case of traditional land-man-relations in the Zeme Naga society of the North Cachar Hills based on my own empirical experiences.

Part I

To understand the land management and land-man-relations in the hill areas of the North Eastern region in their proper perspectives, it is necessary to have a background knowledge of the history and the people inhabiting this area at least begining from the advent of the Ahoms.

During the Ahom Days

When the Ahom entered into Assam during the thirteenth century by crossing the Patkai ranges and established their kingdom in Assam on a secured footing, they had to face many an encounters with tribal chiefs inhabiting the north-eastern hills in the process of consolidating their kingdom. The Ahoms found that these tribal chiefs having their own territorial jurisdiction had more or less sovereign powers. Each ethnic group had more than one chiefs who were known with different names. These chiefs were virtually governing their own people with their customary laws and through their democratic socio-political institutions. The chiefs were the custodians of the landed property of the people of the entire community. In other words the land belonged to the community but its manner of utilization was not uniform. The methods of utilization of land differed from community to community.

The Ahoms evolved rather a distinct policy of peaceful co-existence while dealing with the tribes some of which had been living within their territorial jurisdiction and some inhabiting the bordering areas. This distinct policy of the Ahom had three main aspects, namely, (i) non-interference with the internal affairs of the tribes, (ii) supply of essential commodities to meet their day to day economic needs, and (iii) regulation of trade between the plains people and the tribal people living in the neighbouring hills (Dutta, 1988). Since the management of land was an internal affair of the tribal communities, the Ahom rulers, therefore, had not imposed any land reform measures which they had initiated for the plains people.

During the British Days

As a result of the Treaty of Yandaboo in 1826 between the Burmese and the British, Assam became a part of the British India.

During the East India Company's days, the hill areas of the present North-East India formed a part of the Rongpur district. Following the recommendation of Mr. David Scott who was sent to Assam with a contingent of soldiers by the East India Company to put an end to the atrocities perpetrated on the people of Assam by the Burmese soldiers, the North-Eastern Hill areas were separated from the Rongpur district. The administration of these areas were then placed under the special charge of an officer called Civil Commissioner of North-East, Rongpur. The newly conceived administration of these area was known as the Non-Regulated system. Under this system the powers of the collectors, Magistrates and Judges were in the same hands. Management of land is a very important aspect of administration. Since the north-eastern hill areas was brought under the Non-Regulated system of Administration, naturally the question of bringing any measures so far land management was concerned did not arise.

The Government of India Act 1919, however, had brought a substantial change into the administration in the Non-Regulated system areas. Section 52 A (2) of the above Act provided that the Governor General in Council might declare any territory in British India to be a Backward Tract and on such declaration being made, further direct that any Act of Indian legislature shall not apply to the territories in question or shall apply subject to such exception or modification as was thought fit. Under the above section of this Act, almost all the hill areas of the then Province of Assam were declared as Backward Tracts. These areas being most backward were wholly excluded from any reforms banning the Central as well as Provincial Legislature enacting any laws for these areas. Proposals for expenditure in these areas were not required to be submitted into the Legislature for voting. Not only that, in the Provincial legislature nothing regarding these tracts could either be discussed or questioned. Some portions of the Backward Tracts were, however, not wholly excluded from the applicability of any Act of the Provincial Legislature. But here also this would be determined by the Governor in Council and the Governor of the Province.

The Indian Statutory Commission commonly known as the Simon Commission, recommended more or less the same line of administration for the Backward Tracts as was contemplated under Section 52 A(2) of the Government of India Act 1919. The Government of India Act 1935, based on the recommendations of the Simon Commission, had done away with the terminology of Backward Tract and rechristened these areas as "Excluded Areas" or "Partially Excluded Areas". So far as the administration of the above two areas was concerned, the Governor of the Province was entrusted with very high powers. The "Excluded Areas" were completely kept outside the purview of the Provincial Legislature and these areas were to be administered by the Governor of the Province himself at his discretion.

So far as the "Partially Excluded Areas" were concerned, the administration of these areas was the special responsibility of the Governor of the Province. First he had the right to accept or reject the advice of the concerned Minister in his individual judgment. Secondly, the advice of the Minister was not necessary in matters within the discretion of the Provincial Governor. Thirdly, no Act of the Central or Provincial Legislature could apply to these areas unless the Governor would apply with such modifications and exceptions which he deemed fit. Lastly, the Governor with the prior approval of the Governor General was also empowered to make regulations for the peace and good government in these areas.

In pursuance of the Section 91 (1) of the Government of India's Act, 1935, the Governor General promulgated the Government of India (Excluded and Partially Excluded Areas) Order, 1936. As per this Order the following areas were included in the schedule dealing with Excluded Areas :

i. North-East Frontier (Sadia, Balipara, Lakhimpur) Ditricts.
ii. Naga Hills District.
iii. Lushai Hill District.
iv. North Cachar Hills Sub-division of Cachar District.

The following were included in the partially excluded areas :

i. Garo Hill District.
ii. Mikir Hills in Nagaon and Sibsagar District.
iii. The British portion of the Khasi and Jaintia Hills District other than Shillong Municipality and Cantonment areas.

Now from the above analysis it has now become clear that the territories which had earlier formed a part of modified backward tracts under the Government of India Act 1919 were regarded as "Excluded Areas" or "Partially Excluded Areas' under the Government of India Act, 1935.

Now let us see what led the Simon Commission (1930) for recommending a special provision so far as the administration of the hill areas of the then Assam was concerned. The Commission had mentioned three important grounds in this connection :

(i) According to the Commission the stage of development reached by the inhabitants of these areas would prevent the possibility of applying to them the methods of representation adopted elsewhere.

(ii) Secondly, the people did not ask for determination but for security of their land.

(iii) And thirdly, the people also wanted freedom in the persuit of traditional methods of their livelihood and reasonable exercise of their ancestral customs (Hansaria, 1983).

The British policy towards the hill tribes of the North-East was more or less similar to that of the Ahoms so far as the principle was concerned. But in practice it was rather a mixed one. For the more ferocious tribes like the Akas, Daflas (now called Nishis), Miris, Abors, Mishimis, Khamptis, Singphoes and the Nagas their policy was subjugation of their kingdoms but at the same time they were allowed to manage their own internal affairs. For the numerically stronger tribes like the Garos, Lushais, Khasis and the Jaintias their policy was full annexation of their kingdoms but minimal interference in their internal affairs. The inner line system introduced by the British in 1873 for some of the areas of the North-East inhabited by hill tribes restricting free intercourse between the plains people and the hill tribals had kept the people isolated and ignorant so far as the administrative reform measures were concerned.

The Assam Land and Revenue Regulation 1886 was primarily meant for the Plains districts only excluding the hill districts. For Hill districts, therefore, there was no land Revenue and the British administrators collected house tax only (Gait, 1905).

Constituent Assembly Debate on Draft Sixth Schedule and Founding Fathers' Views

The Constituent Assembly of India had set up an Advisory Committee on fundamentals rights, Minorities, Tribal and Excluded Areas under the Chairmanship of Sardar Ballavbhai Patel. For the North-East Frontier Tribal Areas and Assam Excluded and Partially Excluded Areas a sub-committee with five members was set-up under the chairmanship of Gopi Nath Bordoloi, the then Chief Minister of Assam (called Premier at that time). The other four members of this sub-committee were J.J.M. Nichols Roy, A.V. Thakkar, Rup Nath Brahma and Iliba Imti. Later on Iliba Imti opted to remain out of the sub-committee.

The Sub-Committee while formulating the main provisions of the Sixth Schedule always kept in mind the following basic facts:

i. The Excluded and the Partially Excluded Areas of the North Eastern Region of India were not brought under the regular administrative system of the British Government.

ii. Situations-political, economic and social obtaining in these areas were quite different from those prevalent in the rest of the country.

iii. For the tribal people inhabiting these areas the manage ment and the security of land were the two primary concerns .

This Sub-Committeee had submitted its report on 28th July, 1947. Since the drafting of the Constitution had already begun, the recommendations of the Sub-committee were directly incorporated in the Draft Constitution (Saksena,. 1981).

In the Constituent Assembly debates the draft provisions incorporated in the Sixth Schedule were discussed thoroughly. These debates revealed the founding fathers' views clearly and precisely. The reasons for suggesting special provisions for the administration of the tribal areas of the North-Eastern Hill Regions of the country. In the Constituent Assembly debates, Gopi Nath Bordoloi, the Chairman of the Sub-Committee explained in clear terms the background in which the draft of the Sixth Schedule was prepared. He stated that the problems of the hill areas of Assam which were entirely excluded areas in the sense that none from the Plains could go there and contact the tribal people, were quite different from the problems of those areas which were brought under the regular administrative measures of the British Government. During the Second World War, some of these were under war-zones. During war times some military officers engaged in these areas to fight against the Japanese and the British administrators posted there infused in them a sense of separation and isolation. They assured the tribals that as soon as the war was over they would have their independent states managing their own affairs according to their own way. Bordoloi strongly argued that instead of using brute military force, a method should be used in which willing co-operation from the people could be obtained by the Government for the purpose of governing these areas. Drawing the attention of the Hon'ble Members he had also pointed out the manner in which even the murder cases had been decided by the Village Panchayat. Democracy prevailing in village administration and the manner in which the different community works were distributed among the people of different age groups in the village were simply marvellous according to Bordoloi. He strongly argued that the tribals should be allowed to develop themselves in their own way.

Mr. J.J.M. Nichols Roy, a Member of the Sub-Committee participating in the Constituent Assembly debate on the draft of the Sixth Schedule stated that the hill districts inhabited by tribal hill people would under the Constitution of India be able to develop themselves in their own way without disturbing the main purpose of unity underlying the Constitution presented in the draft. He further stated that these tribes had been self-governing bodies, though small, from time immemorial.

A.B. Thakkar, who was also a Member of the Sub- Committee headed by Gopi Nath Bordoloi, participating in the Constituent Assembly debate on the draft Sixth Schedule supported the views adduced by Bordoloi. He said that the best way to keep the frontier people satisfied was to give them certain measures of self-government so that they might develop according to their own genius and culture. He opined that the advancement of the hill tribes could not be achieved by force. He further argued that advancement would be accepted by them only when they would see something more than what they had. Appreciating the Village Panchayat he said that they were better than the regular courts. The hill tribes, therefore, should not be deprived of the things which they considered to be good for them according to their own way.

Even a politician like Syed Mohammed Saadulla, who headed the Council of Ministers of the Province of Assam during the pre-Independence days twice and who vehemently expressed his disliking to the Sixth Schedule itself in the Constituent Assembly debate, had highly praised the hill tribals. According to him, hill tribals are the most democratic of all democratic people. Their native chiefs are elected by all the people in their territory by adult franchise. These chiefs are only territorial chiefs. They have no right over land. The land belongs to the people. Thus Syed Saadullah had pointed out two major aspects of the hill tribals of Assam, namely, the practice of democracy and the community ownership of land (Constituent Assembly Debate; Official Report, 1989).

From the above discussion it has now become clear that the founding fathers had given utmost importance to the management of land by the hill tribal communities of the North East. Under the provision of the Sixth Schedule to the Constitution the autonomous District/Regional Councils have been provided wide range of Legislative, Executive, Financial and Judicial powers. Under the Legislative powers, management of land, forests other than reserve forests, shifting cultivation, etc., have been entrusted to the District/Regional Councils.

How the hill tribal communities manage their land and all activities relating to the land differ from community to community. Whether the entire community retains the command over the land or such a command has been delegated to the village community or kinship organisation or both depends on the socio-political organisations of the community itself. There are, however, some common factors like the abundance of land, topography, the ول land use pattern, migratory characteristics, ethos like fellow-feeling, brotherhood and thinking in terms of community rather than individual and so on, which had led to the idea of community ownership of land. In other words, the natural resources are the properties of the entire community and their fruits are to be harvested by all the people of the community.

Now let us take up the question of density of population which I consider to be one of the principal factors determining land-man relations in the North East India. The density of population per square km. as per 1981 Census taking into consideration the projected population of Assam was 104 compared to 221 at all India level (N.E.C., 1985). The position of different States is shown below :

	State	*Area (in sq. km.)*	*Total Population*	*Density*
(i)	Arunachal Pradesh	83,743	631,839	8
(ii)	Assam	78,438	19,896,843*	254
(iii)	Manipur	22,327	1,420,954	64
(iv)	Meghalaya	22,429	1,335,819	60
(v)	Mizoram	21,081	439,757	23
(vi)	Nagaland	16,579	774,930	47
(vii)	Tripura	10,486	2,053,058	196
	Total	255,083	26,607,199	104

*Projected population of Assam in 1981.
Source : Basic Statistics of N.E. Region, 1985.

Assam shows the highest density of population because the figure includes the valley areas of the Brahmaputra and the Barak where the density of population is much higher than that of the two hill districts. The density of population in 1981 based on the projected figures of the Karbi Anglong and the North Cachar Hills was 50 and 21 respectively. This aspect has been made more clear by Dr. B.K. Roy Burman (1988) while pointing out to the fact that the population per Sq. km. of gross cultivated areas was much higher in North-East India (587) than that of the India (398) as a whole.

Apart from the fact that the hill people's thinking in terms of community, fraternity and brotherhood, the abundance of land at their disposal, as has been evidenced from the foregoing figures, gives very little scope to go for privatization of ownership of land. That was why in the Karbi Anglong district the Karbis did not have village boundaries in the earlier days as has been pointed out by Mr. Stack (1908).

According to the Law Research Institute, Guwahati High Court (1982) in the North Cachar Hills all lands belonged to the rulers, the Kachari Kings and in the Diyng and Jatinga valleys, the people were supposed to have heritable and transferable rights on the lands under permanent cultivation, subject to the overriding rights of the Kings. However, we feel that these facts need further scrutiny as well as indepth study. Because it is not clear whether the Kings exercised their absolute rights or they were simply custodian of landed property on which only the people had the absolute rights.

Although the Karbis had to live under the suzerainty of the Ahoms and the Kacharis, they had their own system of administration headed by a King called *Lingdokpo*. This institution of Kingship is still present and the present King lives in Niz. Rongkhong in the Hamren subdivision of the Karbi Anglong district. Under him there are three regional Kings called *Lingdok* at Amri, Socheng and Chinthong. The territorial divisions where the King now lives is called Rongkhong. These four territorial divisions are called *Artu*. a group of villages constitute a *Longri* and the old Karbi kingdom had 12 such *Longris*. The administration of a *Longri* is called *Hawai*. While the village council is called *Mei*, the traditional village headman is called *Sarthe*.

The King called *Lingdokpo* had no absolute right over land although tributes from the *Longris* were paid to him in cash and kind. The Kingship is not hereditory and the King was rather nominated by all the officials of the State. The virtual powers so far as land matters were concerned were with the village council, *Mei.* This council decided whether the village was to be shifted to a new *jhum* site and it alloted *jhum* land to each family for cultivation. Apart from the shifting of villages to new *jhum* sites, the Karbis shift their villages because of two other reasons also. Since a Karbi village is named after the village headman and since this post is a very respectable and coveted one, a new aspirant for this post shifts a part of the village along with his supporters to a new site where he establishes a new village and declares himself to be the *Gaonbura* or *Sarthe* (Bordoloi, 1989). If the village is considered to be visited by ghosts or evil spirits, the entire village is shifted.

Part II

Perspectives

Since the Sixth Schedule to the Constitution of India authorises the District/regional councils to make laws in respect of allotment, occupation or use or setting apart of land for agricultural, grazing or residential or non-agricultural purposes or in respect of shifting cultivation, and management of forests other than State Reserved Forests, now let us see the changes and reforms brought about by the District Councils of Karbi Anglong and the North Cachar Hills in respect of management of land, forests and shifting cultivation.

Management of Land : Karbi Anglong District

The Mikir Hills (Land and Revenue) Act, 1953 :

For the assessment and collection of land revenue within the Jurisdiction of the Mikir Hills District Council (present Karbi Anglong District Council) the Assam Land and Revenue Regulation 1886 was adopted for application in the District Council area with suitable modifications.

This Act was amended in 1960 which specifies that any appeals against the order of a Revenue Officer under the administrative control of the Council shall lie with the Chief Executive Member of the Council.

The Mikir Hills District (Transfer of Land) Act, 1959

So far as the land management in the Karbi Anglong district is concerned, this is the most important Act protecting and promoting the interests of the Scheduled Tribes (Hills) on land.

The Act specifies that no land under the District Council shall be sold, mortgaged, leased, bartered, gifted or otherwise transferred by a tribal to a non-tribal or by a non-tribal to another non-tribal except with the previous permission of the Executive Committee. The Act also provides for recording the reason for refusal of transfer.

While the Act provides for maintenance of *status quo* in respect of right on land already acquired, provision for ejectment of such persons other than tribals who are in possession of land other than in accordance with the provisions of the Act is also incorporated. But the penalty fixed for an offence for not obeying the orders of ejection is in monetary terms only and it is quite nominal.

Although the main purpose of this Act is to prevent transfer and alienation of tribal land, none-the-less, unscrupulous people have found the loopholes in the Act and made the Karbi people inhabiting the plains portion of the Karbi Anglong district to alienate their land temporarily but with a tendency to perpetuate for an indefinite period. The manner in which this has been done is described below :

Although there are several devices like *Paikas, Khoi, Bandhak, Sukti Bandhak, Mena, Adhi*, etc., responsible of temporarily alienation of tribal land, nevertheless, the most important one is the *Paikas* system. Incidence of these devices are, however, confined into those plains areas of the district where large number of East Bengal (present Bangladesh) refugees are found to have settled in these regions.

Paikas System

Under this system a tribal settlement holder takes an advance from a cultivator, usually a non-tribal, and in lieu of the advance taken he alienates his land temporarily to the non-tribal cultivator for a period of one year or two years. At the end of the specified period the non-tribal cultivator is required to vacate the occupied land. But in practise it does not so happen since the tribal settlement holder takes another advance from the non-tribal cultivator even before the stipulated period comes to an end. Once a tribal enters into this vicious circle he can hardly get out of it and the alienation of cultivable land becomes perpetual. While the non-tribal cultivator cultivates the land held on *Paikas* and reaps the harvest the actual owner gets nothing but the advance received in cash which is in fact one eighth of the value of the produce obtained from the *Paikas* land. Informal agreements signed by both parties showing the year/years of temporary alienation and the amount involved are prepared as deeds.

It is true that successive years of cultivation do not confer any right to an non-tribal holding land under *Paikas* system. Nevertheless the actual owner becomes a mere spectator while the non-tribal tills the land and reaps the harvest year after year as if he were the actual owner of the land. This system has rendered many Karbi families paupers and their condition is worse than those of the landless people.

Under the provisions of the Mikir Hills District (transfer of Land) Act, 1959, *Paikas* cannot be considered illegal since hiring of tribal land by non-tribals has not been prohibited. It cannot be called 'mortgage' also since there is no question of paying back the cash advance taken from the *Paikas* holder at the end of the stipulated period. The unscrupulous non-tribals, therefore, have been taking the full advantages in the loopholes of the provisions of the Land Transfer Act.

It is found from a survey conducted by the author in a few tribal villages inhabited by the Karbis within the Jurisdiction of the Howraghat Tribal Development Block in the year 1973 that about 70% of the Karbi families did not cultivate their land. They had allowed the neighbouring non-tribals to cultivate their land year after year mainly on *Paikas* system.

The Karbi Anglong District Council, however, had become alive to the situations created by the temporary alienation of tribal land and had enacted a law to prohibit *Paikas* and mortgage forms of alienation.

The Karbi Anglong District (Land Reforms) Act, 1979

This Act envisages a few important aspects in respect of land reforms :

(i) It provides that all kinds of encumbrances land existing by way of *Paikas* or mortgage shall be void upon coming into force of this Act.

(ii) If the period of *Paikas* is not over, the *Paikas* should be converted to *Adhi* system meaning share-cropping.

(iii) Eviction of the cultivator as soon the land of the settlement holder is released at the end of the stipulated period.

(iv) Cancellation of the *Patta* of the settlement holder if he is found to have resorted to *Paikas* or mortgage after the release of his land.

(v) The Act allows the settlement holder to resort to *Adhi* system if he considers it essential. And thus in a sense *Adhi* has been legalised.

(vi) No restriction is imposed on mortgaging land to financial institutions to obtain agricultural loan.

Now let us see how far these land reforms measures are effective in practise or in the practical field. The Assam Institute of Research of Tribals and Scheduled Castes had conducted a survey in 5 Karbi inhabited villages in the plains areas of the Karbi Anglong District in the year 1987 in order to find out the extent of alienation of tribal land. The findings of this survey, however, presents a very dismal picture. The main findings are stated below :

(i) 18.83 per cent of the Karbi families has alienated their 64.33 per cent of their total land holdings by way of transfer to the non-tribals inspite the existence of an almost blanket ban on such transfer.

(ii) While *Paikas* accounts for 26.41 per cent of the alien ated land, *Adhi* alone accounts for 66.76 per cent of the alienated land.

We have now seen that inspite of Land Reforms Act of 1979 prohibiting *Paikas,* this system of temporary alienation of land is still continuing. Prior to this enactment there were written agreements on stamped papers between the settlement holders and *Paikas* holders. Now the *Paikas* holders do not insist on written documents regarding the terms and conditions of *Paikas.* The *Paikas* holders are now being introduced as *kamlas* meaning wage-earners working in the field of the settlement holders and such devices have made it difficult to detect *Paikas* incidence unless one uses the participant observation method as a tool of collecting data.

The incidence of temporary alienation of land under the *Adhiar* system has become so high (66.76 per cent of the total land alienated to non-tribals) because of the fact that a good many of the *Paikas* holders fearing detection declare themselves to be *Adhiar* or share-croppers.

Land Settlement Policies

Land settlement policies are a part and parcel of the entire process of land management. The Karbi Anglong District Council has formulated a set of land settlement policies keeping in view the safe-guarding of the interests of the scheduled tribes (Hills) in land. These policies are as follows :

(i) In the matter of settlement of land in Karbi Anglong first preference is given to the *bonafide* scheduled tribes such as the Karbis, Dimasa Kacharis, Rengma Nagas, etc. The plains tribes are not scheduled in the Autonomous Districts.

(ii) Second preference in respect of land settlement is given to the scheduled tribes coming from other autonomous district.

(iii) Resolution number 9 of the Executive Committee held on 25th October, 1954 runs as follows : "No settlement of land shall be made with any non-tribal who has come into this district after the 15th August, 1947 and all such persons coming after that and found to occupy land in Mikir Hills without any authority shall be evicted forthwith".

(iv) The District Council may, in special cases relating to the victims of unusual natural calamities such as, floods, earthquake, etc., who are already in occupation of land in the district, order settlement of land with the affected non-tribal people on recommendation after due enquiry from the Deputy Commissioner.

Although the District Council has not changed this land policy so far, still it has followed a more realistic policy in respect of settlement of land with the non-tribals considering the merit of each case.

As a piece of further safeguard, waste lands in the district which are suitable for permanent wet-paddy cultivation after reclamation are reserved for the people belonging to the Scheduled Tribes of the district only.

Management of Land in North Cachar Hills

The North Cachar Hills District Council, however, has not adopted the Assam Land and Revenue Regulation 1886 in toto unlike the Karbi Anglong District Council. It adopted a few sections in53, then a few sections in 1954 and all the sections under Chapter V in 1964. Such sections concerning the mutation procedure, declaration of the rights of the land holder and Chapter on Registration of the Assam Land Revenue Regulation 1886 have not yet been adopted.

A. Executive Instructions Prohibiting Transfer of Land from Tribals to Non-Tribals

In the North Cachar Hill District the non-tribal population constitutes slightly more than 30 per cent and the density of population was 16 as per 1971 Census. The incidence of alienation of tribal land in this district, therefore, is quite low. The District Council Authority of the North Cachar Hills has not enacted any law in regard to prohibiting transfer of tribal land to non-tribals. The District Council has issued some executive instructions only in this respect vide Memo No. GA/REV/5/14/62/21, dated 6th July, 1962. So far as land under periodic lease is concerned the tribal settlement holder cannot transfer his land to a non-tribal without prior permission of the District Council Authority. In according permission, the District Council sees whether the person to whom the land is proposed to be transferred is a permanent resident in the district and secondly whether he has enough land in his possession already even if he is a permanent resident.

B. Land Settlement Policy

According to Land Settlement Policy Resolution of 1954, the first preference goes to the indigenous local tribals in settlement of government land. The second preference is given to the permanent non-tribal residents of the district who are electors in the District Council Constituencies. A tribal belonging to the same community but hailing from another village may also get settlement of land in the village provided the other people of the village where the person is proposed to be given settlement do not object.

Management of Jhum Cultivation in North Cachar Hills

The North Cachar Hills District Council has not so far enacted any laws or issued any executive instructions so far the matters connected with shifting cultivation are concerned.

Management of Jhum and Forests in Karbi Anglong District

Now let us have a look at the management of *Jhum* and forests. As per provisions of the Sixth Schedule, the District Councils have the full powers in respect of management of forests other than the State Reserved Forests.

It is very pertinent to mention here that the Karbis practising *jhuming* or shifting cultivation has a tendency to shift their villages to the *jhum* sites. From the point of view of development this is a very harmful practice. The Mikir Hills District (*jhuming*) Regulation, 1954 prohibits the shifting of the villages from the present sites without the previous permission of the Executive Committee of the District Council. Since the villages in the hills have no boundaries, the Regulation provides for the fixation of boundaries of each village. Within a radius of half a mile from the boundary of the village cutting of forests or to do shifting cultivation is totally prohibited. This regulation has thus deprived the traditional village councils of the rights of selecting *jhum* sites and their distribution among the individual families in accordance with the requirement and capacity of each family. According to the provisions of this Regulation, it is the Executive Committee which shall determine the rotation, period of *jhuming* by the people of a village and also the area to be *jhumed* by an individual cultivator. Any person contravening any provision or provisions of this regulation shall be required to pay a penalty which might extend upto Rs. 500.00.

Since the provisions of this Regulation had centralised, all, powers relating to the regulation of the *jhuming* to the Executive Committee of the District Council, the people had a great resentment. The decentralise matters, the Mikir Hills District (*jhuming*) Regulation of 1954 was amended in 1966.

The following are main provisions of this amendment:

(i) *Jhuming* shall be gregarious and restricted to one particular area for a village irrespective of number of fami lies *Jhuming* and shall be selected by villagers in consul tation with *Sarkari Gaonbura* and local *Mouzadar* in accordance with provisions of this Regulation.

(ii) Any disagreement about selection of *jhuming* site among the villagers, *Sarkari Gaonbura* and *Mouzadar* shall refer this to the Executive Committee and decision of the Executive Committee in this respect shall be final.

(iii) Individual plots within the selected area may be selected by the people themselves in consultation with the local *Sarkari Gaonbura.*

(iv) The villagers shall be jointly responsible for any damage to areas not selected for *jhuming* by spreading of fire from *jhumed* areas.

(v) *Jhuming* within two gunter's chain of any perennial stream on either or within one gunter's chain of any State Public Works Department and District Council roads respectively is prohibited.

(vi) Any area which is covered by *Sal* or other valuable trees shall not be selected or allotted for *Jhum.*

(vii) The District Council reserves the right to dispose of the felled stuff in *Jhum* areas in any manner it considers suitable without interfering *Jhuming.*

The Mikir Hills District (Forest) Act, 1957

So far as the management of forests other than the State Reserved Forests is concerned, this is the most important Act.

This Act empowers the District Council to constitute any forest land at the disposal of the Council to a reserved forest after proper inspection and verification by the District Council Officers including the Executive Member in charge of forests and subsequent notifications thereof. All matters concerning inspection, verification, proposed boundaries, compensation if any to be paid, etc., are required to be placed before the Council Forest Board prior to notification in the Assam Gazette. Provision has also been made in the Act allowing an aggrieved person to appeal against the order or decision of the Council Forest Board to the District Forest Tribunal within 30 days from the Notification constituting District Council Reserved Forests.

The Act also prohibits trespass and damage to the District Council Reserved Forests by way of trespassing for cutting and felling trees, burning of fire endangering the forests and pasturing cattle. Collection of minor forest produce by unauthorised persons from the Council reserved forests is also prohibited.

One of the most important provisions of this Act is, however, the constitution of village forests by the Council for the collective benefit of any village community or group of communities. These collective benefits include collection of minor forest produce and pasturing cattle. But the people have to protect, preserve and improve the village forests in lieu of the benefits extended to them.

The Act also provides for penalty of Rs. 500.00 for violating any provision or rules made under this Act.

It is now obvious that the Karbi Anglong District Council has taken some major steps through legislations to control *jhum* or shifting cultivation and also to dissuade people from shifting of their villages to *jhum* sites. This has led to the fixation of permanent boundaries for villages. Secondly, the powers entrusted to the traditional village councils in respect of management of *jhum* sites and allotment of *jhum* land to the individual families have been taken away and now these powers have been vested to a new set of leaders like the village *Gaonburas* and *Mouzadars* appointed by the Councils. The people have also been deprived of collecting minor forest produces from the forests other than the village forests only on which they have been given such a right. In fact the community ownership of land on the hill forests has now been replaced with the District Council ownership which rather infringes the traditional rights of the people on forest land.

Part III

Traditional Land-Man Relations in the Zeme Naga Society of North-Cachar Hills

In this part I would like to highlight some important facts in regard to the land-man relations in the Zeme Naga society of North Cachar Hills based on a few specific case studies. In August, 1970 I accompanied Prof. F. von. Haimendorf of the School of Oriental Studies, London University, in his visit to the Zeme inhabited areas of North Cachar Hills lying on the border of Manipur and Nagaland and both of us toured a good number of Zeme Naga villages for about a fortnight and conducted extensive field studies on various aspects including their traditional land system. The facts stated below are based on my own specific case studies and although more than 21 years have already elapsed since my visit to those areas, the situations have hardly undergone any change except the death of a few *Kadepeos* and succession of the dead by new ones.

The Zeme Nagas of the North Cachar Hills District of Assam have a peculiar system of land ownership which is totally uncommon among the other tribes of Assam. The Zemes have six exogamous clans, namely, *Npame, Nkume, Heneume, Ndriame, Pneume* and *Sogame*. Each of these six clans has it own private land and its ownership is confined to the members of the clan only. Apart from the clan ownership of land, the Zemes have traditional land owners also. These traditional land owners are called *Kadepeo* and the *Kadepeo's* land is called *Heteuram* in Zeme.

It is not definitely known when the Zeme *Kadepeo* system had actually originated. Since there has been no system of private ownership of land among the other Naga tribes, it can be assumed that this system had originated after the migration of the Zeme Nagas to the North Cachar Hills via Manipur.

According to the *Gaonbura* of Laisong, there were no *Kadepeos* among the Zemes till they came under the Kachari suzerainty. The most influencial name of each Zeme village was made a *Kadepeo* by the Kachari kings. This might have been done with two purposes. First, it was one of the ways by which the Kachari kings could keep the Zemes under their control. When the most influencial man of the village was made the owner of all the lands belonging to the village including the *Jhum* sites, the Kachari kings surely expected his unreserved loyality. And through *Kadepeo* the king expected the loyality of other villagers. Secondly, it was an easier way to collect revenue of the Zeme villages through the most influencial villagers.

The second probability of the origin of the *Kadepeo* system may be stated as follows :

The Zeme Nagas migrated to the North Cachar Hills in several batches. Each batch was led be a Chieftain. Each batch had started settling in the uninhabited hills. The settlements were established several kilometers apart. The Chief of each settlement assumed the full control of the village site and the neighbouring hills and his ownership was recognized by his followers. Thus the first Chieftain of each settlement had also become the first *Kadepeo*. Besides each of the clans of the settlement was also allowed to possess some well-marked hills as clan-land. *Kadepeo's* authority over all the land of the settlement except clan-lands was undisputed. The *Kadepeo* system is hereditary. At the death of the *Kadepeo* his sons automatically become the new *Kadepeos*. In case the *Kadepeo* does not leave any male issue, his next male relative automatically inherits the *Kadepeoship*.

Being the most influencial person of the village, the *Kadepeo* had been selected as the village headman also. He was given official recognition by the Government too by presenting him with a red blanket.

But the *Kadepeoship* and village headmanship are not combined together in all the Zeme settlements. In some Zeme villages I have found that the *Kadepeo* and the *Gaonbura* (village headman) are two different persons. In Laisong, the *Kadepeo* is also the village headman. In Hajaichak, the *Kadepeo,* is not the village headman. But he is also the village priest. In Kepeilo, the *Kadepeo* is aslo the village headman.

In some Zeme villages, there are two or three *Kadepeos.* In Natun Neonglo, I have found three *Kadepeas.* The first *Kadepeo* is also the village headman. The three *Kadepeos* of Natun Neonglo are the sons of the same father. In Hajailo, the *Kadepeo* and the *Gaonbura* are two different persons. In Chota Laisong, the *Kadepeo* is also the *Gaonbura*. From the above analysis it can be seen that the *Kadepeo* needs not necessarily be the village headman also. The *Kadepeoship* and the village headmanship are combined together whenever such a combination is practically feasible.

The *Kadepeo* being the most influencial and wealthiest man of the village, authority is surely undisputed. But does the *Kadepeo* act like an oppressive landlord or a dictator ? The answer is surely not. He does not extract revenue indiscriminately from his tenants like a landlord of the mediaeval period of the modern civilized society. For the village sites occupied for homesteads the villagers need not to pay anything to the *Kadepeo*. For the cultivation of the *jhum* land belonging to the *Kadepeo,* each family has to pay a basketful of paddy (about 5 kg.) per annum to the *Kadepeo* as land revenue.

In case of failure of crops owing to drought or untimely rain, the payment of revenue is generally exempted by the *Kadepeo*. There are other humanitarian considerations also for which the *Kadepeo* might exempt the concerned families from the payment of annual land revenue.

The *Kadepeo* virtually rules over the village with the help of a village council. All the village disputes are settled by the *Kadepeo* with the help of this council and the verdict given or the decision arrived at is always final. There is no going back from the decision and the concerned parties have either to accept it or to leave the village for good. Although the *Kadepeo* exerts such powers and authority, he is not a dictator. Because in each Zeme village the Village Council is the supreme body and the decision of the *Kadepeo* can be overruled by the village council provided the latter is strongly supported by the opinions of the other villagers. Anyway, the *Kadepeo* plays a very important role so far as the Zeme polity is concerned.

The *Kadepeo* generally allows his co-villagers to cultivate the land owned by him on payment of a basketful of rice per year per family. But he may allow people from other villages also to cultivate in his land provided sufficient land is left after making provision for his co-villagers. In course of my investigation, I have found such instances. A few Zemes from Hajajilo are found to have cultivated land at Laisong belonging to *Kadepeo* of Laisong. The distance between the two villages through the briddle path would be about 10 kms. In any case the first preference must be given to the villagers where the *Kadepeo* resides.

It may be mentioned here that each of the big Zeme settlements has one or more than one colonies. In some cases it so happens that *Kadepeo* of a big settlement is also the *Kadepeo* of its colony or colonies or its village sites. As for example, Chota Laisong is a colony of Laisong and Laisong Bangan which is another village site of Laisong, is a colony of Hajaichak. Whereas Chota Laisong has its own *Kadepeo*. Laisong Bagan does not have its own *Kadepeo*. But the *Kadepeo* of Laisong is also the *Kadepeo* of Laisong Bagan. In such a case the *Kadepeo* allows the people of the colony to cultivate his land. People from the original village are also allowed to cultivate land in the colonies provided there is enough land.

It has been mentioned earlier that each Zeme clan has got its own private land and the members of the respective clan has exclusive right on the clan-land. In course of my investigation it has been observed by me that each village is inhabited by two or three clans. As all the clan-lands of a village are confined into the hands of the members of two to three clans only, the chances of inter-clan disputes arising out of boundaries, etc., are very little.

The clan-land is collectively owned by the members of the clan. There is well demarcated boundaries for land possessed by each clan. But there are no such boundaries for the members of the clan. Now, does it mean that a family can cultivate any plot of land in the clan land according to its wish ? The answer is definitely 'No'. The elders of each clan decide each year which plot of land should be cultivated by each family.

Thus, it can be clearly seen that the Zemes have three types of land, viz., the land owned by the *Kadepeo,* land owned by each clan and the *jhum* land owned by all the families of the village and on which each family has a right to cultivate. So far as the cultivation of the first two types of land is concerned the decision of the *Kadepeo* and the clan elders respectively is final. So far as the cultivation of the last type of land is concerned the decision has to be taken by the council of the village elders. Just before opening up of new patches of *Jhum* land, generally in the month of December and January, the council of the village elders in its sitting decides which are the hills that are to be taken up for *jhum* cultivation for the particular year. The new *jhum* sites for a particular year are selected in such a manner so that they suffice for the whole village. A newly opened *jhum* sites is cultivated for three consequtive years generally.

Another important thing that was observed by me in course of my investigation is that a few people from one village may be allowed to cultivate in the *jhum* land of another village with the consent of the Council of the village elders of the latter. As for example, a few families of Hajailo are found to have cultivated *Jhum* land belonging to the people of Laisong village. Similarly, some families of Laisong are found to have cutlivated *jhum* land belonging to the people of Chota Laisong. If some families find that the *Jhum* land allotted to them is not quite sufficient or not good enough to produce a good crop, they may appeal to the Council of the elders of another neighbouring village for allottment of *Jhum* land for their cultivation. Such a prayer is granted generally on humanitarian ground. Anyway, such mutual help and understanding have been playing a great role in the socio-economic life of the Zeme people.

So far I have discussed the system of land ownership of the Zemes. Their peculiar system of cycle-migration will be taken up for discussion now.

It is a well known fact that the Barail range which falls within the jurisdiction of the North Cachar Hills district is extremely steep with abounding cliffs and crags. In between there are gorges and deep ravines. Land suitable for *Jhum* exists only in scattered patches and to maintain in such a terrain a village must have an abnormally large territory at its disposal. At the initial stage of their settlement in the North Cachar Hills, the Zemes might have selected several village sites for each village, after taking into account the topography of the terrain and future needs. Because each stretch of *Jhum* land by itself is too small to maintain a large settlement indefinitely. When in course of time a stretch becomes exhausted, they shift the whole village or the part of it to one of the preselected sites. When the whole village is shifted to a new site, there is every likelihood of the village being shifted to the original site again when the regeneration of vegetation in the *Jhum* lands of the old site is complete. So leaving of a particular village site by the people of the village for another site does not mean its abandonment. Because the original village site with its ancestral graves, and their hallowed memory, the rights of the *Kadepeo* and other paraphernalia has a most potent influence on Zeme life. Hence to give up the original village site for good is unthinkable. Sooner or later they would come to the original village site from the other village sites and a rotation would be complete. In this way the difficult topography of the terrain of the Barail range has compelled the Zemes to develop a cycle-migration. But this cycle-migration is too slow a process and it can be measured in terms of generation rather than years. Sometimes the abortive colonies disturb this pattern. Instances of such colonies are not lacking. In course of my investigation I have found that the Zeme village Hajailo has an abortive origin. The village was established as an abortive colony of Boro Neonglo only in the year 1961. The celebration of the festival called *Hgangi* (the Zeme New Year's festival celebration in the mid of January) is a costly proposition. The village council of Boro Neonglo headed by the *Kadepeo* decided to discontinue the celebration of *Hgangi* because of economic reasons. It has already been mentioned that the village councils of the elders headed by the *Kadepeo* virtually rules over each village community and the decision of the village council is always final and binding. And those who disobey or do not want to abide by the decision of the village council must leave the village for good. Now, there was a dissident section of the people of Boro Neonglo. This section did not like the idea of giving up the celebration of such an important festival like *Hgangi*. But it could not go against the decision of the village council. Hence the dissident families had no other alternative rather than to leave the village voluntarily and established a colony at Hajailo, about one kilometre away from Boro Neonglo.

The following facts have been observed by me in regard to the cycle-migration of the Zeme Naga villages visited by me.

Laisong is one of the oldest Zeme settlement of the North Cachar Hills, the others being Hangrum, Asalu, Guilong, Hajaichak, Thunje and Baladhan. Laisong has village sites at two other places. Although Laisong proper has not been migrated to these village sites in toto, these sites have already been inhabited by families migrating from Laisong. Chota Laisong, one of the village sites, was established as a colony of Laisong in the year 1930 by about 30 families who migrated to this village site from Laisong. The other village site Hogokulo was also inhabited by some Zeme families who migrated from Laisong. However, information in regard to the actual number of families who first inhabited Hogokulo and the year in which it was first inhabited could not be obtained.

Like Laisong, Hajaichak is also one of the oldest Zeme settlements. At present Hajaichak has two colonies, namely Natun Neonglo and Kapeolo. Natun Neonglo, as a colony of Hajaichak was established only in the year 1960 and it has at present 37 number of families. The families migrated to the site of Natun Neonglo from Hajaichak.

It has been an established fact that the present village Hajaichak was shifted from its present site to the site where the village Natun Neonglo stands today about three to four generation back. About 50 years back it was again shifted to the present site.

Kepeolo, as a colony of Hajaichak was founded in the year 1935. Originally about 30 families from Hajaichak migrated to Kepeolo when it was felt that Hajaichak had become overpopulated and it could no longer support the growing population.

The new Zeme colony Laisong Bagan has, of course, a different history. It was established only in the year 1959 and at the time of my visit there were 14 families in total. Laisong Bagan, which is situated about 12 km. north of Laisong, belong to the *Kadepeo* of Laisong and is a village site of Laisong, though smaller in area. Laisong Bagan is colonised by Zeme families from Hajaichak and not from Laisong itself. The village site Laisong Bagan was allowed to be colonised by some Zeme families of Hajaichak by the village council of Laisong presided over by the *Kadepeo* when an approach had been made in this regard. The families of Laisong Bagan have to pay usual rent in kind to the *Kadepeo* of Laisong.

A man from the original settlement is allowed to settle in any of its colonies provided he willingly desires to leave the village or he is forced to leave the village by the village council because of crimes committed by him. Similarly, a man from any of the colonies is also allowed to settle in the original settlement if he desires to do so and if the village council of the original settlement approves it.

Thus, we have seen that Zeme Nagas of the North Cachar Hills have an interesting system of land ownership which is unique in character and their cycle-migration, which is well planned, is indirectly related to *Kadepeoship*. Spread of literacy and their contact with the modern world have virtually brought no effect at all to their traditional system of land ownership and cycle-migration (Bordoloi, 1978).

Conclusion

The history of the North East India specifically the areas inhabited by the hill tribes shows that the land-man relations in hese areas were governed by the customary laws of the societies prior to Independence. By keeping these areas as Excluded and Partially Excluded from the regular administrative systems, the British Government followed the policy of least interference so far as aspects like land management were concerned. The founding fathers of the Sixth Schedule to the Constitution of India were quite alive to the prevailing situations in this part of our country. Community ownership of land was a prime factor of their consideration and that was why management of land was made an entrusted subject to the Autonomous District/Regional Councils so that due respect could be shown to the traditions while enacting any laws on land management.

For the management of land, control of *Jhum* cultivation and also for the management of forests, other than the State Reserved Forests, several legal measures and executive measures including land settlement policies have been taken up by the District Councils of Karbi Anglong and North Cachar Hills since 1953 and onwards some of which rather appear to have infringed the traditional rights of the people on land and forests.

The specific case studies among the Zeme Nagas of the North Cachar Hills show that land-man relations among hill tribal societies of the North East India are not uniform. Private ownership of land by the chieftain or the most influential persons among them is a truth and this has belied our pre-conceived idea that among the hill tribals of North East India land ownership rests with the communities only.

REFERENCES

BORDOLOI, B.N., 1978. Land Ownership and Cycle Migration among the Zeme Nagas, In *North East India-A Sociological Study*, Edited by S.M. Dubey, New Delhi : Concept Publishing Company

BORDOLOI, B.N., 1989. Tribal Development Plans and Programmes in the Sixth Schedule Areas of Assam with Special Reference to Management of Land-A Critical Appraisal. Paper presented in the National Seminar on 'Nehru and Evolution of Tribal Policy in India'. New Delhi, September, 1989.

CONSTITUENT ASSEMBLY DEBATES., 1989. *Constituent Assembly Debates-Official Report*, Lok Sabha Secretariat (Reprint), New Delhi.

DUTTA, P.N., 1988. *Glimpses into the History of Assam*, Shillong.

GAIT, E.A., 1905. *A History of Assam*, London (Revised edition, Calcutta : Thackers Spink and Co. 1963).

HANSARIA, B.L., 1983. *Sixth Schedule to the Constitution of India-A Study*. Guwahati.

LAW RESEARCH INSTITUTE., 1982. *A Study of the Land System of North Eastern Region*, Volume I Assam. Law Research Institute, Eastern Region, Gauhati High Court : Guwahati.

NORTH EASTERN COUNCIL., 1987. *Basic Statistics of North Eastern Region, 1985*, Shillong : North Eastern Council.

ROY BURMAN, B.K. 1988. Problems and Prospects of Tribal Development in North East India. Paper presented in the Seminar on Constraints of Tribal Development in North East India, organised by the Tribal Research Institute, Assam, held in June 1988.

SAKSENA, H.C. 1981. *Safeguards for Scheduled Castes and Tribes-Founding Fathers' Views*, Delhi.

STACK, E. and C. LYALL., 1908. *The Mikirs*, London : David Nutt.

12

Land Alienation Among the Tribes in North Cachar District of Assam

TANMAY BHATTACHARJEE

North Cachar lives a sequestered existence. It is cut off from the valley of Assam by language, culture and also by the constraints of economy. The political compulsion has made it a connecting link between the Brahmaputra and the Barak valleys. The hoardes of migrations into this State touched this district slightly and it remained aloof from the enactments of history of this region. Only the later part of the sixteenth century saw some activities in the form of the Dimasa occupation of the hills and it spilled over to the subsequent centuries. The British occupation of these hills remained an 'outside' factor for the people. It hardly touched the inner mechanism of the tribal people living here.

The population was very small and the whole district was a desolate and isolated place and it did not attract the outsiders in large numbers. The Naga population in the North-east of the district might not be a spill over from the territories of present day Nagaland. In the pre-British days, the political boundaries were unsettled and undemarcated and the inter-tribal skirmishes were a regular phenomenon. The Naga presence perhaps is here for a longer timescale. The Kuki tribes too had the same story of migration. Although their 'route of migration' suggests an eastern and southern connections.

The Dimasa came here as a 'royal group' having a king over their head. That was a phenomenon unknown to other tribal groups of the district. The Karbis perhaps stayed here in strength for some centuries prior to the Dimasa colonisation of the district. But due to the continuous opposition of the Kachari kings, they took a further western route of migration and got sheltered in the Jaintia territories. The Karbis were a non political tribes which lived under the Ahoms and the Jaintias and had shifted their habitats many times.

The British authority demarcated the inner territories of Assam rather arbitrarily and the plains territories of the Kachari ruler Tularam Senapati were attached to the districts of the Brahmaputra valley. North Cachar became only a sub-division of the Cachar district.

The territory fell under this new sub-division was the Borail hill range and its slopes. The vegetation was the rain forest. The whole area is drenched regularly by the monsoonic rain for many months. It does not have wide plain valleys where the plain people can do wet cultivation. On the whole, the territory was uninviting for the new migrants.

In the recent past, the British perhaps made a survey of the economic possibility of the area and they left it untouched. Only the hill section railway line which crossed the present district in the north south direction. The British made two railway survey in the second half of the last century. Under the British, a large amount of capital flowed into making the tea gardens in upper Assam. Timber and coal too were extracted by the colonists there. But soon the snag developed. How to export the merchandise. The present Lumding-Badarpur railway line was the product of the thought which resulted in the creation of the railway system in the region. The railway carried the merchandise to the Chittagong port through the hill section.

The railway lines through these hills did not remove the isolation of the district largely due to the policies of the British rulers. The district did not really 'opened up' and remained in the same shape upto the time of Independence. The excluded area provisions under the Government of India Act 1935 made it a closed and secretive entity during 1937-1947 period. Something like the inner line permit system was introduced and it was enforced very effectively. The old time-timers still recollect the incidents and never it was the coveted heaven for different groups.

So, the alienation of the tribal lands was never a serious point of debate in this district because the problem was non-existent. The physical features of a given territory is to be considered. In the neighbouring tribal district of Karbi Anglong, the distribution of lands into hills and plains is approximately in the proportion of 65 : 35. So the non-tribals get their natural environment for wet cultivation. This actually accentuated the problem of land alienation in that district. So is the case of Tripura State, where the tribal land alienation problem has laready attracted national debate.

Backwardness is a difinite insurance against the land alienation. The tribals of North Cachar are very backward in technology and they do not have much idea about the modern industrial innovations which are being introduced elsewhere. The absence of it saved them from the competition of such organised groups. Except for forest, the district does not have any great economic product to offer and this has made it a unsought after place for commercial exploitation.

The Sixth Schedule Provisions

The Sixth Schedule provisions of the Indian Constitution stand as the surest guarantees against the tribal land alienation. The tribal lands cannot now change hands in favour of non-tribals. The main thrust of this provision is to prevent the tribal lands from the surreptitious transfer to the non-tribals. The North Cachar district Council adopted the old Assam Land and Revenue Regulations and Rules 1886 and it was christened as the North Cachar Land and Revenue Act, 1953. It clearly stated that no land shall be sold, mortgaged, leased, bartered, gifted or otherwise transferred by a tribal to a non-tribal or by a non-tribal to a non-tribal except with the previous permission of the Executive council. This has kept the area totally isolated from the rest of the country and few people really came here for settlements.

The people never come and settle down in a territory unless the latter ensures a steady flow of income from living there which is either for export or for their own subsistence. The tribal group which lived here had a very low level of economic demands and their demands did not cross the level of subsistence. They did not have any definite idea of market economy. As reported by informants, in earlier days, the Dimasa had to travel almost sixty kilometres to reach a market at Barkhola in Cachar district. In the nineteenth century there was no market in the area and the population was minuscule.

North Cachar did not have any industry worth the name during the British time like the large tea gardens of upper Assam and Barak Valley. So there was no question of importing labour from outside. Luckily no British ingenuity preferred the district for any kind of economic activity. If the British capital was invested for anything like coffee plantation, the district would have a majority population of imported labourers by now. It is assumed because, this territory is only recently found suitable for commercial cultivation of coffee. But this is a hypothetical situation because North Cachar is saved by the the non-involvement of the British capital in these hills. The situation never came to pass.

Inhospitable terrains are difficult for the people to settle. So the tribal settlements are always in a state of flux. The territory is truely a 'transit point'.

The Land and Land Revenue Act, 1953, conferred upon a landholder a right to occupy the land for a period of thirty years. But a settlement holder other than landholder is granted the period of occupancy for one year only. An annual lease confers no right of transfer or of subletting. Even the right of inheritance is limited to the year of issue. He has only the right of user for the year of issue. It shall be liable to cancellation for any transfer or subletting even during the year of issue.

A landholder has the permanent heritable and transferable rights of use and occupancy in his land subject to the payment of all revenue taxes, cesses and rates from time to time legally assessed.

The council has the right to extract minerals (quarries, mines, minerals, buried treasure) within the land held by the landholder. In North Cachar, the Tenancy Act was not extended and therefore, a landholder cannot engage under law any tenant in his land. In these hills, the strict classification of land-occupants under the Assam Land and Revenue Regulation, 1886 is never maintained. Here landholder generally means the periodic lease holder. His period of lease is 30 years. The second category (settlement holder other than landholder) is given lease for one year which is popularly known as *ek-sona patta* (one year lease).

The provisions of 1886 Regulations as adopted by the council in 1953 are not strictly enforced. It is seen that the one year lease holder transfers or sublets his lands to another person and sometimes, it has a stamp of official sanction. All the land settlements within the district has come to an endon 31.3.1990. The extension of different types of leases within the district is now made by the council thereafter.

The district council has issued an order prohibiting the transfer of tribal lands to the non-tribals. The members of the council attracted the attention of the executive committee on this issue. An interesting discussion was held in the council on 14.8.1972 on this issue. Mr. T. Nampui, an influencial member of the district council raised the issue in one council meeting about the settlement of the non-tribals in the district. The members showed keen interests in the question of land alienation. Almost all the members irrespective of party affiliations demanded that the tribal lands should not go out of their hands. But in spite of the general disapproval of land transfers, the tribal lands did change hands in some areas. But these transfers are very small in number and they do not warrant any serious consideration.

The Nepali, in the north-east India are mainly engaged in cattle rearing, particularly in the interior. The present writer saw in western Karbi-Anglong, the presence of a large number of the Nepali *Khutiwalas* (cattle rearers). They themselves established some sort of a milk cooperative among themselves and they took milk to the greater Guwahati market through Jagiroad. In the Sangbar and Vaithang areas of the district, 20 such *Khutiwalas* were there and out of them 19 were the Nepalis. One person was a tribal Dimasa. There was also an allegation that the *Khutiwala* established a small Panchayat among themselves which collected taxes from their own members. The district council however, denied the charge.

The alienation of tribal lands is not a major and serious issue in the interiors but the district council declared some areas as the 'urban areas' where the non-tribals are found to acquire lands and settled down. Haflong, Maibong, Harangajao, Mahur, Langting and Garampani have the 'settled' non-tribal populations. In north Cachar the alienation problem was non-existent in the pre-British days and now whatever settlement that occured after 1947 that was in the vacant lands both in the unclassified forest and the reserved forest areas of the district.

In 1959, some East Pakistan refugee families tried to settle down in the Dayungmukh area. This area had large vacant lands. The settlement was given by the council. The allegation was that there were 50 refugee families settled in the area. The council in reply said there was only 14 such families and they were given settlements to teach the tribals the better mode of cultivation. But the opposition wanted the cancellation of land lease to the non-tribals. The pressure of the opposition arguments forced the council to reconsider the issue.

In North Cachar, the land alienation problem even if it occures, it would occur among the tribal themselves. It is worth mentioning that, no attempt was so far made to differentiate between a 'local' tribal and an 'outside' tribal. Sometimes, a feeble attempt is made to differentiate between a north-eastern tribal and a tribal from the other parts of India. There are altogether 414 'accepted' tribes of India under the Presidential Notification, 1956 and very large number among them live within the geographical limits of the North-East. These was an attempt to settle some Chakmas in Maibong area but the council did not approve it and they left the place. In North

Cachar, time has come to take a definite census of local tribal population so that their rights and interests can be protected properly. The land alienation between groups occur on different plains. A tribal-tribal land alienation problem is qualitatively and quantitatively not much different from tribal-non tribal land alienation problems. As many anthropologists have suggested-the tribals differ among themselves very widely in habitat, acculturation, levels of development and mode of living. These differences tend to put them into opposing political camps.

The district council in North Cachar do not like to invite controversy in matters of determination of the 'locals' among the tribals but it is important for the district. The council may constitute a committee to go into the whole question or it may accept the decennial census figures. Some influencial leaders of the district strongly express their feelings in the meeting of district council held on 14.8.1972, that the Dimasas, the Nagas, the Biates, the Hmars, the Kukis and the Hrangkhols should only be declared as the indigenous tribes of the district. They opines the Mizos, the Khasis and some other tirbes came here for jobs and business and they should be debarred from being declared as the permanently settled tribes of the district.

The problem did occur in the district when a Thadou village was established near Hatikhali in the north of the district. The Thadous were not considered as an indigenous tribe of the district. The council in its meeting held on 15.2.1960 declared this village as unauthorised. But still the availability of land in the district is abundant and the tribal-migrants are easily absorbed. Saran village in Mahur area and the Jinam valley are the two places where the settlers mainly came from the neighbouring Manipur State. But the District Council is aware of the danger from the influx of people from outside.

The North Cachar hill District Land and Revenue (Adoption of Land and Revenue Regulations and Rules) Act was made afresh by the council, which got the Governor's assent on 2.12.1982, and the 1953 Act was repealed. The 1982 Act further empowered the council to preserve interests of the tribal population. By an administrative order, the appellate jurisdiction in regard to land disputes was given to the Chief Executive Member of the District Council.

So far as the adoption of the Assam Land and Revenue Regulation, 1886 is concerned, it was universally introduced in the hill areas of the north-east India. But in the old Khasi and Jaintia hills district, the complicated land tenure system was in vogue to the presence of *Syiemship* in Khasi hills and *Langdoh* or *Dolloiship* in Jaintia hills. In North Cachar hills, the Assam Land and Revenue Regulations, 1886 was nothing new and even as part of the old Cachar district, it was in operation here. Only change was that the tenancy Acts of the State were not extended to this hill district. The district council took the responsibilities of the Deputy Commissioner of the district.

From the above discussion, it is clear that the interests of the tribal population of the district are protected by the provisions of the Sixth Schedule and also by the Regulations. But the tribal mind is always fearful and thus, the council issued an order (the District Council order number REV/5/16/75/19, dated 31.7.1975) 'to better safeguard the interests of the local tribal people of North Cachar and to prevent alienation of their lands'. This order came into effect immediately. Main feature of this order were :

(i) Settlement, transfer, or mutation of land to the members of different tribes within the village boundary shall not be allowed.

(ii) Transfer, mutation or sale of land from tribal to non-tribal shall not be allowed.

(iii) No non-tribal shall transfer, sell or mortgage land to any other non-tribal without permission of the council.

It is interesting to note that the above order restricts even the inter-tribal settlements and the tribal villages are sought to be made homogeneous. A Dimasa village is homogeneous in the sense that no person belonging to another tribe is allowed to purchase lands or settle down in that village. This exclusive character of a tribal village is a significant aspect which should attract the attention of the anthropologists. The concept of 'one village-one tribe' is more or less a perfect reality in this district.

Conclusion

North Cachar with tribal 'ethnic diversity' accentuated by the geographical constraints may save itself from the conquest by the outsiders by the skin of its teeth. The possibility of commercial cultivation of coffee is said to be quite feasible in the slopes of these hills but the inevitable importation of workers from outside is a forbidding aspect of the whole operation. As the concept of 'wage earning' is foreign to the local tribals, they generally shy away from big enterprises. The enterpreneurial skills among them are all too limited to start enterprises of their own engaging the workers available within the district. Therefore, the extension of 'the industrial process' is a hindrance to tribalism and the possibility of alienation is related to that. Only the strict preservation of forest lands and the systematic exploitation of forests products can ensure the tribal identities.

13

Physical Anthropology of the Deoris of Assam

SARTHAK SENGUPTA

HARKA BAHADUR CHETRY

The Deori forms one distinct tribal group, who are traditionally engaged in priestly activities and are associated with the magico religious rituals in the royal temples of the Chutiyas-a numerically dominant mongoloid population of upper Assam. (Gait, 1905). According to Kakati (1967), the word Deori is originated from Sanskrit word *'Deva Grihika'*. Thus, the word Deori means incharge of a temple or the priest. Now-a-days, they however, prefer to identify themselves as *'Gimasaya'*, meaning 'the children of the Sun and Moon'. They are at present recognised as one of the plains scheduled tribe of Assam. The total population of the Deori in 1971 Census enumeration was 23,080 (11,901 males; 11,179 females). They mainly concentrated in the districts of Lakhimpur (undivided), Dibrugarh, Tinsukia, Sibsagar and Darrang districts of Assam. The original habitat of Deori, however, were in Lohit district of Arunachal Pradesh (Brown, 1895). The Deori tribe comprises of four main subsections or *khel* (territorial group), namely the Dibongiya, the Tengapaniya, the Borgonya and the Patorgonya. It is reported (Saikia, 1976) that the last group have almost become extinct. There is no bar against inter-marriage among these sub-sections of Deori. But in practice, inter-marriage is not frequent.

The population under study, the Dibongiya, is a populous *khel* of the Deori tribe, who are very conservative in their social system. Only they could able to preserve their traditional dialect and at present most of them are bilingual. They are mostly confined in the Lakhimpur district of Assam, particularly in Narayanpur, Bordoloni, Bihupuria and Bangalmara Gram Panchayat areas. Few of them also inhabit in river island 'Majuli' in Brahmaputra river of Assam.

The initial objective of the present study has been concerned with the biological relationship between the present Dibongiya sample and other sub-sections of the Deori reported so far. An attempt has also been made how each of these sub-sections is related with the Deori population as a whole. For this purpose, the data on different sections of Deori have been pooled together to form a single unit of the Deori for comparative study. As already mentioned, it is often said that the Deori population are priestly section and one of the major sub-division of the Chutiya population. The other sections of the Chutiyas are known as Hindu-Chutiya, Ahom-Chutiya, Miri-Chutiya, Moran-Chutiya, Matak-Chutiya, Barahi-Chutiya, etc., which suggests admixture between Chutiya and others. One more concern of the present study is thus, to identify the biological relationship between the Deori and the Chutiya population of Assam.

Material and Method

The anthropological data of the Dibongiya population were collected from seven different villages (Barbam, Gotapather, Upper Chenia, Maj Chenia, Thaigerguri and Kadamguri) of Bordoloni block of Lakhimpur district, Assam in 1991. Proper care was taken not to include closely related individuals in the samples. Somatometric measurements were taken on males only following Martin and Saller (1957) : The other anthropological variables (viz. ABO blood group, finger and plam prints) were collected from both sexes following the standard techniques. In collecting and analysing the dermatoglyphic data, the usual scheme proposed by Cummins and Midlo (1961) is followed. For comparisons, the data on various sections of Deori and the Chutiya population were taken from the published works of other scientists whose method and approach are the same as those of the present worker. In this connection, it is to be mentioned that data on Tengapaniya Deori and Hindu Chutiya (hereinafter called Chutiya) population only available in published literature (Das *et. al.*, 1985). Chi-square and t-test were performed to see the inter-group differences.

Results and Discussion

The Dibongiya are medium in stature (165.04 ± 0.61) characterised by brachycephalic (81.36 ± 0.41), hypsicephalic (76.85 ± 0.72) and acrocephalic (94.22 ± 0.85) head. Their face is leptoprosopic (92.76 ± 0.51) with a tendency towards hyperleptoprosopic and of leptene (55.26 ± 0.42). The nose is mesorrhine (73.66 ± 0.54). On the other hand the Tengapaniya Deori are characterised by below medium (163.86 ± 0.48) stature. The head is mesocephalic (79.31 ± 0.35), hypsicephalic (74.37 ± 0.80) and acrocephalic (93.71 ± 0.95). Their face is mesoprosopic (85.28 ± 0.46) and of mesene (51.65 ± 0.46) type. They also have mesorrhine (73.63 ± 0.86) nose. The mean values of all these measurements and indices have been given in Table 1.

Somatometric features that set apart the Dibongiya from the Tengapaniya include the former's significantly higher sitting height and broader head. The variation between the pair of groups also manifested for having significantly lower mean values of head length and bizygomatic breadth in the Dibongiya than in the Tengapaniya. The head of the Dibongiya is brachycephalic and seen to differ from the Tengapaniya who possess a mesocephalic head. Both the populations show hypsicephalic mean, however, with a higher mean values of length height index, the Dibongiya stand significantly apart from the Tengapaniya. The total facial height of the Dibongiya belong to medium category as reveal by its mean and strickingly differ from that of the Tengapaniya who exhibit comparatively low total face. With regard to total facial index also, both the population differ significantly. With respect of upper facial height, with a higher mean value, the Dibongiya stand significantly apart from the Tengapaniya. The Dibongiya show that they have leptene upper face, and in this regard too, they stand significantly apart from the Tengapaniya who exhibit mesene type of upper face.

Therefore, both in size as obtained by the measurements and in shape, as revealed by the indices there is significant differences between the Dibongiya and the Tengapaniya Deori. One is distinguishable from the other on the basis of mean values of the characters concerned.

Now let us see how each of the sub-sections is related to the Deori population as a whole. Can each of the sub-sections individually represent the Deori population ? For this purpose, the two sets of data available on Deori population have been pooled together to have a picture of the average Deori population and are set out in Table 2.

It is revealed from the Table 2 that only in four somatometric characters the Deori show real distinction with the Dibongiya and the Tengapaniya. The total facial index of the Dibongiya show a mean of leptoprosopic group while in the Tengapaniya it is mesoprosopic. Thus, the Dibongiya and the Tengapaniya being at extreme and differ significantly from the Deori. Significant variation also exists in them with regard to total facial height. From the mean values of upper facial index, it is apparent that the Dibongiya and the Deori belongs to leptene category while the Tengapaniya belong to mesene. Here too, both Dibongiya and the Tengapaniya are significantly different from the Deori. Upper facial height of the Dibongiya also deviate significantly from the Deori, however, the Tengapaniya do not differ from them in same magnitude.

A comparison of the serological characters of the two Deori samples may now be made in order to find out whether there are differences between the populations or not. percentage frequencies of ABO blood groups of the populations under consideration are summarised in Table 3. It is evident from the table that the frequency of phenotype 0 is highest in the Dibongiya whereas frequency of A seen to be the highest in the Tengapaniya. Test of significance also record marked statistical variation (Table 4) between the two populations. However, both the Dibongiya as well as the Tengapaniya are not statistically different from that of the pooled Deori population.

Since bisexual variation is an established fact in most of the dermatoglyphic characters, therefore, in the present comparative study dermatoglyphic characters are compared separately sexwise with regard to each dermatoglyphic variables.

The male Dibongiya are characterised by having comparatively more loops (50.37%) than the whorls (46.03%), while reverse is true in the case of the Tengapaniya male sample (whorl = 54.56%; loop = 43.51%). A higher frequency of arches (3.58%) exhibit by the Dibongiya is in contrast to the Tengapaniya who exhibit only a frequency of 1.93%. Statistical analysis show that both the male samples are significantly different from each other (Table 8). In this regard the Deori samples show close affinity to both the Dibongiya and the Tengapaniya Deori however.

With regard to female samples, it is observed that the Dibongiya are characterised having more loops (57.44%) than whorls (35.74%) while Tengapaniya show a reverse picture in the percentage distribution of patterns (whorl = 54.14%; loop = 42.24%). Further, the Dibongiya females show a higher frequency of arches (6.80%) than the Tengapaniya who possess 3.62% of it. The above mentioned variation in percentage distribution of different patterns in both female populations also show significant variation as revealed from chi-square values (Table 8). The difference between the Deori and the Dibongiya and that between the Deori and the Tengapaniya are also found to be significant.

While considering the finger pattern indices in the Table 6, it is noted that the Dankmeijer's index is higher in the Dibongiya male (7.78) while the Tengapaniya shows the same index as 3.54. On the contrary, in the case of Furuhata's index the Tengapaniya male shows a higher value (125.40) than the Dibongiya (91.38). Thus with regard to these two indices, the two male samples exhibit almost contrast picture. However, no attempt can be made to statistically evaluate the above variation exhibited by the two male samples under consideration. With regard to pattern intensity index, the Dibongiya male stand significantly apart exhibiting a lower mean (14.14 ± 0.53) than the Tengapaniya who possess a mean of 15.51 ± 0.41 (Table 8). The value of pattern intensity index in Deori males show equal consistency and do not deviate significantly from both of them.

In case of females the Dibongiya (19.04) shows a remarkably higher value of Dankmeijer's index than the Tengapaniya (6.69). On the other hand, a completely reverse picture is true in the case of Furuhatas index (Dibongiya = 62.22; Tengapaniya = 128.16). With regard to pattern intensity index too, the Dibongiya show a lower mean (12.73 ± 1.07) than the Tengapaniya who possess 15.08 ± 0.55 as the pattern intensity index. The above index in Deori closely approximate with the Dibongiya and the Tengapaniya sample.

With regard to Wilder's three main line formulae, concentration of greater percentage frequency in the formula 9.7.5 is seen in the case of the Dibongiya male (34.90). While in the case of the Tengapaniya, the formula 7.5.5 is most predominant type (28.57%). Type 11.9.7 is exhibit in higher frequency (20.40%) by the Tengapaniya than the Dibongiya (13.20%). Statistically this difference in percentage distribution in palmar main line formula reveals non significant results (Table 8). The Dibongiya and the Tengapaniya male sample also show statistically non-significant difference with Deori sample.

Almost similar picture in this regard is observed in the case of female sample of both the populations. Occurrence of 9.7.5 is higher in the Dibongiya (35.10%), while 7.5.5 is higher in the Tengapaniya (34.00%). There is no much difference, however, in the frequency of 11.9.7 type in both the populations. The two female samples show their closeness as statistical analysis turned out to be non-significant. The Dibongiya and the Tengapaniya females also exhibit a good deal of similarity to the pooled sample of Deori in this regard.

In the preceding paragraphs we have already examined the nature and range of inter-division variability with regard to somatometric, serological and dermatoglyphic trait and have noted that the inter division variability is quite significant. Thus, there can hardly be any justification for treating the Deori tribe as a single biological unit, because each of the constituent *khels* has its own distinctiveness and differs from the others in a number of characters. The samples from the two sub-sections also deviate considerably from the pooled Deori population in a number of morphological as well as dermatoglyphic characters. In this connection it is worthwhile to be mentioned that almost similar type of biological differentiation process reported earlier by Das (1981), while dealing with different segments of the Rabha and the Khasi populations of north east India. Distinct intra-tribal variation was apparent.

It has already been mentioned that the Deori were considered as the priestly section and one of the major sub-division of the Chutiya. At present, the Deori are recognised as one of the plains scheduled tribe of Assam while the Chutiyas have been recognised as 'other backward classes'. The Deori preserve their traditional culture and are very conservative in their social system and known for their animistic religiocity. The Chutiyas on the other hand are completely Hinduised and much liberal in establishing matrimonial alliance with other communities. With this background, let us examine the pattern of biological relationship between these two cognate populations.

Metric features of the body that set apart (6 out of 16 characters) the Deori from the Chutiya includes the following traits, i.e., nasal length, total facial height, upper facial height, bizygomatic breadth, total facial and upper facial indices.

A mean of leptoprosopic total face which found in the Deori (89.03 ± 0.48) is in stricking contrast to that found among the Chutiya (85.83 ± 0.60) who possess a mesoprosopic total facial mean. The Deori (11.81 ± 0.06) with a higher mean of total facial height also differ significantly from the Chutiya (11.59 ± 0.08). The bizygomatic breadth is of narrow type in both the populations, yet, with a lower mean value the Deori (13.13 ± 0.05) differ significantly from the Chutiya (13.44 ± 0.06). Similarly with a mean of leptene type of upper face, the Deori (53.46 ± 0.43) differ significantly from that of the Chutiya (50.24 ± 0.48) who possess mesene type of face. With regard to upper facial height, with a higher mean the Deori (7.14 ± 0.05) tend to vary significantly from that of the Chutiya (6.76 ±0.06). Both the populations also seen to differ from each other significantly with regard to length of the nose, which is comparatively higher in the Deori.

In ABO blood group system the Deori differ significantly from the Chutiya chiefly in their low phenotype O. Moreover, they also show a relatively high phenotype A and B in comparison to the latter.

Comparative distribution of principal finger pattern types reveals a close degree of similarity between the male samples of the Deori and the Chutiya populations. However, chi-square results reveals that the variation exists in females is statistically significant. Barring Dankmeijer's index in females, with regard to various other finger pattern indices, both the populations exhibit a good deal of similarity. Wilder's three principal main line formula in the males of both the populations shows a tendency of having more 9.7.5 type. However, concentration of people in 7.5.5 and 11.9.7 categories also not negligible. In females, type 11.9.7 is seen to occur in higher frequencies in the Chutiya than the other formula, while 9.7.5 type does so in the Deori. Test of significance reveals that both the populations stand significantly apart in respect of palmar main lines.

From the above comparative account of the two populations, it is evident that there is significant differences in anthropometric, serological and various dermatoglyphic characters between the Deori and the Chutiya. However, only in certain finger dermatoglyphic characters the differences are not apparent. Therefore, keeping in view the limitations of the present study, perhaps it could be said safely that though the Deori and the Chutiya have a common ancestral group, they are showing a tendency to deviate significantly from one another to form two distinct biological units.

As regards the Deori we have already mentioned about their conciousness to preserve their traditional socio-cultural identity. They are strictly endogamous. This may have helped to keep them insolated both socially and biologically from other sub-sections of the Chutiyas. The Chutiyas on the other hand are a bit liberal in this matter.

Hence, besides the role played by a host of other factors, perhaps gene flow is a very potent factor to cause biological variation in the case of the Deori and the Chutiya. This is however an assumption only, as we are not in a position to offer definite explanation of such behaviour of the Deoris and the Chutiyas.

REFERENCES

BROWN, W.B., 1895. *An outline grammar of the Deori Chutiya language spoken in upper Assam.*

CUMMINS, H; C. MIDLO., 1961. *Fi gerprints, Palms and Soles : An introduction to dermatoglyphics.* New York : Dover Publication.

DAS, B.M., 1981. *Micro-Evolution,* New Delhi : Concept Publishing Company.

DAS, B.M.; P.B. DAS; R.DAS; H. WALTER; H DANKER-HOPFE 1985. Anthropological Studies in Assam, India 1. Observation on five mongoloid populations. *Anthropologischer Anzeiger,* 43 : 193-204.

GAIT, E., 1905. *History of Assam,* London (3rd revised edition) Calcutta : Thacker Spink and Co.

KAKATI, B.K., 1967. *Mother Goddess Kamakhya,* Guwahati : Lawers Book Stall.

MARTIN, R.; K., SALLER 1956. *Lehrbuch der Anthropologie,* Stuttgart : Gustav Fischer Verlag.

SAIKIA, P.C., 1976. *The Dibongiyas,* Delhi : B.R. Publishing Corporation.

Table 1

Mean Values of Somatometric Characters

Characters and Indices	*Dibondiya N = 100 Present study*		*Tengapaniya N = 99 Das et.al., 1985*		*Deorj (pooled) N = 199*		*Chutiya N = 83 Das et. al., 1985*	
	Mean	*±S.E.*	*Mean*	*±S.E.*	*Mean*	*±S.E.*	Mean	*±S.E.*
St.	165.04	0.61	163.86	0.48	164.45	0.54	164.11	0.55
SH.	84.67	0.33	83.42	0.50	84.04	0.41	84.92	0.68
HH.	14.00	0.12	13.69	0.15	13.84	0.13	13.63	0.18
HL.	18.20	0.05	18.38	0.05	18.28	0.05	18.38	0.07
HB.	14.80	0.07	14.63	0.05	14.71	0.06	14.68	0.07
NL.	5.24	0.03	5.21	0.05	5.22	0.03	5.04	0.05
NB.	3.83	0.03	3.80	0.03	3.81	0.03	3.78	0.03
TFH	12.19	0.06	11.44	0.06	11.81	0.06	11.59	0.08
UFH	7.28	0.05	7.00	0.06	7.14	0.05	6.76	0.06
BZB	13.14	0.06	13.54	0.05	13.13	0.05	13.44	0.06
CI	81.36	0.41	79.31	0.35	80.34	0.38	80.36	0.41
LHI	76.85	0.72	74.37	0.80	75.61	0.65	74.05	0.90
BHI	94.22	0.85	93.71	0.95	93.96	0.89	92.66	1.24
TFI	92.76	0.51	85.28	0.46	89.03	0.48	85.83	0.60
UFI	55.26	0.42	51.65	0.46	53.46	0.43	50.24	0.48
NI	73.66	0.54	73.63	0.86	73.64	0.69	75.59	0.90

Table 2

Test of Significance : SomatometricCharacters.

Character and Indices	*Dibongiya Vs Tengapaniya*	*Deori Vs Dibongiya*	*Deori Vs Tengapaniya*	*Deori Vs Chutiya*
St	1.51	0.72	0.81	0.44
SH	2.08*	1.19	0.95	1.10
HH	1.61	0.90	0.75	0.94
HL	2.54*	1.13	1.41	1.16
HB	1.97*	0.97	1.02	0.32

NL	0.51	0.47	0.17	3.08*
NB	0.70	0.47	0.23	0.70
TFH	8.83*	4.47*	4.36*	2.20*
UFH	3.58*	1.97*	1.79	4.86*
BZB	5.12*	0.12	5.79*	3.96*
CI	3.80*	1.82	1.61	0.03
LHI	2.30*	1.19	1.13	1.33
BHI	0.40	0.21	0.19	0.85
TFI	7.89*	5.32*	5.64*	4.16*
UFI	5.79*	2.99*	2.87*	4.99*
NI	0.02	0.02	0.01	1.71

* Indicates statistically significant at 5% level of probability.

Table 3

Percentage and Allele Frequencies of ABO Blood Groups

Population	*N*	*O*	*A*	*B*	*AB*	*p*	*q*	*r*
Dibongiya	100	44.00	30.00	21.00	5.00	0.194	0.140	0.666
Tengapaniya	200	28.50	44.00	19.50	8.00	0.309	0.149	0.542
Deori (pooled)	300	33.66	39.33	20.00	7.00	0.272	0.152	0.576
Chutiya	184	47.30	31.50	16.90	4.30	0.200	0.112	0.688

Table 4

Test of Significance : ABO Blood Groups

Groups Compared		*Chi-square* Values (*d.f.=3*)
Dibongiya	x Tengapaniya	8.98*
Deori	x Dibongiya	4.43
Deori	x Tengapaniya	1.82
Deori	x Chutiya	9.25*

*Indicates significant at 5% level of probability.

Table 5

Percentage Distribution of Digital Dermatoglyphics

Population	*Sex*	*No.*	*Whorl*	*Loop*			*Arch*
				Ulnor	*Radial*	*Total*	
Dibongiya	Male	53	46.03	49.62	0.75	50.37	3.58
	Female	47	35.74	55.74	1.70	57.44	6.80
Tengapaniya	Male	57	54.56	40.70	2.81	43.51	1.93
	Female	58	54.14	40.34	1.90	42.24	3.62
Deori (pooled)	Male	110	50.45	45.00	1.81	46.81	2.72
	Female	105	45.90	47.23	1.80	49.03	5.04
Chutiya	Male	62	49.19	45.16	2.10	47.26	3.55
	Female	58	41.55	55.69	2.07	57.76	0.69

Table 6

Finger Pattern Indices

Population	*Sex*	*No*	*Dankmeijer's Index*	*Furuhata's Index*	*Pattern intensity Index*
					Mean ± S.E.
Dibongiya	Male	53	7.78	91.38	14.14	0.53
	Female	47	19.04	62.22	12.73	1.07
Tengapaniya	Male	57	3.54	125.40	15.51	0.41
	Female	58	6.69	128.16	15.08	0.55
Deori (pooled)	Male	110	5.40	107.76	14.84	0.46
	Female	105	10.99	93.59	14.02	0.78
Chutiya	Male	62	7.21	104.10	14.79	0.48
	Female	58	1.66	71.94	14.09	0.37

Table 7
Percentage Distribution of Palmar Main Line Formulae

Population	*Sex*	*No*	*11.9.7*	*9.7.5*	*7.5.5.*
Dibongiya	Male	53	13.20	34.90	27.36
	Female	47	12.76	35.10	22.34
Tengapaniya	Male	49	20.40	24.48	28.57
	Female	50	16.00	32.00	34.00
Deori (pooled)	Male	102	16.66	29.90	27.94
	Female	97	10.30	25.25	23.19
Chutiya	Male	51	24.50	33.32	24.50
	Female	49	36.73	30.61	15.30

Table 8
Test of Significance : Dermatoglyphic Characters

Groups Compared		*Digital Pattern (Chi-square Values)*		*Pattern Intensity Index (t Values)*		*Main Line Formula (Chi-square Values)*	
		Male	*Female*	*Male*	*Female*	*Male*	*Female*
Dibongiya	x Tengapaniya	9.45*	36.60*	2.04*	1.95*	3.40	0.42
Deori	x Dibongiya	3.21	14.05*	0.99	0.97	1.05	0.06
	x Tengapaniya	3.09	10.54*	1.08	1.11	17.84*	0.18
Deori	x Chutiya	1.00	27.29*	0.07	0.08	12.47*	19.08

*Indicates statistically significant at 5% level of probability.

14

The Mao and Maram Nagas of Manipur : A Morphogenetic Study

MAYANGLAMBAM MANIBABU

Introduction

The Mao and Maram are the two endogamous populations of the Naga tribes of Manipur, an easternly State of India bordering Myanmar. They are mainly concentrated along the rugged hills of the Senapati district of Manipur. The two tribes, whose respective populations are 50,715 and 6,544 (1981 Census) form 3.57% 0.46% of the total population of the State respectively. The *Mao* or *Memi* (or *Sopvoma* as it is called by themselves) and Maram Nagas 'derive their name from the two most important villages in their area' (Hodson, 1984: 2). The two tribes, with other Naga tribes, viz., Angami, Sema, Lotha, Tangkhul and other Naga tribes of Manipur shared the same legend of their origin at Meikhel, a village between the Mao and

Maram areas, situated at about ten miles south east of Kohima town, Nagaland (Horam, 1975 : 30; Shimray, 1985). The Mao and Maram who 'claim to have a common origin, but perpetually at feud with each other...are nevertheless closely allied by inter-marriage' (Grierson, 1987 : 498). George Watt (1887) surmises that the Mao and Murram (Maram) are included among the eight clans of Kolya Nagas. The Kolyas are the non-kilted Nagas according to Woodthrope's (1882) classification of the Nagas. But according to Hutton's (1969) classification, the two tribes are included within the Western Naga group. The two Naga populations 'claim to have descended from the Angami's (Watt, *op. cit.)* and the title *quasi-Angami* has been given by some writers to both the populations 'on the ground that they are more closely connected with the Angamis than their fellow subjects the Tangkhuls and the Kabuis' (Hodson, *op. cit.* : 2). Linguistically, both the Mao and Maram Nagas belong to the Naga-Kuki sub-group of the Naga group of Tibeto-Burman family within Assamese-Burmese branch (Grierson, 1967).

The two patri-oriented Naga groups are mainly cultivators and practised both shifting and terrace forms. The Mao Naga is divided into two exogamous groups *(Khel)*, the 'separation being according to tradition-religious rather than social' (Hodson, *op. cit.*), whereas, Maram has three exogamous divisions (Bose, 1980 : 21). Polygamy is rare in both these Naga groups and 'is not encouraged by public opinion' (Hodson, *op. cit.,* 94). Though prevelent, cross-cousin marriage is also not preferred among the Mao (*ibid.*, 63) on the ground that the two sexes are descended from the same blood. Junior levirate is sanctioned in the Mao Naga society but the senior levirate is absolutely forbidden (*ibid.*, 85).

It is generally referred that 'no Naga tribe is of pure blood' and each tribe 'has combined elements due to immigration from three directions : north-east, north-west and south, the people having been pushed up from the plains of Assam and Burma' (Horam, 1975 : 28). And 'though grouped as Indo-Mongoloids, the Naga tribes are not typical Mongols; the caucasoid element is present among them in a remarkable degree (*ibid.*, 29). However, the assimilation of fresh genes in each Naga appears to be incorporated 'from neighbouring areas and of nearly the same ethnic group '(Das, 1981 : 81). He also remarks 'if admixture among the tribes (Naga) continues freely, one day there may be one bigger Naga 'unit' in biological sense also' (*ibid.*, 81-82).

In the present study the Mao and Maram Naga have been studied for the frequency of the different types of hand clasping, arm folding, handedness, dominant eye and the ear lobe types; and to examine if they show any similarities or differences with each other, and the other neighbouring populations.

Method and Material

Data on hand clasping, arm folding, handedness and dominant eye types have been collected according to Mani Babu, *et. al.*, (1987); while for the earlobe types the method of Chattopadhyay (1968) has been followed. The material consists of 268 Maos (205 males and 63 females) and 195 Marams (150 males and 45 females) from different villages of Mao-Maram sub-division and Sadar Hills East sub-division of the Senapati district, Manipur during the period of September, 1990 to March, 1991. Care was taken to include in the study unrelated subjects only. The age of the subjects ranged from 12 to 48 years.

Results and Discussion

The results of the right type of hand clasping (HC), arm folding (AF), handedness (Hnd), dominant eye (DE), and attached type of earlobe (AE) of the Mao and Maram are given in Table 1. The frequency of right type of hand clasping, handedness and dominant eye is higher than that of the left type in both the populations, and the reverse pattern in arm folding. In earlobe attachment, Mao and Maram show 63.81% and 60.51% of attached-type respectively. The remaining frequency of earlobe types of the Mao (36.19) and Maram (39.49%) are of free type. The lobeless condition (Chattopadhyay, 1968) has not been found in any of the subjects tested in the two populations. It is seen from Table 1 that Mao males have a higher incidence of attached type (66.34%) than that of females (55.56%), and a reverse pattern of sexwise distribution among the Maram Naga. However, not statistical bisexual difference occur in this trait and also in all the characters under study (Table 2). So far as the earlobe types are concerned, the two Naga tribes fall within the mongoloid range which have a frequency of the attached type of ear lobe between 44.87% to 67.1% (Chattopadhyay, 1968).

The available data on the distribution of the above mentioned five morphogenetic traits among different populations of north-east Indian States are tabulated in Table 3. It is apparent from this table that the Mao and Maram Nagas, having the respective percentage frequencies of 65.67 and 66.67 of right hand claspers show closeness with each other, and also with that of Manipuri Meithei (64.02%), Nocte (64.76%) and Kabui Naga (68.62%). The frequency of right type of armfolding shows a wide range of variation on different populations of north-east India with a lowest of 31.24% among the Andro of Manipur, and the highest of 66.03% among the Muslim of Assam. The Mao and Maram having the respective percentages of 33.9 and 35.4 of right arm folders do not differ much from Andro (31.24%), Meithis (32.5%), Phayeng (33.88%), Nocte (36.19%) and Khasi (36.19%). The Mao and Maram Nagas also show closeness with Kabui Nagas of Manipur and Aka tribe of Arunachal Pradesh in respect of handedness and dominant eye respectively. Again, attached type of earlobe in Mao (63.81%) and Maram (60.51%) can be comparable with those of Kabui Naga (57.54%), Phayeng (59.54%), Tangkhul (60.84%), Ahom (62.00%) and Sema (63.0%).

The calculated chi-square values for evaluating the degree and directions of difference in respect of all the five characters under study between the Mao and Maram Nagas, and the two with other populations of allied or diverse racial affinities of north eastern India are summarized in Table 4. It is observed that the difference of the Mao and Maram Nagas in insignificant for the various characters considered in the present study. Findings on dermatoglyphics patterns (Mani Babu, *n.d.*) also show homogeneity in between the two populations. It strengthens the view that they are descended from the same stock, probably the Angamis. It seems probable that the separation has taken place in none too distant past; otherwise the Marams with such a small population strength could not have shown such close similarities with the Mao.

It is also apparent from the Table (Table 4) that the Mao and Maram Nagas show highly significant differences with Gallong, Tangsa, Wancho, Jugi, Khangabok-Hairok, Tangkhul-both from Assam and Manipur, Assamese Hindu and Sema in respect of hand clasping. Significant difference is also seen with Aka and Mao with regard to this trait. However, in arm folding both the Naga populations show highly significant differences with almost all the populations reported from Assam except Sema and Nepalee. The same is true with Jugi, Tangkhul, Manipuri Muslim, Manipuri Brahmin, Manipuri Meithei also. Further in this trait, significant differences are seen between Mao and Gallong and Maram with Tangsa, Wancho and Khangabok-Heirok. A highly significant chi-square value of Mao and Maram is observed with Aka, Khasi, Andro, Phayeng, Tangkhul, Manipuri Muslim and Assamese Hindu in respect of handedness. Similarly, Maram also shows highly significant difference with Khowa in this trait.

In respect of dominant eye, Mao Naga shows highly significant differences with Khasi, Kaibarta, Keot, Assamese Muslim and Assamese Hindu. On the other hand, Maram Naga shows heterogeneity with Khasi, Kaibarta, Baishya, Keot, Assamese Hindu and Assamese Muslim. The two Naga pupulations show greater heterogeneity with populations, viz. Manipuri Brahmin, Meithei, Manipuri Muslim, Nepalee, Baishya and Keot in respect of earlobe attachment.

Form the Table 4, it is apparent that the Mao and Maram Nagas agree with the two *loi* populations reported from Manipur, viz. Andro and Phayeng in all the traits except in handedness. There are homogeneous pattern of the Mao and Maram Naga with Nocte and Kabui in all the respective traits under study. The Mao and Maram also do not differ from another Naga counterpart-the Sema, except in hand clasping. The heterogeneity with the Tangkhul Naga (except in earlobe attachment) further substantiates the assumption of a loose closeness of the Mao and Maram with the Tangkhul (Hodson, 1984 : 2). However, further studies embracing more genetical characters is needed to elucidate this presumption. Within the limitations of the morphogenetic traits considered in the present study, Kabui is not enough to pull apart from its two Naga counterparts-Mao and Maram. It is interesting to note that with regard to hand clasping particularly, there is farthest relationship of the two Naga tribes with the Tangsa (Tengsa), who is categorised to belong to the Central sub-group of the Naga group of Tibeto-

Burman linguistic family (Grierson, 1987 : 375) and also 'seems to be very closely connected with the Aos' (Hutton, 1969 : 371). Similar result of heterogeneity of the Tengsa with Kabui Naga were also reported (Mani Babu et. al., 1987).

On the basis of the present study, it can be concluded that the Mao and the Maram do not differ from each other significantly in any of the morphogenetic characters considered. They however, show differences with the other Naga tribes and the populations from the plains of Assam and the caste Hindu populations of Manipur.

Acknowledgement

I am grateful to Professor Dr. P.K. Chattopadhyay, Head of the Department of Forensic Science, Punjabi University, Patiala for critically going through the manuscript, and for his valuable suggestions for its improvement.

REFERENCES

BOSE, J.K., 1980. Glimpses of Tribal Life in North East India, Calcutta : Institute of Social Research and Applied Anthropology.

CHATTOPADHYAY, P.K., 1968. A note on the earlobe attachment among the Jats and Ahirs, *Acta. Genet. Basel*, 18 : 277-282.

DAS, B.M., 1981. *Microevolution*, New Delhi : Concept Publishing Company.

GRIERSON, G.A., 1967. *Linguistic Survey of India*, 3 : 3 (reprint) Delhi : Motilal Banarasidas.

GRIERSON, G.A., 1987. *Languages of North East India - A Survey*, Vol. II (Reprint). Delhi : Gian Publishing House.

HODSON, T.C., 1984. *The Naga Tribes of Manipur*, (third reprint), Delhi : Neeraj Publishing House.

HORAM, M., 1975. *Naga Polity*, Delhi : B.R. Publishing Corporation.

HUTTON, J.H., 1969. *The Angamis* (Second reprint), London : Oxford University Press.

MANI BABU, M. ; CH. SUNITIBALA. ; K.S. SINGH., 1987. Hand clasping, arm folding and handedness and dominant eye among the Kabui Nagas of Manipur, *Indian Jounal of Physical Anthropology and Human Genetics*, 13, 1 : 51-56.

MANI BABU, M., *n.d.* Finger dermatoglyphic study of the two Naga populations of Manipur. (Sent for publication),

SHIMRAY, R.R., 1985. *Origin and Culture of Nagas*, New Delhi.

WATT, G., 1887. The Aboriginal Tribes of Manipur, *Journal of Anthropological Institute*, 16 : 346-370.

WOODTHROPE, R.G., 1882. Note on the wild tribes inhabiting the so-called Naga hills on our North-East Frontier of India, *Journal of Anthropological Institute* 11 : 56-72.

Table 1

Percentage Distribution of Right Type of Hand Clasping, Arm Folding, Handedness, Dominant Eye and Attached Earlobe Among the Mao and Maram Nagas of Manipur.

	Mao Naga			*Maram Naga*		
	Male	*Female*	*M + F*	*Male*	*Female*	*M + F*
	(N=205)	*(N=63)*	*(N=268)*	*(N=150)*	*(N=45*	*(N=195)*
Hand clasping	64.39	69.84	65.67	68.00	62.20	66.67
Arm folding	32.68	38.09	33.96	36.67	31.11	35.38
Handedness	81.46	80.95	81.34	80.00	77.78	79.49
Dominant eye	65.85	58.73	64.18	62.67	57.78	61.54
Attached earlobe	66.34	55.56	63.81	59.33	64.44	60.51

Table 2

Test of Significance for Bisexual Variation

	Mao Naga	*Maram Naga*
	Chi-square value (d.f.-1)	*Chi-square value (d.f.-1)*
Hand clasping	1.58	0.52
Arm folding	0.63	0.47
Handedness	0.008	0.10
Dominant eye	1.06	3.22
Earlobe attachment	2.43	0.34

Table 3
Percentage Distribution of Right Type of Hand Clasping, Arm Folding, Handedness, Dominant Eye and Attached earlobe in some Populations of North East India

Population	*Sample size*	*HC*	*AF*	*Hnd*	*DE*	*AE*	*Sources*
ARUNACHAL PRADESH							
Aka	180	54.44	40.00	73.30	65.00	-	Das and Buragohain, 1972
Khowa	149	72.48	43.6	73.15	67.79	-	-do-
Gallong	244	52.87	44.26	-	-	67.21	Das and Choudhury, 1975
Nocte	210	64.76	36.19	-	-	-	-do-
Tangsa	207	49.28	48.31	-	-	-	Das, et. al. 1976
Wancho*	117	71.79	36.61	-	-	-	-do-
ASSAM							
Ahom	100	62.00	59.00	-	-	62.00	Dutta & Phookan, 1978-79
Baishya	361	63.7	48.1	-	70.9	24.2	Das, et. al., 1972
Keot	227	63.8	47.1	-	69.6	18.1	-do-
Hindu (A)	(A)	89.14	48.3	90.2	71.9	-	Das, et. al., 1978-79
Muslim	318	86.2	66.0	82.4	72.64	-	-do-
Nepalee	100	70.0	36.0	-	-	28.0	Phook and Begum, 1976
Sema	100	51.0	43.0	-	-	63.0	-do-
Kaibarta	200	62.5	50.0	-	52.0	57.0	Das & Das, 1978-79
TRIPURA							
Jugi	165	52.70	54.37	-	-	-	Dutta and Ghosh, 1988
MEGHALAYA							
Khasi	201	69.15	36.19	92.50	49.52	-	Das and Barua, 1974
MANIPUR							
Andro	234	70.50	31.24	97.86	-	-	Singh, 1978
Manipuri Meithei	214	64.00	56.90	-	-	55.50+	Singh and Malhotra, 1970, 1971

Population	N	1	2	3	4	5	Source
Manipuri Brahmin	113	75.50	54.40	-	-	22.35++	-do-
Meithei	160	70.00	32.50	-	-	-	Singh, 1973
Muslim	(B)	35.00	57.40	100.00	-	44.70	Chakravarty, 1986
Khangabok-Heirok	272	56.90	49.50	-	-	-	Singh, 1973
Phayeng	304	70.39	33.88	96.40	67.10	59.40	Mani Babu and Sunitibala, 1989
Kabui Naga	341	68.60	40.20	78.60	68.90	57.50@	Mani Babu, *et.al.* 1987
Tangkhul	(C)	53.90	47.70	95.80	-	60.80	Chakravarty, 1986
Mao Naga	268	65.70	33.90	81.30	64.20	63.80	Present study
Maram Naga	195	66.70	35.40	79.50	61.50	60.50	Present study

Note :
- * Sample size includes only the males.
- (A) Respective sample sizes for HC, AF, Hnd, and DE are 1206, 1205, 1209 and 1208.
- \+ Sample size = 217 (Singh and Malhotra, 1970).
- ++ Sample size = 116 (*ibid.,*).
- (B) Sample size for HC, AF, Hnd and earlobe attachment are 360, 408, 134 and 234 respectively.
- (@) Sample size = 749 (Mani Babu, *n.d.*)
- (C) Sample size for HC, AF, Hnd, and earlobe attachment are 269, 262, 191 and 263 respectively.

Table 4

Values of Chi-Square Test for Inter-Population Differences

Groups Compared		*HC*	*AF*	*Hnd*	*DE*	*AE*
Mao	x Maram	0.05	0.10	0.24	0.33	0.52
	x Aka	5.71*	1.70	4.04*	0.03	-
	x Khowa	2.04	3.82	3.79	0.55	-
	x Gallong	4.86*	5.71*	-	-	0.65
	x Nocte	0.04	0.25	-	-	-
	x Tangsa	12.93*	1.00	-	-	-
	x Wancho	11.08*	2.82	-	-	-

	x Khasi	0.63	0.74	12.05*	7.33*	-
	x Jugi	7.33*	18.83*	-	-	-
	x Manipuri Brahmin	3.36	14.46*	-	-	55.52*
	x Manipuri Meithei	0.15	23.63*	-	-	3.61
	x Meithei	0.82	0.009	-	-	12.85*
	x Khangabok-Heirok	4.32*	0.46	-	-	-
	x Andro	1.34	0.06	34.94*	-	-
	x Kabui Naga	0.59	0.28	0.70	1.51	0.16
	x Phayeng	1.46	0.00	29.87*	0.54	1.09
	x Tangkhul	7.73*	10.38*	21.14*	-	0.49
	x Manipuri Muslim	57.89*	35.47*	28.55*	-	22.35*
	x Sema	6.63*	2.57	-	-	0.02
	x Nepalee	0.61	0.13	-	-	37.59*
	x Kaibarta	0.50	12.20*	-	7.51*	2.22
	x Ahom	0.04	18.91*	-	-	0.17
	x Baishya	0.25	12.80*	-	3.20	18.32*
	x Keot	0.17	8.89*	-	6.05*	13.86*
	x Assamese Hindu	94.03*	18.17*	17.22*	6.35*	-
	x Assamese Muslim	34.27*	59.92*	0.10	4.85	-
Maram	x Aka	0.36	0.08	39.87*	0.46	-
	x Khowa	1.34	2.04	38.72*	1.43	-
	x Gallong	8.53*	3.55	-	-	2.11
	x Nocte	0.16	0.02	-	-	-
	x Tangsa	12.44*	6.88*	-	-	-
	x Wancho	13.97*	5.36*	-	-	-
	x Khasi	0.28	0.24	14.38*	3.86*	-
	x Jugi	7.25*	14.14*	-	-	-
	x Manipuri Brahmin	2.48	11.11*	-	-	42.46*
	x Manipuri Meithei	0.31	19.99*	-	-	1.14

x Meithei	0.45	0.23	-	-	5.87*
x Khangabok-Heirok	4.47*	3.89*	-	-	-
x Andro	0.73	0.29	38.25*	-	-
x Kabui Naga	0.21	1.20	0.06	3.01	0.56
x Phayeng	0.77	0.11	36.95*	1.61	0.04
x Tangkhul	7.62	6.95	23.61*	-	0.01
x Manipuri Muslim	51.34*	25.47*	31.29*	-	13.49*
x Sema	6.84	1.62	-	-	0.14
x Nepalee	0.33	0.01	-	-	27.92*
x Kaibarta	0.74	12.86*	-	9.63*	0.50
x Ahom	0.63	19.13*	-	-	0.06
x Baishya	0.42	8.45*	-	7.86*	32.48*
x Keot	0.49	6.83*	-	8.36*	24.21*
x Assamese Hindu	7.85*	11.25*	31.17*	8.72*	-
x Assamese Muslim	27.46*	45.78*	0.67	6.89*	-

* Indicates statistically significant at 5.0% level of probability.

15

Opportunity of Selection in the Pnar of Jaintia Hills District, Meghalaya

MRINMAYI BANERJI
DIPESH CHOUDHURY
DIPAK KUMAR ADAK

In Meghalaya, the district of Jaintia Hills, with its considerable hilly area, is inhabited by a large number of tribal populations. The district is situated between 28°-8' and 26°-8' north latitude and between 92°-0' and 92°-51' east longitude. The altitude of the district varies from 1220 meters to 1830 meters from the sea level. Pnar, the sub-tribes of the Khasi is mostly predominated in this district. The tribe Pnars are still able to retain some of their ancient culture and language is thought to be Mon-Khmer origin and linguistically they belong to the Austro-Asiatic language speaking group. They are matrilineal and cross-cousin marriage is practised by them. The Pnars firstly influenced by Hindus, but during the British rule the waves of Western culture influenced the Pnar (Deb Roy, 1981). So, this change affect the socio-economic condition of the people. The wave of Christianity and the activities of the missionaries have improved the economy, education and hygienic condition of the Pnars considerably, yet the old tradition and culture habits are not gone totally. The tribe practice the agriculture though, many of them have taken up their jobs like basket making, business and day labour, etc. The average size of the family is very small and the impact of the family planning programme seems to be insignificant. So, these diverse situations regarding socio-economy, transitional position of the way of life of the Pnar, may affect the forces of natural selection to operate in an unmitigated manner. Hence, it would be interesting to study the intensity of the natural selection as proposed by Crow (1958), on the basis of fertility and mortality variables.

The chief concern of the present study is to compute the index of selection intensity of the Pnar of Jaintia Hills district. Furthermore, an endeavour is made to compare and portray the nature and extent of the variation of the values of selection intensity (I) with the published data of the North Eastern tribes, studied earlier.

Material and Method

To collect the reproductive performance of the evermarried women concerning the tribe Pnars, the first author (M.B.) carried out field investigations in the village Nongbah of Jaintia Hills district during November 1991 to January 1992. The village is situated at a distance of 13 km. west from Jowai town which falls under Thadlaskein Block of Jaintia Hills district. Considerable number of cases of tuberculosis, influenza, diarrhoea, anemia, dysentery, malnutrition are reported at the Primary Health Centre, though the centre is far away from the village Nongbah. Minimum amenities like Primary Health Centres and private doctors at the time of need relating to health problems are not at all available in the village Nongbah of the Jaintia Hills district.

Selection Intensity

Any differential in fertility or mortality is Natural Selection and this helps to measure the fitness of a particular population in a particular environment. Population geneticists (Spuhler, 1973) have regarded it as a genetic phenomenon that has been operating in all human populations through differential fertility and mortality. Spuhler (1973) has suggested that selection operates at three different levels-total or individual selection, phenotypical selection and genotypical selection.

Crow (1958) called this index as an index of Total Selection Intensity (now called index of opportunity for selection) in a population. This index can be partitioned into two components, namely, index due to fertility and index due to mortality.

In short, the main concept of natural selection is that of fitness, which means, "the reproductive capacities of an individual or class of individuals in terms of numbers of offspring they contribute to the next generation" (Spuhler 1973).

In order to estimate the total selection intensity of the Pnars we have followed the method proposed by Crow (1958) and his later modifications by Johnston and Kensinger (1971) which takes care of embryonic deaths.

The statistical formula proposed by Crow (1958) is as follows:

$$I = I_m + I_f \backslash P_s$$

$$I_m = P_d \backslash P_s$$

$$I_f = I_f \backslash (x)^2$$

where, I= index of total selection intensity = 0.4162

I_m= index of selection due to infant mortality = 0.1057

I_f = index of selection due to fertility = 0.2808

X = average number of live births per women aged 40 years and above = 4.3832

V_f = variance in the number of live births due to fertility =5.3944

P_d = premature deaths (died before 15 years of life) =9.56%

P_s = proportion of survivors from 15 years and above =0.9044

Results and Discussion

From the analysis it appears that, among the Pnars the mortality component (I_m =0.1057) of total selection intensity is lower than the fertility component (I_f=0.2808). The total selection intensity of the Pnar is (I=0.4162). It also reveals that selection is operating in Pnar which is nearer to the lower limit of the range of Indian population (0.24 - 2.25). The higher fertility differential within the Pnar population might be due to not having the proper concept of family welfare methods along with high fertility is also indicate the influence of culture, behaviour ... and environmental factors.

Only a few populations of north east India have been studied in order to find out the effect of selection. The data summarised in the Table 2 shows that the total selection intensity, i.e., (I) is highest among the Singpho (I=1.020) of Arunachal Pradesh (Padmanabham and Jaswal, 1982) and lowest among the Sonowal Kachari (I=0.360) of Assam (Deka, 1980). Comparing the present finding with the tribal population of north eastern region, it is seen that the total selection intensity in all the populations is just in the middle of the above mentioned range. Excepting in the case of the Pnar and the Khampti all other tribes of north east region show the relatively high contribution of mortality component in the selection index. It can be presumed that diseases such as anemia, gastrointestinal parasites, malnutrition and hard work for procuring food and fuel which are the characteristic features of the hilly and forest habitat are responsible for the higher incidence of pre-reproductive mortality in most of the tribes of north east region.

From the above findings thus, it could be summarised that selection is operating with low intensity in most of the tribes of north east India. This may be due to the fact that most of the tribes of this region are living in a more or less same geographical milieu and almost similar cultural environments.

REFERENCES

BARUA, S., 1983. The Hajongs of Meghalaya : A Biodemographic Study, *Human Science*, 32 : 190-200.

CROW, J.E., 1958. Some possibilities for measuring selection intensities in man, *Human Biology*, 30 : 1-13.

DEKA, A., 1978. Reproductive performance and selection among the Jaintias of village Sa-Phai, *Genetical Demography of Indian Population*, Calcutta : Anthropological Survey of India, pp 6-11.

DEKA, R., 1980. Selection potential among Sonowal Kachari of upper Assam, *Bulletin of the Department of Anthropology, Dibrugarh University* 9 : 136 - 140.

JOHNSTON, F.E.; K. M. KENSINGER., 1971. Fertility and mortality differentials and their implications for micro-evolutionary change among the Cachinahua, *Human Biology*, 43 : 356 - 364.

PADMANABHAM, P.B.S.V.; I.J.S. JASWAL., 1982. A demographic study of Apatanis, *Proceedings of the Seminar on Biological and Cultural Variation of the People of North East India*. Guwahati : Anthropology Department, Guwahati University.

SPUHLER, J.N., 1973. 'Anthropological Genetics : An Overview', In *Methods and Theories in Anthropological Genetics*, Edited by M.H. Crowford and P.L. Workman. Albuquerque : University of New Mexico Press, pp. 623-651.

Table 1

Indices of Selection Intensity of the Pnar

Crow, 1958 (Calculated from birth)			*Johnston and Kensinger, 1971* (Calculated from early embryonic stage)			
I_m	I_f	I	I_{me}	I_{mc}	I_f	I
0.1057	0.2808	0.4162	0.1270	0.1057	0.2808	0.5960

Table 2

Indices of Selection Intensity : The Pnar and other population groups

Population	*Area*	I_m	I_f	I	*Source*
Apatani (Guchi)	Arunachal	0.435	0.190	0.170	Padmanabham and Jaswal, 1982
Apatani (Guth)	"	0.440	0.312	0.889	do
Singpho	"	0.437	0.406	1.020	do
Khampti	"	0.388	0.398	0.934	Choudhury (Unpub.)
Sonowal Kachari	Assam	0.192	0.141	0.360	Deka, 1980
Hajong	Meghalaya	0.443	0.131	0.631	Barua, 1983
Jaintia	"	0.456	0.125	0.638	Deka, 1978
Pnar	"	0.106	0.281	0.416	Present study

16

Finger Dermatoglyphics of the Lakher of Mizoram

N.N. SENGUPTA

The Lakher, who are synonymous with Mara form one of the major scheduled tribe of Mizoram. They are distributed in about 60 villages in Chhimtuipui District of Mizoram. The villages are mainly concentrated in the eastern and south eastern part of the district. In 1971 Census, the population of Lakher was 11,625. The major occupation of the population is agriculture, *Jhum* cultivation is the main form of cultivation. They have their own district council, known as 'the Lakher District Council', which came into existence since 1972.

Material and Method

The present paper deals with the finger dermatoglyphics of the Lakher. Material for the present work were collected from different educational institutions of Saiha, the district head quarter of

Chhimtuipui district, during the month of March 1988. The material comprises bilateral inked impressions of fingerballs of 121 unrelated individuals (61 males and 60 females). The data have been analysed according to the methods described by Cummins and Medlo (1961).

Results and Discussion

Table 1a and 1b show the frequency of finger patterns on the different digits of the Lakher males and females respectively. It appears that among females total frequency of whorls (49.33%) is slightly higher than the males (45.57%) while the percentage figure of loops for females (49.16%) is slightly lower than that of males (51.15%). Likewise the females have lower occurrence of arches (1.50%) than males (3.28%). It is also observed that ulnar loops occur almost equally in males (48.36%) and females (48.33%). However, the radial loop show a higher percentage in males (2.79%) than the females (0.83%).

It is apparent from the table that, of all the patterns, ulnar loops occur in highest frequency in males, whereas whorls does so in females. The next highest frequency in case of males and females are whorl and loop respectively. Ulnar loops show the highest frequency in the fifth finger whereas the highest number of radial loops are observed in the second finger in both hands and in both sexes. As regards arches, the simple arches are more frequent than tented arches in case of females whereas both the types are almost similar in case of male. Highest frequency of arch occurs in the first finger in case of females and second finger in case of males.

In the Table 2, the frequencies of various digital patterns briefly classified into whorls, loops and arches following Galton in both the sexes are shown. It is revealed from the table that whorls are more frequent in the right hand in males and while it is left hand in females. Reverse is true in the case of loops. The loops are more frequent in the left hand in males and right hand in females. The arches shows higher frequency on the left hand in both the sexes.

There is no statistically significant bimanual differences in both the sexes. Sex difference is also not significant as revealed from the value of chi-square (Table 3).

The occurrence of symmetrical and asymmetrical combination patterns in all digits are given in Table 4. It is seen from the Table that the trend of symmetrical combination in male is I = V > II > IV > III, while in female it is IV > V > I = III > II.

Table 5 shows the frequency of monomorphic hands of both the sexes. It is revealed that the monomorphic hands occurs in a much higher frequency (50.00%) in females than that of males (44.26%). Right hand is more monomorphic than left hand in both the sexes. It is worth mentioning that there is no monomorphic hand having arches in both the sexes. As regards total monomorphism, males show comparatively higher (13.11%) frequency than that of females (10.10.%).

It is evident from the table 6 that pattern intensity index does not show much difference between males and females, whereas Dankmeijer's index exhibit much higher value in males than the females. Similarly Furuhata's index also show much sex difference.

Difference between mean ridge count for individual fingers in two sexes are shown in Table 7. In general, means for individual digits as well as total ridge count are higher in females than males. There are however, exceptions in digit I of the both right and left hands. Further, excepting digit I the differences in means in all the other digits are too small. Digit III and V show a lower mean value on the right than on the left. Bimanual differences for males and females show higher total ridge count on right hand than on the left in males, inspite of the disparity of the digits III and V. Reverse is the case of females, where higher total ridge count is on the left hand than on the right, inspite of the disparity of digits I and IV. The total mean ridge count for female is 127.16 and that of males is 123.16.

Table 8 summarizes the principal papillary pattern types and indices of some tribes of Mizoram and Manipur. In respect of papillary patterns male Lakher seem to be closer to the Veiphei and Gangte (Chakravatti and Mukherjee 1962), while the female are closer to Pawi (Sengupta, unpublished). The frequency of arches is relatively lower as in all populations under consideration. The Lakher male sample show slightly higher frequency of arches and seems to be close with the Bawm community of Mizoram (Sengupta, unpublished). On the whole, the Lakher are well within the broad range of variations of Mongoloids. According to World summaries (Chamla, 1962-1963) whorl and loop vary among the Mongoloids between 43% to 59% and 38% to 59%. The arch frequency and pattern intensity index variations among Mongoloids is of the order 0.0% to 5.5% and 13.45 to 15.90 respectively. Similarly they are also well within the Mongoloid fold with regard to Dankmeijer's arch/whorl index too. According to Dankmeijer (1938), arch/whorl index below 10 is typical for Mongoloids. The index of pattern intensity displays almost similar pattern in all the populations under consideration, except the Pawi of Mizoram. The Lakher male shows a close tie as regards Dankmeijer's and Furuhata's index with the Bawm community of Mizoram, while female shows closer relationship with the Pawi community.

ACKNOWLEDGEMENT

I express my thanks to Shri S.K. Bhattacharjee and Late N.N. Kundu for their help during the field work.

REFERENCES

CHAKRAVARTTI, M.R., 1962. The first report of dermatoglyphic studies of tribes and castes of Manipur and Nagaland, *Bulletin of the Department of Anthropology, Govt. of India*, II.

CHAMLA, M.C., 1962-1963. La repartition geographique des cretes papillaries digitales dans le monde : nouvel essai de synthese, *L'Anthropologie* 67; 1-2 : 1-48.

CUMMINS, H. C. MIDLO., 1961. *Finger Prints, Palms and Soles : An Introduction to Dermatogl yphics*, New York : Dover Publication.

DANKMEIJER, J., 1938. Some anthropological data on finger prints, *American Journal of Physical Anthropology*, 23 : 377-388.

Table 1a

Distribution of finger pattern in individual digits

Patterns	RIGHT						LEFT						Combined
	I	II	III	IV	V	Total	I	II	III	IV	V	Total	Total
Whorl	35	36	21	38	13	143	35	33	22	32	13	135	278
%	5.74	5.90	3.44	6.23	2.13	23.44	5.74	5.41	3.61	5.25	2.13	22.13	45.57
Loop Ulnar	24	15	37	23	47	146	22	15	36	28	48	149	295
%	3.93	2.46	6.07	3.77	7.70	23.93	3.61	2.46	5.90	4.59	7.87	24.43	48.36
Loop Radial	6	6	2			8		8	1			9	17
%		0.98	0.33			1.31		1.31	0.16			1.48	2.79
Arch Tented		2				2	2	3	2	1		8	10
%		0.33				0.33	0.33	0.49	0.33	0.16		1.31	1.64
Arch simple	2	2	1		1	6	2	2				4	10
%	0.33	0.33	0.16		0.16	0.98	0.33	0.33				0.66	1.64

Table 1b

Distribution of finger pattern in individual digits among female Lakher

Patterns	RIGHT						LEFT						Combined
	I	II	III	IV	V	Total	I	II	III	IV	V	Total	Total
Whorl	34	31	23	41	15	144	30	35	33	43	11	152	296
%	5.67	5.17	3.83	6.83	2.50	24.00	5.00	5.83	5.50	7.17	1.83	25.33	49.33
Ulnar loop	23	26	37	19	45	150	26	22	26	17	49	140	290
%	3.83	4.33	6.17	3.17	7.50	25.00	4.33	3.67	4.33	2.83	8.17	23.33	48.33
Radial loop	—	3	—	—	—	3	—	2	—	—	—	2	5
%		0 50				0.50		0.33				0.33	0.83
Tented Arch	—	—	—	—	—	—	—	1	—	—	—	1	1
%								0.17				0.17	0.17
Simple Arch	3	—	—	—	—	3	4	—	1	—	—	5	8
%	0.50					0.50	0.67		0.17			0.83	1.33

Table 2
Percentage Distribution of Principal Pattern Types of Finger Among the Lakher

Sex	Hand	Whorl	Loop	Arch
Male	Right	46.89	50.49	2.62
	Left	44.26	51.80	3.93
	R + L	45.57	51.15	3.28
Female	Right	48.00	51.00	1.00
	Left	50.67	47.33	2.00
	R + L	49.33	49.17	1.50

Table 3
Values of Test of Significance: Digital Pattern Distribution

	Chi-square value (d.f. = 2)	*Probability*	*Inference*
Bimanual variation			
Male	1.10	0.70 >p>0.50	Insignificant
Female	1.64	0.50 >P>0.30	-do-
M + F	1.76	0.50 >p>0.30	-do-
Bisexual Variation			
Male x Female	5.13	0.10>p>0.05	-do-

Table 4

Percentage Distribution of Symmetry- Asymmetrical combination in Finger Pattern Types Among the Lakher

Digit	Male		Female	
	Symmetry	*Asymmetry*	*Symmetry*	*Asymmetry*
I	88.52	11.48	71.67	28.33
II	70.49	29.52	66.67	33.33
III	63.93	36.07	71.67	28.33
IV	68.85	31.15	90.00	10.00
V	88.52	11.48	76.67	23.33

Table 5

Percentage Distribution of Monomorphic Hands Among the Lakher

Sex	*Type*	*Right*	*Left*	*R + L*	*Both*
Male	Whorl	11.48	6.56	9.02	3.28
	Loop	11.48	14.75	13.11	9.84
		22.96	21.31	22.13	13.12
Female	Whorl	15.00	8.33	11.66	5.00
	Loop	11.67	15.00	13.33	5.00
		26.67	23.33	24.99	10.00

Table 6

Value of the Indices of Pattern Type in Fingers Among the Lakher

Sex	*Dankmeijer's Index*	*Furuhatas Index*	*Pattern intensity Index*
Male	7.19	83.10	14.23
Female	3.04	100.33	14.78
M + F	5.05	94.56	14.50

Table 7

Mean Ridge Count in Fingers Among the Lakher

Sex	*Hand*	*I*	*II*	*III*	*IV*	*V*	*Combined Digit*
Male	Right	15.80	11.14	12.05	13.10	9.69	61.78
	Left	14.31	10.77	12.57	13.05	10.54	61.24
	R + L	15.06	10.96	12.31	13.08	10.12	61.51
	R - L	+1.49	+0.37	-0.52	+0.05	-0.85	+0.54
Female	Right	14.71	11.97	12.22	14.22	10.36	63.48
	Left	13.24	12.08	13.31	14.12	10.93	63.68
	R + L	13.98	12.03	12.77	14.17	10.65	63.58
	R - L	+1.47	-0.11	-1.09	+0.10	-0.57	-0.20
M + F	Right	15.26	11.56	12.14	13.66	10.03	62.65
	Left	13.78	11.43	12.94	13.59	10.74	62.48
	R + L	14.52	11.50	12.54	13.63	10.39	62.57
	R - L	+1.48	+0.13	-0.80	+0.07	-0.71	+0.17

Table 8

Frequency of Principal digital patterns and indices Lakher and other tribes of Mizoram and Manipur

Population	No.	Whorl	Loop	Arch	Dankmeijer's index	Furuhatas index	Index of Pattern intensity	Source
MALE								
Lakher (Mara)	61	45.57	51.15	3.28	7.19	83.10	14.23	Present study
Pawi	52	60.38	39.23	0.38	0.64	132.92	16.00	Sengupta (Unpubl.)
Bawm	58	44.66	52.59	2.76	6.18	84.91	14.19	do
Lushai	134	41.64	57.01	1.34	-	-	14.02	Chakravarty and Mukerjee 1961
Gangte	100	46.00	52.00	2.00	-	-	14.40	do
Paite	101	51.39	46.93	1.68	-	-	14.92	do
Thado	100	44.00	55.00	1.00	-	-	14.28	do
Vaiphei	148	45.54	52.84	1.62	-	-	14.49	do
Hmar	100	49.00	50.00	1.00	-	-	14.75	do
Tanghkul	270	53.54	45.15	1.40	-	-	15.21	do
Meithei	118	51.95	46.19	1.86	-	-	15.01	do
FEMALE								
Lakher (Mara)	60	49.33	49.17	1.50	3.04	100.33	14.78	Present study
Pawi	47	48.09	50.64	1.28	2.65	94.96	14.68	Sengupta (Unpubl.)
Bawm	51	33.33	63.33	3.33	10.00	52.63	13.00	do
Lushai	124	41.13	55.64	3.23	-	-	13.79	Chakravartti and Mukherjee 1961

Population	No.	Whorl	Loop	Arch	Dankmeijer's index	Furuhatas index	Index of Pattern intensity	Source
Gangte	100	45.00	54.00	1.00	-	-	14.40	do
Paite	150	47.20	52.40	0.40	-	-	14.68	do
Thado	124	40.48	56.62	2.90	-	-	13.75	do
Vaiphei	86	46.28	52.33	1.40	-	-	14.48	Chakravartti and Mukherjee, 1961
Hmar	148	41.62	57.98	0.41	-	-	14.12	do
Tangkhul	172	55.70	42.79	1.51	-	-	15.42	do
Meithei	128	43.36	55.15	1.48	-	-	14.19	do

17

Dimensions of Naga Society : The Processes of Cultural Fusion and Fission

N. SAHA

S.S. MISHRA

The Naga is a generic name of the community given to the people by the outsiders since pre-independence period. They are sparsely distributed in the four States of North-East India namely Assam, Arunachal Pradesh, Nagaland and Manipur. Ethnically they belong to mongoloid group and linguistically they come under the Tibeto-Burman family of languages. They are scheduled tribes. The various Naga groups migrated to their present inhabitat long back in different waves from places situated in North and South-Eastern part of India. In Assam, there are three Naga communities inhabit namely

Jeme in North Cachar Hills district, Kabui in Cachar district and the Sema in Dibrugarh district. There are two cognate groups of the Naga namely the Nocte and the Wancho inhabit Arunachal Pradesh having the population 33,339 and 33,082 respectively (Census :1981). Manipur is inhabited by the seven major Naga groups (Census : 1971) such as Tangkhul (57,851), Kabui including Puimei (40,257), Mao (33,379), Kacha (13,026), Anal (6,670), Maram (4,539) and Monsang (930). The largest Naga population (4,26,262) having sixteen different groups are found in Nagaland State (Census : 1971). These are Ao (65,630), Angami (38,570), Chakhesang (42,799), Chang (16,007), Chiru (692), Khiemnungun (14,326), Konyak (72,263), Lotha (35,627), Makwari (2,501), Phom (18,005), Rengma (7,828), Sangtam (19,100), Sema (62,984), Tikhir (2,800), Yimchungre (14,086) and Zeliang (13,044).

Due to some political and administrative reasons Zemei and Liangmei of Nagaland are known as Zeliang whereas in Manipur, Rongmei is called Kabui and Zemei and Liangmei are known as Kacha Naga. In Assam they are known as Kabui and the Jeme in place of Rongmei and Zemei. The Zeliangrong is a composite name formed out of three Naga communities such as Zemei, Liangmei and Rongmei. Chronologically the name Zeliangrong was coined only in 1947. But the common ancestry of the Zeliangrong people is embeded in the legends and folklores of the tribes and the idea of Zeliangrong fraternity was implanted by Jadonang and Rani Gaidinliu during Zeliangrong uprising between 1930-1932. The Zeliangrong movement in the first phase was a revivalistic and socio-religious reform movement to achieve unity and soliderity in the face of spreading Christianity. The second phase was marked with political motivation against the 'British Raj' to establish 'Naga Raj' which in the process has taken some armed struggle as well as programmes in the line of nationalistic movement of India in 1946-1947. The third phase which has started since independence, i.e., after the release of Rani Gaidinliu from Jail is marked with the period of ethnic solidarity, socio-cultural and politico-economic development in the three contiguous Zeliangrong area of Nagaland, Manipur and Assam. The underground movement of the Naga people in Nagaland was remarkable in shaping the history of the Naga itself. The formation of cultural as well as political organisations such as Naga Club (1918), Naga National Council (1946) and Naga Nationalist

Organisation (1964) has paved the way for attainment of statehood as well as the Naga Nationhood. The contribution of Naga Peace Council initiated by the Christian Church leaders and Dr. A. Aram the then Director of Peace Council, Nagaland is remarkable in this respect. Even after independence and attainment of statehood a section of the Naga still continues the underground movement under the banner of an organisation called 'Naga Socialist Council of Nagaland' which perhaps does not receive popular support from the mass Naga population of North East. As a matter of fact, the detailed account of the Naga solidarity and political movements has been narrated in the publications of Robinson (1841), Holcombe (1874), Hodson (1911), Hutton (1921), Bower (1950), Butler (1955), Bareh (1970), Choube (1973), Yonuo (1974), Saha (1984) and others.

Land and forest are the primary resources of the Naga people. Agriculture, both shifting and terrace cultivation, is the basis of their agrarian economy. About 80 per cent of the total working force is engaged in agricultural activities. It is interesting to note that the Naga maintain four types of land owning system unlike other plain societies. These are : (i) family land, (ii) village or *khel* land, (iii) clan land, and (iv) land owned by chief. The system of owning land by family is prevalent among the Angami and the Chakhesang Naga of Nagaland whereas land owned by the chief is found among the Sema, Konyak, Nocte and Wancho. The Naga belong to patrilineal society and inheritance of property goes through male members. The position of women in Naga society is lower than that of man. But the contribution of Naga women in agricultural operation and household management is considerable. All the Naga communities have their traditional village control system maintained through village council and *khel* under the supervision of a traditional chief of *Gaonburah*. The roles of *Ang* among the Konyak and *Kekami* among the Sema of Nagaland; *Lowang* among the Nocte, *Wangham* among the Wanchoo of Arunachal Pradesh and *Awunga* among the Tangkhul of Manipur are most remarkable as regards their socio-economic and politico-religious roles are concerned. The modern administrative system is applicable only when there are cases of murder and serious land disputes. The *Dobhashi* (tribal judge) system of social justice is found to exist among some Naga communities of Nagaland who settles disputes as per traditional laws. Two important institutions namely ; 'Area Council' and 'Village Development Board' are prevalent since Independence in Nagaland to facilitate the development of the Naga people.

The every Naga community has an identity mark mostly represented by its unique, colourful shawl design weaved skillfully and laborously by the women of that community. These shawls have also commercial value in present days. The Naga people are craftsmen and their artistic and aesthetic expressions are displayed in varied and colourful ceremonial dresses, ornaments, house designs, wood curvings, tatoo paintings, engravings, bamboo and cane basket making. The *Morung* institution (bachelor's dormitory for boys and girls) of the Naga occupy a pivotal position in their socio-cultural and economic life as it preserves the deep seated moral social value of the Naga society. The Naga life and joy becomes more vibrant and meaningful while they observe and participate in festivals and dances related to harvest, fertility, feast of merit and head hunting. The harvest festivals invariably observed by every Naga community named differently in different communities such as *Liekhwenyi Keva Kete* and *Tseikranyi* (Angami), *Khilunyie* (Chakhesang), *Ngadha* (Rengma), *Meleingi* (Zeliangron), *Tsatekhu* and *Kate* (Pochury), *Aolingmonya* and *Oniebu* (Konyak), *Moatsu* (Ao), so on and so forth. A general account of the socio-cultural life of the different Naga groups is available in the ethnographic publications of Hudson (1911), Hutton (1921) Heimendorf (1946), Barch (1970) and Saha (1984). About 80 percent of the Naga people accepted Christianity as their religion. A considerable section of the Nocte Naga profess Vaishnavism while 'Heraka' religion is prevalent among a small population of the Zeliangron Naga. The remaining others believe in animism or traditional religion.

Cultural Fusion and Fission

The process of cultural fusion and fission is in existence mainly among the four tribes of Nagaland namely Chakhesang. Pochury, Zeliangrong and Yimchunger. This process of fusion and fission among the tribes revolve around two important aspects like 'political power' and 'economic benefit'.

The Chakhesang of the Phek district of Nagaland is formed out of three subgroups of the allied ethnic groups called Chakro,

Kheza and Sangtam although they have separate and distinct moieties like *Chuzo* and *Thevo* in addition to number of clans and lineages. But due to some politico-economic pressure from within and outside their own group they were compelled to be merged together for their own socio-cultural and political existence. Since the formation of Phek district, the Chakhesang participated in the political field and represented in the State assembly. This could enable them to be established as a single and powerful political and ethnic force to preserve their identity and culture.

The Pochury were once called as 'Eastern Angami' but dissociated themselves from the Angami tribe both socially as well as politically. The word Pochury is an acronym formed by combining three clan names namely *Sapo, Kechuri* and *Khury*. Although the Government of India has not given any recognition to them as an independent tribe. Here also the same process of cultural fusion and fission is going on for some ethnic, political and economic reasons to safeguard their interest. It is to be noted that in the process of cultural fusion some different ethnic groups like Sema, Sangtam and Rengma Naga, who had immigrated in the Pochury area, had been absorbed in the Pochury group. Now they have organised themselves into a formidable socio-political force claiming political power in the State assembly, so as to safeguard their interest.

The Zeliangrong tribe live in the contiguous areas of Nagaland, Manipur and Assam. This tribe is formed by the fusion of the three subgroups namely *Zemei, Liangmei* and *Rongmei*. Once they were separate ethnic groups. They were united by Rani Gaidinlieu through a politico-religious ideology, called 'Heraka Cult', with a view of social solidarity, ethnic identity and to achieve the freedom. Apart from this three groups they have other allied small groups of Manipur namely *Chiru, Anal, Chothe, Kom, Koiro* and *Koirang*, who are still remained dissociated as a result of socio-cultural differences and dominance of the Zeliangrong. At present Zeliangrong has formed a strong development council for their ethnic, political and cultural solidarity.

The Yimchunger, once a single tribe is now divided into three subgroups namely, *Tikhir, Makwoore* and *Chirr*. Each of these groups claims itself as an independent ethnic group for deriving socio-political, economic and political benefits from the government. This cultural fission has created an ethnic instability among the different groups and the Yimchunger itself. During election and changing political scenario these groups sometimes unite themselves for certain politico-economic gain and again dissociate themselves with one another on certain occasion to achieve temporary politico-economic benefit.

Conclusion

The Naga society as a whole is under the process of rapid change. The multifarious transformations brought about by the Christian Missionaries and philanthropic agencies are intricately related to the developmental processess of the Naga people prior to the Independence. Since evangelization has been going on along with the welfare schemes of the converts, the Naga people have accepted Christianity as the basis of their all round progress social, cultural, economical, political and religious. The Christianity alone could bring the Nagas from social and religious disillusions. The new religion offered them enough food to satisfy their religious bent of mind. The superstitious belief and practices like the head hunting, inter-tribal and intra-village feuds were replaced by new faith, festivals and worship. Their fatalistic attitude towards life has been turned into a life of faith and hope. After independence more and more socio-economic developmental schemes have created a sense of belongingness to the Naga people. Education is highly valued. The people are more interested to maintain societal peace, harmony and solidarity. Modernity and technological advancement along with modern administrative system provided them social, political and economic security. With the advancement of road and transport communication system it became easier for the Naga people to maintain socio-cultural and commercial linkages with the neighbouring communities of the other States. The Naga of the North East are now peace loving people. The cultural process of fusion and fission are very much in existence and revolves around the changing socio-political and economic situations of the concerned community involved.

REFERENCES

BAREH, H., 1970. *Gazetteer of India : Nagaland Kohima District*, Kohima : Government of Nagaland.

BUTTLER, J., 1875. Rough Notes on the Angami Nagas and their Languages, *Journal of Asiatic Society of Bengal, Calcutta*, Volume XL. IV.

CHOUBE, S.K., 1973. *Hill Politics of North East India*, Calcutta : Orient Longman.

HALCOMBE, W.A., 1873. *Exploration Survey in Naga Hills East*, London.

HODSON, T.C., 1911. *Naga Tribes of Manipur*, London : MacMillan and Company Ltd.

HUTTON, J.H., 1921. *The Angami Nagas*, London : MacMillan and Company Ltd.

ROBINSON, W.A., 1841. *A Descriptive Account of Assam*, London.

SAHA, N., 1984. 'Ethnographic Study of the Zeliangrong Tribe of North East India, In *The Tribes of North East India*. Edited by S. Karotemprel, Shillong : Vendrame Missiological Institute.

YONUO, A., 1974. *The Rising Nagas*, New Delhi : Vivek Publishing House.

18

Religion : A Factor of Culture Change amongst Angamis in Nagaland

JOGAMAYA K.K. SAIKIA

Nagaland, the land of Nagas, has derived its name from her inhabitants. It is situated in the eastern frontier of India, Bordering Assam in the North, Myanmar and Arunachal Pradesh in the East and Manipur in the South. Kohima, Mokokchung, Tuensang, Wakha, Zuneboto, Phek and Mon are the seven districts of this State.

Nagaland exhibits racial inter-mixtures in a great range as it is a meeting-centre of the Himalayan, Burmese, Japanese, Thai and Malaysian cultures. The Gazetteer mentions that they belong to the Mongoloid race. She has different tribes residing in different parts of the State. They are mainly Angamis, Ao, Chakhesang, Chang,

Konyak, Khenmungan, Kuki, Lotha, Phom, Rengma, Sema, Sangtham, Yimchunger, and Zeliang. Besides these, Kachari, Nepali and people from different parts of India are also living in the State. The majority of the tribes have similar cultural background and history. All the different tribes and sub-tribes amongst Nagas have their own individual dialects which are distinctive from the rest.

In the present study, amongst the tribes, an attempt has been made to focus the Angami, a major tribe of Kohima district and their religion in the their past and present. The religious impact on the socio-economic and cultural life in transition from tradition to modernity will be the focal theme to examine the various social structure of customs, marriage, family pattern, etc.

Land of Angamis

Before discussion, let the readers have knowledge of the land of Angamis and their mode of life first. Kohima (old) district, the abode of Angamis, like Nagaland, forms an irregular plateau, with elevated ridges and peaks. Agriculture is the mainstay of the Angami which is totally dependent on the mercy of monsoon.

Kohima, the district head quarters as well as the Capital town, is situated in the heart of the district along with its panoramic natural beauties excelled with peaks, slopes, ridges, valleys and terraces in and around. Besides these, the beautiful Angami land presents unity in diversity of race, religion, language, culture and other ethnological considerations. With all these qualities, the area plays a distinctive role in the civilisation which is further printed as the factors of change and transition. Religion, a unique blessing of any given society on per tradition, change, development of the time, will be referred here with these background history of the land.

Angamis have reverred quality of possessing love, affection for their culture-based society and tied up with their traditional life. Tradition is a learned behaviour and is practised in the day to day life to reckon with their socio-cultural life. This life is again learned by the youngsters along with elders and thus transmitted generation after generation. It is of course, not an exceptional case with Angami alone, but an universal phenomenon. Due to the growth of Statehood mixture of heterogeneity in tribes, other people pouring in from different States, religions, cultures help Angamis to procure more exposure to the outside world. This area, being the seat of Capital, district head quarter, sub-divisional head quarters, etc., feeds the heads of all administrative departments. With these multiple developmental scopes being placed to seat-up, again in return, open the opportunities for the Angamis to learn others without facing any difficulties and naturally get interacted with other population along with their own.

Religion

Religion is entwined with culture and is interrelated with social institutions and maintains the social relationships that prevails in society. Religion countributes towards social integration and group solidarity and strengthens social control. Society for its existence depends on the certain system of sentiments by which the conduct of the individual is regulated with the society's need and demand. Here, the sentiments are regulated by peoples' intellectual, emotional and practical life. These are given colour by the religion one professes. Moreover, personal, family and community life in general are dominated by religion that moulds person's behaviours, actions and faiths for conducting social norms and ethics. Absence of the religious knowledge etiolates judgment of holding the right action in proper time. Religion assures conscience from abstaining from wrong action. Around religion, people take food, provide decision-making, organise institution, exercise socio-economic life. Internal and external changes are motivated by religion to different organisations of society. Religion shows the reality in ideas, modes of living, ways of thinking and patterns of acceptance. This is why religion as Mair (1972 : 210) says "a system of belief as well as a system of relationship and action..........which is directed towards entities the existence of which is not open to observation". Different authors have different views about religion but it is common fact that it concerns supernatural order of beings, forces, entities, behaviour, welfare and connected the individual and private, and collective and social life-demanding duty, participation, interaction to socio-cultural life as a process for further diffusion. Action takes shape acknowledged by religion. Hence, religion is the mirror of the society, it regulates the social order authority, legitimate the way of life, regulates social activities for meaningful living. Therefore, religion is accepted as belief and practised by maintaining the relationship between man and environment that crops up amongst different human groups.

Religious Background of the Angami Naga

Angamis religion concerns beliefs and rituals directed at a supernatural realm of forces, powers and deities. It has profound impact on everyday occurrences including economy. Religion mobilises the people to perform economic role. At every stages of agro-economic activity, i.e., selection of land, sewing seed, transplantation, before and after harvest, before testing new product of the field, Angamis worship their appropriate deities, observe *gennas* (taboo), consult omens which are related to their daily life. All these are accepted as "a way of life", "a way of worship".

Gazetteer of India, Nagaland, Kohima District (1970 : 61) says "Naga religion is described by sociologists to be animistic which lays emphasis on the existence of the deified manifestations of nature and propitiation of spirits both benevolent and melevolent. The Angamis believe in supernaturalism with reference to deity or god or creator. They believe that troubles, calamities are caused by influence of evil spirits. According to them all nature is alive with unseen forces. They offer up sacrifices of *mithuns,* cows, dogs, cocks, liquor to get rid of their social, personal calamities and bad luck. For the success of an undertaking in daily occupation, an offering is made to the benevolent spirits. Though Angamis perform these rites, yet they do not have an established form of worship, temple, priest. The ceremonies and practices are handed down to them by traditions and a knowledgeable person works as community priest known as *Kemevo* which is hereditary and maintains genealogical, traditional facts related to village, *Khel*, etc. He directs the *gennas*. On the eve of all important projects, omens are consulted.

This traditional background gives a picture of the Angami religion. But in recent years, a great number of Angamis have embraced Christianity. For this, many of the traditional aspects will be discussed later after having a discussion on the conversion to the new faith.

Conversion to Christianity

The change regarding traditional life and independent religious views were introduced in the Angami society with the advent of the Americans in the early twentieth century. With the British administrators, American missionaries started evangelic work in this hilly region. Conversion amongst the Nagas had began in the early 19th century. But in Kohima District, it was started by Rev. C.D. King in 1878. His successor Dr. Rivenburg opened schools and printed the first Angami booklets. Even after independence, foreign missionaries continued their works. Only in 1953-56 foreign missionaries withdrew from the State. During the pre-and post-independence period and even after inauguration of new statehood within the Indian Union, preaching conversion to Christianity is being carried out by the local Christian leaders.

The conversion to Christianity is the main factor causing the change in all the vital aspects of socio-economic, religious and cultural life. It touches even further, i.e., their political life. As late as 1901 Census, 96% of the total population was animistic and followed their own traditional religion. But we may surmise that within a period of 70 years a vital change of religion from their traditional animistic one to a new western oriented Christian religion. The American missionaries converted the Angamis to Christianity in the denomination of Baptism. American Baptists were interested in higher education and increased steadily educational institutions. Conversion to a western religion preached by western people, has touched all aspects of life, which will be discussed here briefly. The discussion will help us to go into the depth of change in attitude and tolerance among the two religious groups, those who follow the traditional and the Christianity.

The Census data of 1972 shows the conversion pattern-where more rural conversions in both the sexes than those from urban area. Out of my total sample of 400 government Angami employees, it was found that 373 (93.25%) had embraced Christianity. When we look at the actual number and a comparison is drawn between the urban/rural background and between the sex, it is seen that males have higher conversion rate in urban background and females have a higher conversion rate from rural background. It should be noted that all females from rural background are Christians. Mostly amongst the samples, majority falls under the category of being the first to be converted to Christianity in their family where urbanities have been first to be converted than the ruralities, who still follow traditional (animistic) religion. It is further observed that in these families, there is no rigidity regarding the religious worship of the converts and the non-converts. There seems to be a parallel observances of the new and the old faith. In some cases parents were converted first to Christianity, hence my respondents were born Christian being in second generation. In some, grand-parents of 12 respondents (6 urban and 6 rural) were first converted in the family and our respondents are the third generation Christian. Out of these, 3 respondents (2 urban female and 1 rural male) further informed that their grandparents were converted to Christianity prior to World War I and were working with Dr. Rivenburg and his party in order to spread Christianity. It further proves that local Angami Christian started the work of conversion from World War I along with the foreign missionaries in their own areas.

Besides, the informations provided by my respondents, I was informed that there are many other members in the respondents family, who converted first to Christianity. These are less in number, yet they are the initiators in their respective families. This aspect was focussed by the respondents, where we find brothers, sisters, mother, wife or uncles to be the first initiators of the new faith in the family.

Participation and Interaction

In regards to participation in their religious activities like Easter, Christmas, etc., majority of the converts regularly celebrate the Christian festivales. It reveals that the converted Angamis are accepting the new faith whole heartedly. From this, we can definitely assess that considerable cultural change has taken place in the religious outlook of the respondents. However, these respondents also perform the traditional festivals in which participation of rural respondents were more than urban. It is due to the reason that in the rural settings, traditional norms, values and beliefs are more conservatively observed than in the urban area. Moreover ruralities are close knit with their kin group and have ties with their religious beliefs which cannot be erroded even with conversion to Christianity. Ruralities in fact are more attached to their native and indigenous religious practices and therefore find it difficult to completely cut themselves off from it. Change in religion does not prevent them from participation in their "traditional way of life", "pattern of living", customs, belief which are well knotted in their day-today life. Collectivism, Cohesiveness are the basic characteristics in the rural areas-even though they may give up some of the religious aspects of animism due to their conversion, which is only "in part" and not "wholly". On the other hand, in urban areas due to perceptual awakening caused by change in ideas, education and urban life in general, the converted Angamis are prone to change easily. As such, age-old well knotted customs, beliefs, festivals are gradually on a decline from day to day living. Regarding the performance of *Sekrenyi* many converted Angamis celebrated *Sekrenyi* omitting the traditional ritual of worship as a part of cultural pattern of Angamis "way of life". Many converts do not perform *Sekrenyi* as they feel that this traditional native religious practice was completely against the norms of Christianity, and hence alienated from the traditional form of worship. Opinions regarding the performence and non-performance of the traditional religion and practices vary. Though most of the Christians do not perform the traditional festivals yet attendance at festivals was made. It is mainly due to the cause, though they are converted to Christianity, but reside with the non-converted and participate in the activities of other Angamis. Likewise, non-converted Angamis participate in Christian festivals whole heartedly as both the sections live in close proximity but not in the prayer or service part of the religion. As Christians and non-Christians stay together in the village and sometimes under the same roof, they do not have any compunctions in living together or mixing freely. This is an anti-thesis of customs in other parts of tribal India where converted and non-converted people of the tribe live in separate clusters of houses. Dr. Karve in her extensive work observed this differentiations.

At the time of the ceremony in the family such as birth day, marriage, all members of the family, clan and village and often the whole tribe is invited. Often non-Nagas and other tribal people also are invited on friendly basis. This mixing and interaction points out that the traditional religion is tolerant to Christianity and other religion and vice-versa.

Impact on Marriage

With conversion to Christianity, the traditional marriage pattern is totally changed. After negotiation of marriage, when the date is fixed for wedding, both the parties go to the Church, adorned in western wedding dresses in most of the cases for solemonization. After this, cutting of wedding cake by the couple begins the party-lunch or dinner, according to the marriage-timing in the Church. Sometimes, they invite the priest to their home to officiate. Along with coversion, now, the Angamis go for inter-tribe mate-selection in and outside the state provided they belong to Christianity or willing to converted before or after the marriage. Inter-religious marriage takes place amongst Angamis due to the close association with the other spouse during college days or in working condition. Bambawala (1977) has put up good effort to study the details of such marriages. But though this type of marriage is a practice of the day, yet it is observed that traditional form of marriages are in practice as it is less expensive, can be celebrated without much preparation and does not disturb the pattern of normal life.

Impact on Drinks

Christians refrain from drinking. Even in wedding, etc., they do not take. Now-a-days in Angami areas both Christians and non-Christians try to abstain from this as they accept it social evil. Country liquor *madhu* (rice beer) is taken if offered on special occasions like rituals, festivals or any ceremony or while on a social visit or during group work or social work.

Impact on Socio-economic Life

Religious activities are related to socio-economic life of the Angamis. Festivals are mostly related to economic life which is agro-based. In traditional life, the norms of the festivals for solemonization though is retained with Angamis but it is in declining line as most of the Angamis are now converted to a religion which is alien to this animistic religion. Agro-economic and nature based and pattern of worship, offering, which Angamis were participating, in Christianity they are not accepted. Now-a-days only tradition bound processes conducting the festivals like eating, feasting, singing, merry-making only are made by leaving apart the '*puja*' part related to religion. A totally alien westernised religion has not only converted but influenced all the institutions like family and marriage. Those Angamis who are convert for the first generation live side by side with parents who still observe the animistic religious practices. Perhaps they have yet to be totally absorbed in the new religion. On the other hand, the cultural change as observed in this study is very real when we come to the performance of Christian festivals, we find that great number of the Christians abstain from the ritualistic activity of the indigenous animistic religion. This whole hearted acceptance of the alien religion and the alienation of the traditional religion norms clearly indicate culture change in attitude and acceptance of religious values of the new religion. Though the contact between converts and non-converts is close, yet the converts are not motivated to participate in the traditional ceremonies. This total change not yet come in because of the factor of acculturation. The change amongst non-converts in their participation in Christian festivals shows that they like to maintain the social contacts as well as the secular values in a tradition bound societies.

Conclusion

Changes amongst Angamis or any tribe in Nagaland has essentially due to the conversion to Christianity. Education, employment though are the factors of change in Angamis, yet religion and its impact in education, employment, family life, worship, decision-making are noteworthy and remains vital in culture and culture-change amongst Angamis in Nagaland.

REFERENCES

BAMBAWALA, U., 1977. *Inter Religion Marriage*, Unpublished Ph.D. Thesis, University of Poona.

HUTTON, J.H., 1921. *The Angamis*, London : MacMillan and Co., Ltd.

MAIR, L., 1972. *An Introduction to Social Anthropology*, London : Oxford University Press.

SAIKIA, J.K.K., 1980. *A Study of Culture Change Amongst Angamis in Nagaland*, Unpublished Ph. D. Thesis, University of Poona.

19

The Jamatia of Tripura

DEBABRATA MANDAL

Tripura is a small State in North-eastern India. The State is surrounded on three sides by Bangladesh as well as Assam and Mizoram States. Topographically, Tripura is mainly covered by picturesque hills, forests and dales.

The history of Tripura goes back to the days of Mahabharata. Formerly the territory was a tribals dominated under the Maharajas. Still a good number of population in Tripura is tribal population. There are altogether 19 Scheduled Tribes living in the State. The relation between the tribes and the Kings of Tripura was very old. Among the tribes, particularly the Jamatia was in the army staff of the King.

The Jamatia is one of the important, well organised, dominant tribes in Tripura, still confined within a geographical territory. They are mainly inhabited in the South Tripura district, especially in

Udaipur and Amarpur Sub-divisions. However, they are also found in the other Sub-divisions as well. It is estimated that there are approximately 600 villages inhabited by around 7000 households of Jamatia.

Etymologically the term Jamatia is derived from the word 'Jamat' which means assemblage in Bengali and Urdu. Some believe that they were recruited in the army of Tripura Kings and were called as 'Jamat' and subsequently known as Jamatia. Scholars like Saigol (1978), Deb Barma (1931) have also expressed similar views in regard to the etymology of the term. W.W. Hunter (1876) asserts that the Jamatia are a fighting caste of Tipperah and are well fitted for jungle warfare. Some expressed their views that the term Jamatia is derived from the word 'Jama' which means tax and 'Twiya' meaning free from the burden. Since the Jamatia were serving in the army and were allowed to enjoy these privileges. Jamatia belong to the Indo-Chinese stock with an admixture of Aryan blood. They however, enjoy the Kshatriya status and claim descent from the lunar race. The dialect spoken by them is known as Kak-Barak, (i.e., language of man). According to Hunter (1876), the Tipperas are divided into four classes, viz. Tripuri, Jamatia, Noatia and Riang. Except Jamatia each of the three groups are sub-divided into several sections. E.A. Gait, said that unlike all other tribes of Tripura which have number of *daphas* (sub-division) or clans among them, the Jamatia are a tribe without having any sub-division and clan.

According to the Census 1981, the population of the Jamatia is 44,501. They are living in the high land and forest tracts and some of them also practising shifting cultivation (*jhum*) regularly. Now-a-days of course a good number of Jamatia have settled in the plains and are practising plough cultivation. In the past they were semi-nomadic in nature and used to move for shifting cultivation. They also wonder in the hilly jungle areas for hunting and collection of forest products. They used to inhabit in cluster of bamboo made huts (tong) on lineage basis. But now their houses are built on the ground of high land (*tilla*) and have mud plaster on the floor and walls. The roof is of corrugated sheets or tiles.

Jamatia is an endogamous group. Marriage (*Kolai*) within three generations is strictly prohibited. Spouse from relatives beyond three generations is preferred. Among the Jamatia there is no prescriptive form of marriage but usually bridegroom from affinal side is preferred. Marriage by service (*Jamat Otha*) is most common among the Jamatia. But this practice is disappearing fast day by day especially among the educated as-well-to-do sections. Cross cousin marriage occurs rarely. A man may marry his deceased wife's younger sister. It is customary among the Jamatia that a widower or divorcee can not marry an unmarried girl. They can marry but only with widow or female divorcee. Among the Jamatia usually the marriage is being held by negotiation (*Kaglaimani*), where the parent play the major role. Recently marriage is held by mutual consent (*Hongkoinamain*) of bride and bridegroom. In such case the parent of both accept the couple after performing *Lam-Pra* puja and purificatory ceremony (*Ochai Tui*) conducted by the village priest (*Ochai*). Now-a-days they do not prefer early marriage. Inter ethnic marriage between the Jamatia with other tribes and castes like Noatia, Tripuri, Kola, Laskar and Bengali though accepted by the society under unavoidable circumstances, but such events are not encouraged by the elders. In the past, the parents having a lone daughter without having any male issue, preferred to have a son-in-law who continued to be a member (*Ghar-Jamai*) of their family.

Monogamy (*Nokhum*) is the general rule. Polygamy is rarely found. Polygamous type of family is permitted in case of barrenness. The rate of divorce is quite high among the Jamatia. Divorce can be sanctioned on the ground of madness, adultery, impotence, etc. by the *moyal paneh* (regional council). After divorce the minor children stay with mother and the step children do not get the share of property of their foster father.

Marriage of minor son or daughter usually does not happen but it is permissible. Junior levirate is allowed. Remarriage was widely practised in the past. Now-a-days if a person desires to marry once more, he has to pay fine and take permission from the council. Even if a person remarries second time outside his own society, he will be ostracised in favour of the norms of the society. However, he may be readmitted after paying a fine and performing *Lam-Pra* Puja.

If a household has no extra worker except husband and wife, in such case they even brought an adult bride for comparatively younger son. In cases of marriage by service, the bridegroom stays at brides house where he has to render assistance in agricultural works for a period of three years or till the bride attains maturity. If after working for some period by the prospective groom, the marriage is not solemnised due to unavoidable circumstances then a consolidate amount of money has to be paid for his labour.

Patrilocal residence among them is common. If accommodation is not sufficiently available with the parent, couple follow neolocal soon after the marriage. Now-a-days, instead of bride price, dowry system has been introduced among the educated and cultured families, though the council members are against it. Practice of adoption (*Pusimanibusa*) of a child through religious purification by the *Ochai* is quite frequent among the childless couples. Adoption takes place after performing *Lam-Pra* worship by the village priest and if the child belongs to another ethnic groups, the child is purified by sprinkling holy water (*Ochai Tui*) to the child's head.

Father is the head of the family who controls the family affairs and allocate duties and responsibilities to each member of the family. The unit of Jamatia social organisation is joint family. Frequency of extended family, particularly, vertically extended families are more in number than the laterally extended type.

The position of woman in society is almost equal to their counterpart. However, they are restricted to take part in village council. The Jamatia woman is very active and hard worker in domestic as well as agricultural works. Besides domestic work, women are also engaged in various activities such as agricultural work, collection of firewood, potable water, weaving clothes, looking after the cattles, etc.

To a Jamatia, the belonging of a person having monitary value and which could be exchanged, mortgaged or sold, are considered as property. Property mainly includes land, utensils, furnitures, implements, trees, ponds, ornaments, cattles, cash, etc. Among the Jamatia property is equally inherited among the sons. The sons living with the parents at the time of latter's death usually inherits the residential houses, and some movable articles. When a person dies without having any issue, the property remain under the possession of widow till her remarriage or death. If she is remarried to another man, the property will go to her deceased household's close relatives. Usually father equally divides his property among the sons during his old age. Land is the most valuable property among the Jamatia. If a person likes he may allocate one eight portion of_land to his daughter. The unmarried daughter and widow mother get one share of land for their maintenance. Step son can not claim any property from the step father. But it is permissible to give a plot of land to step son or son-in-law. If any dispute occurs regarding the division of property and could not be solved within the kins, it is referred to the village council. The council come forward to solve the problem according to their customary laws. Council is working as the main key for maintaining harmony of the society. The Jamatia have no right over natural fallow land and jungle. But there is no restriction to collect fruits, fire wood and they could visit for hunting occasionally in the neighbouring jungle.

Hunting was one of the most important aspects for their livelihood and recreation. Now-a-days, due to restriction imposed by the Government, rarely people visit jungle for hunting. Usually kins take part in group hunting operation. Except the first shooter all other gets equal share of the flesh of the game. The first shooter gets the head of the game with an usual share. In the past all the villagers used to participate in hunting.

Jamatia have a well constituted three tiers system of village (*Luko*), regional (*Mayal*) and supreme (*Hada*) councils. The executive members of three councils are nominated by selections in every five years. Beside executive members, educated and elderly persons also participate in the meeting to decide the cases of dispute, offence, and organised religious function. The village, regional and supreme headmen are called as *Chowdhury*, *Sardar* and *Akra* respectively. There are two *Akras* in the overall supreme council of the society. Besides these two *Akras*, there are 26 *Sardars* in 13 *Mayals*. The functions of *Sardars* and *Akras* are to maintain laws and order in the society. *Sardars* are empowered to control within the respective jurisdiction. Besides the judicial function, they also arrange annual religious ceremonies as well as some welfare work for the society.

Besides the traditional council, each Jamatia village comes under a *Gaon Sabha* and under the jurisdiction of *Nayapanchayat* since 1961.

The council members strongly oppose any breach from its autonomous laws. The councils keep record of the cases. If the occurrence of a particular type of breach are more, immediately council members meet together and devise way to control such deviation. It is observed that a new custom which is favourable to the society, is accepted by all members without any objection. The councils are very alert to accept and reject the old and new prac tices. Annual meeting is held on the occasion of *gang puja* and if needed the old custom may be changed or modified according to need of the people.

In the past the Jamatia were animistic in nature. The process of Hinduisation is going on among the Jamatia since last century. Now they profess Hinduism. Many of them became Vaishnav mendicant who are known as *Sadhu.* They worship the *Rakshakali, Durga, Radha Krishna,* etc. In addition to their traditional deities like *Lam-Pra, Garia, Kher, Balongia, Chadda Devata, Geng.* etc., god and goodess of Hindu pantheon are also worshipped.

The *Goria* is the most important annual festival of the Jamatia held in the month of April. The *Goria* is worshipped by the priest who belongs to *Kherpang* lineage. During the *Kher* worship, they do not admit outsiders to their hamlets for nearly 32 hours and trespassers are penalised. Before any festival subscription is collected from each household of the community. Each village has a priest known as *Ochai.* He is the religious head and performs rituals and rites of passage of the villager. Besides *Ochai, Purohit* (Hindu Brahmin) is also employed for performing marriage and death ceremonies and also in worship of the Hindu deities. Each lineage has a *Mandak* (courtyard) for daily worship of the Radha Krishna. Among the Jamatia the male wears sacred thread (*Upanayan*) between the age of 15 to 18 years.

The dead body is cremated near the river side. After cremation an earthen lamp is lighted on the alter. They observe the pollution period for 13 days. On 13th day they observe *Sardh* ceremony and offer money and gift to Brahmin.

The Jamatias prefer to inhabit on the hillocks and practise *jhum* cultivation on hill slopes. A plot of land is cultivated for a year and kept vacant for 4 to 6 years. Now-a-days good number of Jamatia are practising settled wet cultivation on plain lands with improved modern techniques of operation. The principal crops produced by them are paddy, jute, wheat, oilseeds, pulses and vegetables.

REFERENCES

HUNTER, W.W., 1876. *A Statistical Account of Bengal*, Chittagong Hill Tracts, Chittagong, Noakhali, Tipperah, Hill Tipperah, Volume VI, London : Trubner and Company.

SAIGAL, O., 1978. *Tripura : Its History and Culture*, Delhi : Concept Publishing Company.

20

Political Institutions of the Chakmas of Tripura

R.P. ATHPARIA

The Chakmas are numerically insignificant tribe of Nort East India. They are mainly concentrated in Tripura. They are also found in some pockets of Assam, Mizoram and Arunachal Pradesh. It is notified as Scheduled Tribe in all the States of North East India except in Nagaland. Lewin (1869) classes the Chakmas with the Khyoungtha or Jumia Magh who are of Arakanese origin and who speak the ancient Arakan dialect. They follow the Buddhist religion and customs (Hunter, 1973 : 43). Regarding the origin and etiology of the term Chakma, Hunter (1973 : 43). Regarding the origin and etiology of the term Chakma, Hunter (1973 : 43) quotes Lewin (1969 : 62); that "the name of Chakma is given to this tribe in general by the inhabitants of the Chittagong district, and the largest and dominant section of the tribe recognises this as its rightful appellation. It is also sometimes spelt *Tsakma* or *Tsak*, or, as it is called in Burmese, *Thek*". Supporting Lewin (1869), Hutchinson.

(1906 : 89) says that "the Chakmas are undoubtedly of Arakanese origin. They immigrated into the Chittagong district where they were inter-married largely with the Bengalis, whose language they speak. The Chakma is of medium stature and thick set build, with fair complexion and cheerful, honest looking face".

The Chakmas believe that the ethnic name Chakma has been derived from the ruling capital town of Champaknagar or Champanager. They claim themselves to be the descendants of the Kshatriya rulers. There is some controversy regarding the location of Champaknagar or Champanagar. Hutchinson (1906) mentions that Champaknagar was in Bihar. The author says that "the tribe (Chakma) consider themselves descendants of emigrants from Bihar who came over and settled in these parts in the days of the Arakanese king (ibid. : 89)". Lewin (1869) holds that Champanager was a town near Malacca. In the folksong, the Chakmas mention of a place named Noornagar. This Noornagar is situated in Hill Tripura. It is assumed that the Chakmas had been settled in Hill Tripura from very ancient times. This belief still exists among the Chakmas.

Champaknagar or Champanagar as most of the Chakmas claim to be the place of origin is believed to be on the northern region of ancient Magadha (Bihar) and southern portion of Nepal in which part the Kapilavasta or Sakya Rajya was situated. The district of Champaran on the northern border of Bihar might have derived its name from the old Champa Rajya.

Regarding the religion of the Chakmas, Lewin (1869) tried to prove that the Chakmas were once Muslims and their religion alongwith nomenclatures, titles, coustoms and rituals has been changed in course of time. It may happen that the royal family of the Chakmas was influenced by the Mohammedan faith in the later years. It is said by the Chakmas that their rulers had married some well-to-do and beautiful Muslim girls whose desire was to keep Muslim names to her children and the queen introduced the cremation keeping the head towards the west. This practice is still prevalent among the Chakmas.

When the Chakmas came in contact with the Bengalees, the Chakmas accepted the Hindu religion. Ultimately, the Chakmas began to follow the Hindu faith. In this respect Hunter (1973 : 45) states that "The religion practised by the Chakmas is Buddhism; but from their constant contact with the Bengalis, they have now added to their own rites much of Hindu superstition". It is thus clear that the Chakmas were once the followers of animism and then they felt attracted to the Hindu religion and then, finally to Buddhism.

The Chakmas speak Bengali language. This was previously written in a corrupt Burmese script. Grierson (1904) states that the Chakmas speak broken Bengali dialect, peculiar to the locality. The Chakma dialect is based on south-eastern Bengali but it had undergone so much transformations that it has almost become a separate language. It is written in an alphabet which is identical to the Khmer character. Grierson opines that the Khmer character was previously in use in the southern parts of Burma.

It has already been mentioned above that the Chakmas had settled in strength in Arakan of Burma. At one time, the Chakmas heard about Tripura to be a land of milk and honey, hence some of them migrated to Hill Tripura. Seeing the better position, gradually the Chakmas of Arakan (Burma) and Chittagong Hill Tracts (Bangladesh) migrated to Hill Tripura for better avenue of life in the remote past. In the Census of 1901 the number of Chakmas in Tripura was 4501. Hunter (1876 : 492-493) states that "In 1872 about 400 persons of the Chakma tribe emigrated from the Chittagong Hill Tracts, and settled in the territory of the Tipperah Raja. The reason assigned by the immigrants for changing their place of residence was that they had exhausted all the land fit for *Jhum* (shifting) cultivation near their former villages, and that they were tempted to Hill Tipperah by the splendid opportunities afforded to them for *Jhuming*.

The Chakmas are born cultivators. From the remote past the Chakmas have been practising *jhum* cultivation for having food and other crops. Their prime implement is *takhal* which is used for the entire *jhum* cultivation from sowing to harvesting. At present, a good number of them has adopted plough cultivation.

An attempt has been in this paper to highlight the political institutions of the Chakmas who are concentrated in Amarpur, Belonia,

Dharmanagar, Kailasahar, Kamalpur and Udaipur sub-divisions of Tripura. According to 1971 Census, their total population was 28,662 in Tripura.

Traditional Political Institutions

Earlier, the Chakmas had their own tribal council. The council was associated with socio-religious and socio-political affairs of the tribe. Originally, they had a *Maharaja* or *Raja* who was the supreme authority. He used to run the administration with the help of different categories of councillors along with the elderly persons of the Chakma kingdom or Chakma Rajya.

The councillors dealt with all the disputes among the villages and most of the matters were connected with their jurisdiction. The following were the councillors of the Chakma kingdom :

(i) *Dewan* - *Dewan* was the head of the villlage. He used to control all the village affairs under his jurisdiction.

(ii) *Khisha* - *Khisha* was an honorary title conferred by the Chakma Raja to the well-to-do and respectable man of the village. He had little executive function in the village.

(iii) *Karbari* - The office of the *Karbari* was created during the British rule. His main func tion was an over all assistance to *Dewan*.

(iv) Male *Ojhai* - Worshipper of gods and goddesses and witchcrafts. He had no executive func tion.

(v) Female *Ojhai* - Midwife of the village.

Apart from the above mentioned functionaries of the Raja, there were three religious functionaries in the Raja's council. They were :

(i) *Roulilori* - who performed the religious rites of the villages;

(ii) *Bhikshu* - the priest; and

(iii) *Genkuli* - They used to sing the historical facts and love songs with *Behala;* an indigenous musical instruments.

These religious functionaries had no executive role.

The office of the *Raja* was hereditary. It might be held by the members of a particular family. When the *Raja* died, his eldest son would get the office of the father. He then selected the different functionaries of his council. The councillors along with some elderly persons of the village decided all the social, religious, legal and semilegal nature arising in the village. They were the dispensers of justice and custodians of the traditional customs and manners. As such, they disposed off the civil and criminal cases of the village. The Chakmas preferred arbitration by the elderly persons of the village to going to the civil court. Earlier, the Chakmas did not take recourse of law courts for having their conflicts settled. Disputes of the villagers were settled through the intervention of different councils. The traditional political institutions of the Chakmas was a three-tier system, namely, the *Village Council,* the *Anchal Council* (mostly covering a wide area of a sub-division) and the *Sola-ani Council* (the whole territory).

Hunter (1973 : 44) opines that the Chakma rulers who are known to have reigned over the tribe, are the names of Jamaul Khan, Sukdeb Rai and Dharm-Baksh Khan, the first name being Muhammadan, the second Hindu, and the third a compound of both. The author further says that Raja Dharm Baksh Khan belonged to the *Molima goza* or clan. His wife, Kalindi Rani, who succeeded him, was of the *Kura Gotiya* clan. In referring the functions of the *Dewan,* Hunter (1973 : 45) quotes Lewin (1869 : 67) that "over each *goza* there is a *Dewan* or headman, who represents the head of the family from which the clan originally sprang........... He collects the poll-tax, and retaining a certain fixed proportion thereof, pays the remainder to the chief of the tribe, together with a yearly offering of first fruits. He has the privilege of deciding disputes, and for doing so receives certain fees, the amount of which is prescribed by custom. The *Dewan* also receives as a right portion of any wild animal fit for food that may be killed by any of his people. When the *goza*, or clan, is a large one, the *Dewan* appoints several subordinates under him to assist him in the administration ; these officers are called *Khejas*. They are exempted from the payment of revenue, and from the covers, or unpaid labour, to which the rest of the tribe are liable, but every year they are bound to present to the *Dewan*, an offering of one measure of rice, one bamboo tube of spirits, and one fowl".

Now-a-days, the traditional council of the Chakmas has become less important. It deals with some minor affairs such as cases of divorce, adultery, theft, minor cases arising out of love-affairs and breach of social rules or norms. The council also organises annual worships and celebrations of the tribe. It may impose fines on the offenders according to the nature of the offence or may take any other deterrent actions as deemed proper.

Recent changes in Political Institutions

According to the provisions of the Panchayati Raj Act 1947, the Chakma villages of Tripura came under the purview of the *Gaon Sabha*. The *Gaon Sabha* is the statutory body which consists of a revenue village or group of revenue villages as recorded in the revenue records by issuing an official notification in the Gazettee by the State Government. The Government at any time either on its own motion or on the request of the residents of the villages excludes or includes any area from the area of the *Gaon Sabha*. The Gaon Sabha is a bigger and broad institution at the village level and these consist of all adult members of the village whose names are included in the register of the *Gaon Sabha*.

According to 1971 Census, the total number of revenue villages in Tripura is 871 and the number of *Gaon Sabha* is 476. The *Gaon Sabha* has both-executive bodies and judicial bodies-were constituted by adult franchise. In accordance with the principle of Balwantrai Mehta Committee's recommendation, no real transfer of power to the people has yet been made in North East and consequently the main object of transferring the programme of development from a 'government programme with people's participation' to a 'people programme with government participation' is not observed here.

The Naya:a Panchayat

The judicial bodies of the *Gaon Sabha* are constituted covering a jurisdiction between two to five *Gaon Sabhas*. The sub-divisional Magistrate demarcates the jurisdiction of the *Naya Panchayat* circles. The Benches of the *Naya Panchayats* are appointed from amongst the elected members of the *Gaon Sabha* possessing suitable qualification for a period of five years, i.e., the members of the *Nayya Panchayat* are selected members. The members of the *Nayya Panchayat* Circle in turn elect their *Pradhan* and *Sahayak Pradhan* or assistant *Pradhan*. The *Pradhan* is empowered to take cognizance of the cases and distribute, transfer or re-transfer of cases of the benches constituted by him for specific period.

The *Naya Panchayats* have both criminal and civil jurisdiction. The criminal jurisdiction extends to minor offences, such as affray, intimidation, voluntarily causing hurt, assult or use of criminal force, theft (when the value of the stolen property does not exceed Rs. 50/-), receiving of stolen property, mischief and some other minor offence against the individual or the community. The Naya: *Panchayat* may also for keeping tranquility and security call upon a person to show cause why he should not execute a bond for an amount not exceeding Rs. 100/- with or without surety for keeping the tranquility for a period not exceeding 15 days and may confirm or quash the order after hearing of such person or persons.

The new democratic process has brought a new sensation among the Chakmas. The election procedures provides an opportunity in the electorate to take stock of the situation existing in the institutions before exercising their franchise. It is a process of legitimation of power and at the same time a mandate, a verdict and election of leaders.

It is observed that though the traditional political institutions of the Chakmas exist in subdued form, they show interest in election of Panchayats. In many cases the chiefs of the traditional tribal organisations are elected as *Pradhans* of Panchayat organisation. In fact, it is good sign in the matter of the better working of the Panchayat system.

To sum up, it can be said that after Independence, the idea of conciliation and curbing the litigations amongst the Chakmas have been greatly emphasised. The constitution of the *Naya Panchayat* was aimed at bringing of justice nearer to the villagers with least cost and delay. Decentralisation of judicial functions and judicial powers at the lowest level provides ample opportunities to the villagers to express their intimate knowledge in the administration of justice fearlessly and impartially. Fostering of harmoneous relation in village life in North East has been greatly achieved since the setting up of the modern political institutions. The Panchayats hardly find enough time to execute their judicial work besides their development works.

It is a fact that economic development of the poorer section of the society like the Chakmas depends not merely on the invested capital but on human resources. Therefore, for achieving success of the economic growth of the Chakmas, the utilisation of the local manpower is absolutely necessary. It is people's developmental role nor can the justice remain equitable and impartial when it is combined with executive responsibilities. As such, separation of the *Nayya Panchayat* is considerably necessary. This separation is supposed to attract suitable persons in the *Naya Panchayat*. The principle of justice underlying rigidly in the village courts is that it must follow the principle of natural justice, avoid bias, ill-will or affection. It is people's institutions at the lower level that must be activised and used more effectively for the purpose. Environmental impact is recognised as a very important factor in development schemes and programmes.

REFERENCES

GRIERSON, G.A., 1904. *Linguistic Survey of India*, Indo-Aryan Family, Eastern Group, Volume V, Part - I, Calcutta : Office of the Superintendent of Government Printing.

HUNTER, W.W., 1973. *A Statistical Account of Bengal*, Chittagong Hill Tracts, Chittagong, Noakhali, Tipperah, Hill Tiperah, Volume VI. (Reprinted) Delhi : D.K. Publishers. (First published by Trubner and Co., London; 1876).

HUTCHINSON, R.H.S., 1978. *An Account of Chittagong Hill Tracts*, Delhi : Vivek Publishing.

LEWIN, T.H., 1869. *The Hill Tracts of Chittagong and the Dwellers Therein*, Calcutta: Asiatic Society of Bengal.

21

Ethnicity and Identity of Tripura Tribes

J. GANCHAUDHURI

The question of ethnicity and identity of the Tripura tribes has been assuming a serious proportion since 1947. Tripura and the neighbouring States have become a hot bed of politics, communal hatred and violence. This trend has been variously termed. Inspite of administrative response and positive reforms, tribal impatience rises. Provocative neighbours and various organisations are going on exacerbating the tribal resentment.

The Land and Its People

Geographically Tripura consisted of plains and hills. The plains portion was in the western side, while the hills portion is in the east. A division between the fertile plains portion and the hills portion was brought about in 1618 A.D. by the Mughals. The plains portion was subsequently and very unjustly annexed to East Bengal. Its inhabitants were mostly the Bengali Hindus. The Kings of Tripura failed to protect its Kingdom and subjects. So after 1947 these Bengalees have come to the eastern hills. In the eastern hills the Tripuri Kshatriyas, who later come to be known as tribals, have been the main residents. The eastern hills now mean the Tripura State. Today Tripura is a multi-ethnic and multi-lingual State. However, the Bengalees and the tribals constitute two major groups of people. The Bengalees are about 65% and the tribals are about 30% of the population.

Genesis of Communalism

The relations between these two groups have been encumbered on the issues of land, language and the like. Right from 1947 attempts have been made by the easterners to drive out immigrants westerners. Such attempts are recurrent even today occasionally assume dangerous proportions. In this context, riots may be taken as militant minority actions over a passive majority.

Tribal Resentment

The tense situation implies that the easterners have some complaints. Their grievances ventilated in papers, pamphlets, journals, meetings and conferences, may be summarised and catalogued in the following words :

(a) merger of Tripura with the Indian Union is illegal.

(b) merger has brought about all sufferings to the tribals.

(c) tribal lands have been grabbed by the Bengalees.

(d) tribals have been outnumbered by the Bengalees.

(e) tribal language has been neglected.

(f) tribals have been reduced to beggary.

(g) rulers have been turned into ruled.

(h) lowering of social status from Tripura Kshatriya to tribe took place.

(i) scarcity of land led to stoppage of shifting cultivation.

(j) the Bengalees cheat and deceive in offices and markets.

(k) tribal culture is in danger.

(l) tribals are deprived of their legitimate rights.

(m) autonomous District Council is cipher.

(n) infiltration from Bangladesh continues unabated.

(o) political parties are insincere towards tribal welfare.

Obviously, most of the grievances are against the Bengalees. The longer the issues remain unsolved, the quicker the inter-group relations will be bitter and the greater opportunities for the provocative neighbours to provoke the complainants will develop. But formal and meaningful dialogue between the two groups has not taken place; no group did take the initiative for direct dialogue. A Seminar was arranged only recently at the Agartala Press Club by the tribals. But it has not been effective.

Strategies

To redress their grievances, the tribals have adopted multi-strategy approach. They have simultaneously started a multi-dimensional struggle on all possible fronts. The movement manifests itself in the formation of various associations and organisations, in the establishment of *Kak-barak* Schools, in the publication of various books, journals and newspapers, in strengthening inter-tribal communications and marriage, in consolidating different tribes, in the growing identification of the tribals with their *Kak-barak* language, in their demand for a script different from that of the Bengalees, in politicising the tribals to vote for tribal parties, in organising various meetings, in articulating their demands, in launching campaigns against addiction, child marriage, dowry and marriage by physical service, in imparting training in fire arms to the tribal youths in the deep forest, and in committin arson, assassination, genocide, pillage, treason, treachery and ravage.

Tribal Organisations

In order to launch such a gigantic movement they have a number of parties and pressure groups which serve as organisational vehicle for tribal consciousness. The following list will amply illustrate the point : Tripura Jana-Siksha Samiti (1945), Tripura Sangh (1946), Seng Krak (1947), Tripura Ganamukti Parishad (1948), Paharia Union (1951) Adivasi Samiti (1952), Tripura Rajya Adivasi Sangh (1953), Adivasi Samsad (1954), East India Tribal Union (1956), Tripura Upajati Yuba Samiti (1967), Nikhil Tripura Upjati Yuba Samiti (1967), Tripura Upajati Karmachari Samiti (1968), Kakbarak Sahitya Sabha (1968), Tripura Tribal Student's Federation (1968), Barkhi Halam (1974), Tripura National Volunteers (1979), Tripursundari Naribahini (1980), Tribal People's Liberation Organisation (1981), Tripura Hills Peoples Party (1983), Lama Kautal (1985), Tripura Tribal Socio-Cultural Development Organisation (1989), All Tripura Tribal Force (1991).

Relations Among Organisations

It is evident from the above list that these associations have been formed along the lines of ethnic identity. All these associations are equally active and alive. Certain unions like Pahariya Union, Adivasi Samiti, Tripura Rajya Adivasi Sangh, Adivasi Samsad, East India Tribal Union etc., are almost dead now. Tripura Gana Mukti Parishad (TGP) and Tripura Hills People's Party (THPP) are CPI (M) supporting parties. The Tripura Upajati Juba Samiti (TUJS) is probably the most prominent of all parties now active in Tripura tribal politics. In alliance with the Indian National Congress party, the Tripura Upajati Juba Samiti is now (1988-1992) ruling in Tripura. Nevertheless, relations among various organisations were initially cordial. These units were expected to maintain close cooperation and coordination. But relationship among them seems to be not so cordial mainly because of ideological, religious, strategical and personal differences. As the strained relation continues, there are friends and enemies among them; and there are instances of alliances forged and broken.

Nature of Movement

This movement is not follwing a single, uniform pattern and path. Over the last fortyfive years, divisions and diversions have occurred. The movement has both mild and wild, evolutionary and revolutionary, Gandhian and Marxian, centripetal and centrifugal, subnational and national trends. Both ballot and bullet have been used. It is widely believed that many tribal leaders primarily adhere to ethnocentric interests even when they publicly speak of multiracism and mixed culture of Tripura; they bank upon tribal pride and solidarity for mass mobilisation. To the leaders of this movement, the question involved is not one of colour and racial discrimination; it is a question of dispossession of land, and it is a question of intrusion of the Bengalees. So the movement is directed against the Bengali Colonies and against those Bengalees irrespective of caste and class. The reason for making such contradictory remark and apparently confusing assessment about the nature of the movement is that the tribal leaders do not represent a unified front and differ in their aims, objects and strategy.

Administrative Response

The Constitutional directives for rapid tribal development has admonished various departments of both Central and State governments. If the Tripura Tribal Area Autonomous District Council is taken as another government, in Tripura three Governments are active. So almost all the departments of these three Governments are having plans and programmes for tribal welfare and exercising their brains to find, discover, invent or incorporate new schemes. The following list, though incomplete, will illustrate it :

1. The tribals have free access to public academies, bathi ing ghats, cremation grounds, gardens, hotels, hostels, restaurants, roads, shops, tanks, wells, etc. (Art. 15)

2. There are effective provisions for the reservation of ap pointments and posts for them; (Art. 16)

3. They have formed a number of associations and pub lished books and journals; (Art. 19)

4. They have right to establish and administer academies; (Art. 30)

5. Constitutionally Bihar, Madhya Pradesh and Orissa ought to have Tribal Welfare Minister, but conventionally Tripura too has a Tribal Welfare Minister; (Art. 164)

6. Seats are reserved in Parliament, Legislative Assembly, Municipal bodies, District Council, Block and Gaon Panchayat; (Arts. 330, 333, etc.)

7. The Commissioner for Scheduled Caste and Scheduled Tribe has been appointed by the President of India; (Art. 338)

8. Commissions have been appointed by the President of India to report on the state of welfare, problems and prospects of the Scheduled Tribe; (Art. 339)

9. Certain communities gave been specified as Scheduled Tribe by the President of India; (Art. 342). In Tripura t there are 18 such communities. The nineteenth cummunity has been a misnomer.

10. They are exempted from direct Income tax.

11. The All India Radio has been announcing some programme in their *Kak-barak* dialect since 1957.

12. The Tripura Land Regulation and Land Revenue Act of 1960 prohibits transfer of tribal lands to non-tribals all over Tripura.

13. An Ordinance of 1973 has declared void all cases of transfer of land which took place after 1.1.1969. The hilly, jungly, boggy tribal lands made cultivable and fertile by the non tribal purchasers are being taken back by the government at a nominal price and offered to the tribals free of cost.

14. In 1872 only two academies were first opened in Tripura. In 1992 the number of academies will be more than three thousand. In nook and corners of Tripura schools have been established.

15. For admission into all sorts of academies the tribals are getting relaxation in age and marks; even for technical and honours courses this facility has been extended.

16. A good number of tribal boarding houses has been estab lished to provide an ideal atmosphere.

17. The school going tribal students get attendance grant, book grant, dress grant and pre-matric stipend and mid-day meal.

18. Competitive examinees among them get monthly stipend for a period and preparatory coaching.

19. For competitive examinations they have reservation fa cility and relaxation as to age and marks.

20. In Civil Services post entry promotion is given to the tribal employees comparatively rapidly.

21. Tripura Tribal Areas Autonomous District Council has been established in 1979. Abour 70% of Tripura's total area have been brought within the Tripura Tribal Areas Autonomous District Council.

22. The decret and bureaucrat personnel of the Autonomous District Council are largely tribal. They constitute the decision-making authority.

23. Old age pension is given to old and infirm tribals.

24. In the Autonomous District Council area tribals are getting rice through ration shops at an abnormally low and subsidised rate.

25. The ribal weavers get bundles of yarn free of cost.

26. For rearing domestic fowl, goat, swine, cow, duck and pigeon the tribals get financial assistance, loans and subsidies from various agencies like bank, block office, corporation, Autonomous District Council, Tribal Welfare Department, etc.

27. For agriculture and horticulture they get assistance in cash and kind. Seeds, seedlings, implements, manure, training and cash money are offered. Irrigation is arranged.

28. Anti-poverty measures like National Rural Employment Programme, State Rural Employment Programme, Food for work and Jawahar Rojgar Yojana are implemented to check Seasonal unemployment.

29. In the Autonomous District Council area tribal houses are electrified by the Public Works Department free of cost.

30. Various voluntary organisations have been running projects.

Tribal Reaction to Administrative Response

The foregoing outline may be encouraging. A comparison between Pre-1947 situation and post-1947 situation will substantiate the point that there has been a rapid improvement in the tribal life after 1947. But it leaves unanswered the crucial question whether this direction of improvement will satisfy the tribals. There are certain signs that this improvement fails to convince and satisfy the tribal leaders. Though due to administrative measures and political pressures the balance of power is tilting in favour of the tribals, occurrence of insurgency, militancy and riots indicates tribal dissatisfaction. The Bengalees in the interior places are losing life in tribal attacks and ambushes. Such incidents perpetually remind the Bengalees of their traumatic experience of 1980 communal riots.

Historical Perspective

In response to an appeal made through a local daily newspaper (The *Dainik Sambad,* dated 1.2.1992) by one tribal writer asking the people of Tripura to study the past history of Tripura. This particular historical perspective is presented here. Rightly studied, history can provide clue to the origin of many contemporary problems.

Bengal fell into the hands of the Muslims in the first decade of the thirteenth century. The Muslims intrusions into the north-east Indian states began soon. From 1240 to 1765 Tripura was attacked nearly twenty five times by the Muslims. The means adopted by the invaders were uncharitable.

During the reign of Maharaj Amar Manikya, war broke out between Arakan and Tripura. The Mag of Arakan ransacked the capital town of Tripura and returned with a large amount of booty. Being defeated and chased, Amar Manikya committed suicide.

In the army of Amar Manikya the Portuguese pirates of Chittagong were recruited as mercenary. At the time of war between Arakan and Tripura the Portuguese betrayed and joined the Mag army, they jointly ravaged Udaypur. During the reign of Kalyan Manikya, Manipur raided on Tripura and took away about 200 captives.

The Hindu Kings of Bengal never attacked Tripura. The Bengali subjects of Tripura assisted Tripura in times of crisis. During the Arakan-Tripura was the Bengali *zamindars* of plains Tripura sent their forces along with the Tripura army. During Amar Manikya's Srihatta and Tarap expedition, the Bengali army accompanied him.

The King Ratna Manikya and the King Vijaya Manikya brought several *navasak* Bengali families (Gope, Malakar, Teli, Tanti, Modak, Bauri, Kumbhakar, Karmakar and Napit) from Bengal. To fulfil the need of traditional handicrafts and cottage industries such steps were taken by the previous and subsequent kings also. A good number of bureaucrats too were similarly recruited by the Tripura Kings from the Bengali community. A substantial amount of revenue of Tripura would come form the Bengali settled cultivators. To dig the big tanks in South Tripura, the Bengali labourers were forced by the Tripura Kings. The Bengali zamindar of Bhulua protested against the act of assassination and usurption of throne by Udaya Manikya.

Recurrence of Muslim attacks and annexation of the western part of Tripura and the Tripura Kings' inability to protect that fertile part compelled its Bengali subjects to take shelter in the eastern hilly portion which was infested with wild animals, insects and mosquitoes.

What wrecked Tripura was the internal palace politics. Tripura Court was a paradise for the intrigueres.

Disputed succession, fratricide, treason, ambition, mis-appropriation and the like were common features.

Observation

To understand the present trend of the ethnic movements in this State, a few observations about the contemporary forces are made below :

1. Nearly a dozen of the Christian missionary denominations have been making systematic efforts to anglicise and converts the tribal people. The converts have come to the confiction that their culture and existence are at a stake due to the engulfing culture of the ever increasing Bengalees, and that they can trust the missionaries only. The treatment to alien culture by Christianity, Hinduism and Islam is known to the rational scholars of comparative religion. The missionaries have projected themselves as messiah of the tribals. But how far it is genuine has been assessed by the some foreign scholars. It is worth quoting them. Mills (1926) comments, "Of the mistakes made by the Mission the gravest, in my opinion, and the one most fraught with danger for the future is their policy of stranuously imposing an alien western culture on the converts. I think I am right in saying that no member of the Mission has ever studied no customs deeply, but nearly all have been eager to uproot what they neither understand nor sympathise with, and to substitute for it a superficial civilisation". Mecabe (1935) points out, "The papacy

itself made a mockery of its own pretence of political neutrality".

2. Impartial observers of Tripura politics are familiar with the ruthless manoeuvre with which the local communists exacerbate the tribal resentment by blaming the Bengalees. One top ranking leader shocked many when he had remarked. "Had I been a tribal I would also be an insurgent. Since 1948 they are politicising and mobilising the tribal masses along the communal lines".

3. Tripura is surrounded by provocative neighbours. When the neighbouring states are themselves in turmoil, Tripura cannot remain uneffected. The insurgents of Tripura have been getting shelter in the neighbouring Indian States as well as in Bangladesh, China and Burma. The headquarters of the Tripura National Volunteers was in the Chittagong hill tract for a long time.

4. Deception of the tribals by some Bengali touts and imposters constitutes a cardinal charge as well as ground for ethnic movement. Nevertheless, it has to be admitted that some Bengali merchants have cheated some tribals. In course of time similar touts have grown up among the tribals also.

5. The women folk among the tribals continue to constitute the economic backbone. They are more hardworking than the males. Majority of the males used to spend their time in gossiping, smoking, drinking and merry-making. The moment an amount of loan, help, subsidy or assistance is received, many of them first purchase meat, fish, sweetmeats and country liquor. Domestic birds and animals are sacrificed to cure a disease. Several departments of the Government and voluntary organisations have been spending crores of rupees for tribal welfare. Still their poverty remains.

6. The traumatic experience of communal riots before and after 1947 compelled the Bengali subjects to leave their hearth and home in the western part of Tripura itself. A good number of them settled in the interior hills and laboured hard for reclamation of fallowed lands or lands nominally owned by tribals. They are minority in tribal pockets. What is their lot now ? A good number of them have lost their persons and properties in tribal attacks and

ambushes. This situation perpetually reminds them of their traumatic experience of those days of partition.

7. That a significant change in the Bengali thinking has begun can be proved from the fact that a large number of them have already started leaving the hills and interior places and settling in the non Autonomous District Council areas of suburban areas. They admit that in future they will not be able to live peacefully in the hills.

8. It may be foolhardy to predict the future course of events which will influence the ethnic relations in Tripura. However, two contingencies may be apprehended : the tribals of Chittagong Hill Tracts will be ruthlessly and completely driven out by the Muslims from Arakan and Bangladesh; the tribal refugees of Chittagong Hill Tracts will take shelter in Tripura and Mizoram; these refugees will drive out the non-tribals from Tripura's Autonomous District Council area.

9. Even after that, will all these migrations and movements ensure lasting peace ? There is every doubt. Even a microscopic minority either among the Bengalees or among the Tribals do not realise that enemy is within each of us. Chaos and confusion, corruption and crimes persist in both the communities. Some political leaders have been continuing the nasty games of intrigues, bargaining and cheap popularity. Their activities arouse the destructive instincts of the youths.

10. It is indeed difficult to devide the two communities. The two communities are interdependent and intermixed in various ways. There are many instances of marrriage between the two communities. The two communities share common public places, worship common deities and observe so many common customs and rituals. The two communities have a lot in common. Any policy or policies, philosophy or programme which fails to reckon with this interdependence as well as commonness is bound to bring disaster to both. The two communities must not see each other as enemy.

REFERENCES

MILLS, J.P., 1926. *The Ao Nagas*, London : MacMillan.

INDEX